No More Mr. Nice Guy

NO MORE MR. NICE GUY

A LIFE OF HARDBALL

DICK WILLIAMS AND BILL PLASCHKE

HARCOURT BRACE JOVANOVICH, PUBLISHERS

San Diego   New York   London

Requests for permission to make copies of any part
of the work should be mailed to: Permissions Department,
Harcourt Brace Jovanovich, Publishers, Orlando, Florida 32887.

Library of Congress Cataloging-in-Publication Data
Williams, Dick, 1929–
No more Mr. Nice Guy: a life of hardball/Dick
Williams and Bill Plaschke.
p.   cm.
ISBN 0-15-166728-4
1. Williams, Dick, 1929– . 2. Baseball—United States—
Managers—Biography. I. Plaschke, Bill. II. Title.
GV865.W495A3   1990
796.357'092—dc20   90-37418
[B]

Designed by G. B. D. Smith
Printed in the United States of America

First edition   A B C D E

To Norma, who has always stood by me, and to our three children, Kathi, Rick, and Marc, who never complained or questioned when I seemed to miss all the important days. Thank you for standing by me always. —D.W.

To my daughter, who I hope will always remember that "It's a Wonderful Day to Be Tessa Ann." —B.P.

Contents

Acknowledgments

The worst part about writing this book is that there is only room on the cover for two names. Many other people inspired the spirits that created the words. This is their page; we're just glad it's one of the first.

Author Williams would like to thank Bobby Bragan and the late Paul Richards for believing in his managerial ability and Dick O'Connell and the late Neal Mahoney for giving him the opportunity to show that ability. He also thanks his true friends, who have stood by him through the good years and the lean ones; his supportive relatives, who number many; and last here, but first in his heart, is his best friend and biggest fan, mom Kathryn.

Author Plaschke would like to thank wife Lisa Ann Jacobs for, well, every single thing, cover to cover. If she owns his heart, it's because she has worked for it. He would also like to thank a wonderful family who put up with him until, after many long hours on this book, he was no more Mr. Nice Guy: dad Grover and mom Mary, and Brad, Bob, Beth, and newest member Tom. Thanks also to Jim Street for belief, and Gary Piepenbrink, his editor, for understanding, and

Joan and Andrew Fishbein for just being there. And then there is Bill Ward, the best journalism teacher currently walking the earth. Ward may not even know this book was being written, but no word Plaschke writes does not contain his inspiration. Finally, to wise man Blaine Johnson, who very long ago advised that writing a book would be like running a marathon: you're two for two.

INTRODUCTION

I am growing old now. As I grab the sides of my bathroom sink this morning and look straight ahead, I can tell you, I'm growing old.

My glasses are here on the top of the toilet, waiting to fit my face. In a few minutes I'll put them on, and I won't take them off the rest of the day. It was never like this until one day in San Diego while I was managing the Padres. Before one game I put my glasses on, and I found nine innings later that I was still wearing them. I thought then, This is what it's like to get old.

My voice is here, but now it's likely to die if I'm not careful. While managing in a Senior Professional Baseball Association game last winter, I argued with an umpire so loud and so long that I couldn't talk for two days. I tried to remember the last time that had happened. I could not.

My mustache is white. When I sneak a smoke, the top part of it turns a telltale yellow—which is how my wife, Norma, knows to yell at me for keeping up one of my bad habits. I don't know whether anybody else from my Mustache Gang days with the Oakland Athletics has the same problem. But then, maybe most of them have shaved off their mustaches. I never did. I thought mine would keep me young. I was wrong.

My hair, which used to be dark and long, is now gray and neatly cut. I'm not losing it, but maybe it would be better if I did. As it is now, everyone says I look like Wilfred Brimley. I don't want to look like Wilfred Brimley. I want to look like me: face still taut with a constant smirk, shoulders still thrown back, midsection still hard.

I never thought it would happen, but I am growing old. And it's time for us to talk.

My name is Dick Williams, I am 61 years old, and I was a major league baseball manager. You may have heard of me. If so, let me guess what you've heard: that I was one of the most successful managers in the history of baseball, and that I could be one of the game's worst human beings. And you probably heard both things from the same person.

You may have wondered, How can that be? Lately I've wondered the same thing. Because I've realized that it's true.

• • •

For parts of 21 seasons I won acclaim for taking three different teams to the World Series, a record matched by only one other manager in baseball history. Three times I was voted Manager of the Year. In all, I won 1,571 games, which puts me 13th among all managers. Just seven managers have bettered my 12 World Series wins. No manager has bossed more teams—six—since 1900.

But these are just general facts, not tied to any particular team or season. The specifics, people say, are even more impressive. I never thought about it much, because what I did for teams was never more than what I did for myself: turning troubled losers into winners. Here are some specifics:

• The 1966 Boston Red Sox finished ninth in the American League, one game out of last place. The next year, as a rookie manager, I took them to the World Series in a season that became known as "The Impossible Dream."

• The Oakland Athletics had never won a pennant when I arrived as manager in 1971. By the time I left, they had won three straight pennants and two World Series championships.

• When I moved north to Montreal in 1977, the Expos had lost 107 games the previous season. Three years later they had won 95 and were in second place. In five years, a couple of weeks after I was fired, they won the National League East Division.

• Then there were the San Diego Padres, who had had one winning record in their 14-year history when I joined them in 1982. Three seasons later, in 1984, the entire city was silly on champagne. Taking a National League pennant by surprise does that to people.

Through it all I have developed a core of players who would do anything for me, players who understood what it means to win and, more important, what it takes to win. Players like Jim Lonborg, Reggie Smith, Mike Andrews, Reggie Jackson, Sal Bando, Catfish Hunter, Frank Tanana, Nolan Ryan, Gary Carter, Andre Dawson, Goose Gossage, Graig Nettles, Tony Gwynn. Real players.

That's some of the good stuff that lets me lay claim to being one of the most successful managers in the history of the game. Now for the other stuff.

Some people hate me. Some people have threatened to quit when I was hired, and then celebrated when I was fired. Some people seem to hate me so much that they make jokes about it. I remember reading a sports column consisting of funny questions; whoever gave the worst answers was promised a dinner with Dick Williams. Come to think of it, I've seen that kind of column more than once.

I must lead all of baseball as a target for behind-the-back verbal assaults. I've been called mean, cruel, insensitive. I've been called a bully. I've been called a bastard and a son of a bitch. Why, my life's even been threatened, though I think it was at least partly a joke. After I was fired in San Diego, one of my players, Tim Flannery, said, "Dick Williams is the best manager I've ever played for . . . but as soon as he gets out of baseball, I'm going to run him over with my car." I wanted to tell Tim, "Don't worry, I've been run over before."

All of this is because I've supposedly been too tough on players. They say I've screamed at them, spat on them, shoved them, been sarcastic with them, humiliated them. They're right, I've done all of that, but they usually leave one thing out: once I even tackled a player, squeezing him so hard I shit my pants. People say I haven't been "human" enough with players—whatever that means. They say I wouldn't talk to them enough, listen to them enough, compliment them enough, or even dream of coddling them a little when necessary. Again, they're probably right.

Some people say that all of my winning has been fine but that it has come at an awfully high price to my teams. In this they are only partially right. There has been a price, but it's been exacted from *me*. I have paid, and I have won; I have paid, and I have won again, over and over, until sometimes I've felt swallowed by something far too large to fight.

An obsession with winning and the heartbreak involved in feeding that obsession—that is what this book is about. It's about a boy who grew up in St. Louis, blessed with a work ethic and a proud father who would kick his ass if he forgot it. A father who taught him, sometimes crudely, that there is nothing in life but finishing first. It's about how that boy moved to southern California as a teenager and how, all of a sudden, that father was gone. And how the boy thought it was his own fault. And how a simple love for winning became an addiction.

The book is about how that boy became a fairly good baseball player, and made it all the way to Brooklyn and the famed Dodgers. It's about how many of those Boys of Summer weren't really boys but mean-spirited men filled with conceit, and how they made the boy feel like a real bum. It's about how that boy finally became a man, making the starting lineup . . . and then blowing out his shoulder. Blowing out his dreams.

The book is about how that injury still hurts. It's about how the man vowed to make it another way, vowed through 3 A.M. anguish that if he could no longer win baseball games with his body, he would one day win them with his mind and his heart. From there the book travels through the cities that made the manager but nearly extinguished the human being.

First there was Toronto, a triple-A team, my first managing job, the place I first realized that wanting 25 men to win could give me a horrible temper and zero tolerance. Then there was Boston, where I realized winning could drive me crazy. The Impossible Dream season came so quickly and with such intensity that I had to experience it again, immediately, the very next year, and the year after that. That new dream was surely impossible—a sad fact that I spent those two years learning as I nearly drank myself out of my marriage and my sanity. Carl Yastrzemski can tell you about that dream.

Then there was Oakland, where winning became fun, so much fun that everyone wanted to get into the act, including a team owner named Charley Finley and his moron mule, both of whom were so loony that they drove me to George Steinbrenner. And Vida Blue and Blue Moon Odom always thought it was them. The book travels from there to southern California, where I learned with the Angels that even in my foulest and most bitter moods, winning is sometimes truly impossible. Sorry, Nolan Ryan, I tried. And to hell with you, Bill Melton.

Then it's on to Montreal, where the game itself started becoming impossible. After my first 10 years as a manager the players were making more money and I was getting less respect. It was in Montreal that I discovered widespread drug use in professional baseball. And for the first time I experienced genuine, heartfelt disillusionment. Nothing against Gary Carter and Andre Dawson, but Montreal was too much Ellis Valentine and Steve Rogers. From Montreal the book moves back south to San Diego, where for a couple of wonderful years winning was worth it once again, despite more drugs and more disillusionment. And then I learned the old lesson that winners attract backstabbers (anyone who knows Jack McKeon knows what I'm talking about here). It was San Diego that finally broke my heart, a heart I'd been told was made of rock. If only it had been Teflon, as my first baseman's, Steve Garvey's, apparently was.

Having brought me back to reality, the book then goes to Seattle, where the modern-day player finally drove me from the big league game altogether. The egos, the lawsuits, the players like Mark Langston who were afraid to get themselves dirty, the chapel services in the shower room. And George Argyros, the modern-day owner. But, thank goodness, the book doesn't end here.

It ends in West Palm Beach, Florida, with a sweet little idea called the Senior Professional Baseball Association, where I spent a winter learning to feel good about baseball again. Many think that league was a joke, and perhaps by the time you read this it will be out of business. But the players cared. And the players tried. Real baseball, my long-lost friend, came back to sit with me one more time. That's all I ever wanted out of myself and my players. Real baseball. Real caring about real winning. This is the story about that simple wish, how easy it seemed and how costly it became. In that sense this story isn't just about me but about two eras of baseball: my era, and the era I was cast out from—today's era.

• • •

Many of my former players and associates, I have heard, are dreading this book and its revelations. I can't say that they're lacking just cause. This book will not make me friends. But when I set out to write it, I wasn't looking for friends. I was looking for peace. I was looking to explain my life—the good, the bad, and the worse—in hopes of discovering a justification for 23 years of hardball. In hopes of answering questions that have worked their way into my success like a painful splinter, questions of whether it was really all worth it.

This book is for me and for the other person who has always appreciated how I've played and managed—the fan. I swear that I've tried to write as I've done everything else. Head down, running hard, never going around someone when I can go over or through him.

This has made for some painful pages. But in finishing the text, I realized what must be life's greatest feeling, next to a win. My answers. I had found them. For the sake of those who have either loved me or despised me, I sincerely hope this book will share those answers.

Dick Williams
Seattle, Washington
March 1990

No More Mr. Nice Guy

BORN TO HIT AND RUN

The dog didn't have to get that mad. I was only trying to turn this mangy white collie into an animal somebody would want. I was determined to wise him up so that he'd never again be fooled by a mailman with a stick, or by a dog catcher with a secret death sentence.

It was the summer of 1935. I was six years old, playing with this dog—cleverly named Whitey—in the backyard of a buddy who lived across the street from my parents' small brick house in north St. Louis. We were back where his family's tiny garden, like everyone else's tiny garden, came to an abrupt end at the edge of the alley. In my mostly German neighborhood of cramped, single-story houses, everything nice had its boundaries. We were supposed to play either on the thin strip of grass in the front yard or in the backyard garden. Whatever we did, though, stay the hell out of the alley.

But this day it was different. I needed to help this dog. Honest. I had gone into the forbidden alley to play fetch with a stick and soon discovered that I could fake throwing it and Whitey would run down the alley anyway. It wasn't until 50 yards later, when he stopped and looked back, that he would realize I still had the stick. Then he would run back to me and cry.

I was just a kid, but already I had a well-developed soft spot for mutts (a trait that stuck with me, as anybody who ever saw me manage the California Angels would attest). So I could see that this particular dog was a little dumb and very much in need of a lesson. I decided I would teach him to never lose sight of the stick. I would fake the throw and then, after he returned from his futile run, do it again. And again. And again. I kept faking the throw, hoping that eventually he would realize he had to watch my hand before making like Lassie.

But he never did. Whitey got tired, I became frustrated, and finally I faked like I was going to lay that damn stick right down across his dumb nose. I never actually did it, I just faked it. Keeping his eye on the stick, he didn't flinch. And for a moment I thought, Success! I thought wrong. What happened next you can still see today, just next to my left eye. That dumb dog had learned something, all right . . . that Dick Williams could be a jerk. He jumped up and bit a chunk out of my little wise guy face.

My older brother, Ellery, heard the screams and ran over to find Whitey teaching *me* a lesson. Ellery finally managed to chase him off, though, and then carried me home. My mother later said that upon seeing me and hearing the story, she had a premonition. "I knew then," she said, "that my son would go through life being a pain in the ass."

I didn't think I was being a pain in the ass with Whitey. I considered it teaching. After all, isn't that what my father, Harvey, called it when he would crack Ellery's elbows and mine if we were resting them on the table during dinner? Isn't that "teaching"? Or when he would kick our shins if we didn't sit up? Wasn't he really just trying to be a teacher when he would take Ellery down to the basement and, ignoring my mother's tears, tie him up and . . . Well, a bit of background first.

I was born in north St. Louis on May 7, 1929. My first address was 4642 Korte Avenue. My first memories were of the street's big trees and small lawns and garages in back, and the most wonderful geographical phenomenon just five doors down: a dead end. The street stopped and a vacant lot began. It was there we would spend almost every daylight hour. In summer we would come home with dirt in our underwear—the lot was perfect for practicing imaginary big league slides into home plate. In winter we would come home with ice chunks in our long johns—the frozen street in front of the lot made a great makeshift skating rink.

Every child should grow up next to a dead end, especially those like me who needed to escape a house overstuffed with the energies of two young boys, a father, a mother, and my grandfather. But thank goodness for my grandfather, Fred Rohde. It was his house, and for much of my youth our meals were his food.

He owned a grocery store, while my father, although he tried, didn't own much of anything, particularly a steady job. During the Depression my father would spend his days on the city buses, riding around looking for work. Some days it would come from the back of a fish truck as he made deliveries. Other days, from one of the local breweries—a place like Hyde Park or Falstaff—where he would clean out vats.

I would think back to those days many years later when I brought teams into St. Louis's Busch Stadium. All those people in the stands would boo me while spilling beer on each other, and I would think, My father used to clean up some of this beer, and here you are throwing it around and cursing his son . . . My teams always had a pretty good record in St. Louis. I think I know why.

On days my father didn't find work, he would come home in unearned dirt and angry. My grandfather would keep us fed while my father ate frustration. And this wasn't a man used to frustration.

Before he married my mother—when he was 25 and she

was 17—the stubborn man had left high school to join the Navy. He was just what the Navy needed: a redneck. He would show off by diving 50 feet from transport ships into the ocean and then swimming around with the sharks. When he came home, he showed off by swimming across the Mississippi River.

And man, was he bullheaded. He was such a strong Republican that he wouldn't vote Democrat even if it would help protect his brother's livelihood. Case in point: His brother happened to work for the city, holding a job that depended upon political favors. When the Democrat who'd hired him was in danger of being voted out of office by a Republican, he begged my father to vote for the Democrat. The man wasn't trying to make a political statement, he just wanted to save his own ass. But to my father, everything you did in life was a statement. So he refused to vote against his affiliation. His brother, by the way, nearly lost his job.

Friends say I was like that some 50 years later, in Game Five of the 1984 World Series between my San Diego Padres and Sparky Anderson's Detroit Tigers. In the eighth inning, with one out, runners on second and third, and my team down 5–4, I allowed a pleading Goose Gossage to pitch to Kirk Gibson even though I wanted Gibson to be intentionally walked. I gave in to Gossage, not because I had a better strategy but because I was bullheaded. For my entire career I've let the pitcher decide what he wants to do—he could shake off the catcher's signs and even mine. Just because a nation was watching and a world championship was on the line, I wasn't going to change now. Just like my father, who wouldn't change his principles even though they might eventually cause his brother some trouble.

With a pitcher my principle has been: It's his earned run average, it's his win-loss record, it's his butt. If I can help him succeed, fine. But if he fails, he won't be able to live with himself unless he fails his way. Besides, you make a pitcher do something he doesn't want to do, no telling how his arm will react. Guys who want to throw curveballs but are forced to throw fastballs usually end up throwing a fastball so weak and so hanging that it might as well be a curveball—a bad one that's usually knocked out of the park. If a pitcher doesn't want to do something, his brain may subconsciously tell his arm to do it half-assed.

When I went to the mound in that 1984 Series, prepared to tell my pitcher to walk the guy, the gruff-voiced Gossage suddenly sounded like a little boy. "I can get him, Dick," he said. "C'mon, let me get him." So I said fine. Gossage was perhaps the biggest reason we were even in this World Series. More than any pitcher I'd managed before, here was one who definitely deserved to determine his own fate.

If you don't remember what happened next, you can probably make an educated guess. Gibson hit the damn ball into the next neighborhood. It disappeared into the right field upper deck for a three-run homer that gave the Tigers an 8–4 victory and a world championship.

I can still see Gibson rounding the bases with his right fist pumping the air. I can still see Gossage's red-faced anger, even though this wasn't his fault. But I can still see my father too, stomping around the house proclaiming that a man who can't follow his heart goes through life lost, whether he's Democrat or Republican. My father's heart told him to vote Republican *always*, even when there were damn good family reasons not to. My heart has always told me to let a pitcher decide what he wants to do. The heart has its own reasons, good or bad. I can live with that.

It wasn't easy living with my father, all 5-foot-9 of him, with prematurely gray curls but a rock-hard body that wouldn't grow old. Pop had a deep, winding scar at the corner of his right eye, a scar with a face of its own. You never looked my father in the eye, you looked him in the scar. And you cowered. My father was the living definition of the word "blunt." And not only in the way he would teach us table manners.

How about the way Pop taught us to swim? At the time it didn't seem like such a big deal. We thought everybody's father taught his sons to swim by taking them down to the Gasconade River in southern Missouri near the Ozark Mountains, throwing them in against a rushing current, ordering them to stroke, and then standing behind them while the current forced them back downstream. Ellery and I may have been the first brothers to learn how to swim forward by going backward. But wasn't that how everybody did it?

Then there was the way my father attempted to teach me to drive. We needed only one session. With him alongside me in the passenger seat, I tried to start a car for the first time. I flooded the engine. Twice. Three times. At that my father shoved open his door, jumped out, and walked up the street. Ten minutes later a neighbor returned in his place. "Dickie," he said, "I guess I'm going to teach you how to drive."

Not that my brother or I ever said anything contrary. My father wouldn't tolerate insubordination. He didn't mind if we got into trouble. What he minded was when we didn't respect that he knew what the hell he was talking about. He had the loudest whistle in the neighborhood, a shrill Navy blast he made with just his tongue and his teeth. When he whistled, we came. If we didn't, that was disobedience, and that just killed him. And darn near killed us.

Today they would call it child abuse. Back then it was just another case of a father dragging a son down the basement steps, tying him to a pole, and whipping him. The most interesting thing about the special beatings he gave Ellery was that I never hated him for it. I reacted to it the way my mother did, watching and crying. I hoped it wouldn't ever happen to me . . . but I understood that if I went against my father's orders, it would. For order to exist, there must first be authority—one authority. In the case of our household, it was him. Later, in the case of several baseball teams, it was me. And if I seemed more like a stern father than a businesslike manager, maybe that's because I learned it's the best way to exercise authority. I got that from my own father. Maybe it's in my blood.

Pop wanted us to follow him blindly. Funny thing about that was, when we did, like on Sunday afternoons, good things often happened. He'd order us into the car for a boring weekend drive, but then often he'd turn the car into a dusty parking lot next to a local amateur baseball field where players were gathering. "Get out," he'd say, smiling. "We're going to watch a little baseball." Eyes wide, we would clamber out of the car and run for the bleachers. For the next couple of hours, the only thing better than imitating the players on the field and chasing foul balls was watching my father umpire the games, which he sometimes did.

Some of my former players might chuckle to learn that in my first experiences with baseball I actually defied authority. Maybe it was because I was just seven years old at the time. We lived near Sportsman's Park, home of the St. Louis Cardinals and Browns. Ellery, who was three years older than me, belonged to the Knothole Gang, which admitted kids at least 10 years old to 3 P.M. games for free.

Lucky for me, Ellery wasn't that interested in baseball, and elementary school ended every day about 3:15 P.M. So I was able to use his pass, act like I was 10, and sneak into games, arriving by the second inning. Those nights, lying in the same bed with Ellery, just a few feet away from our grandfather's bed, I would clutch my covers and tell him what I'd seen. When it was warm, we'd move our beds to the back-yard and cover ourselves with a mosquito net, and I'd be able to talk without whispering. What wonderful stories I had. And heroes.

I loved all the St. Louis players who got dirty and looked cocky and strutted. All the players who looked like my father. But left fielders were my favorites, and not just because they were a better combination of power and grace than anyone. It was also because our cheap seats were in left field, and sometimes, with people standing in front of us, the left fielder was all we could see. Joe Medwick was my man for the Cardinals, while Chet Laabs was my man for the Browns.

You've probably heard of Hall of Famer Medwick. Laabs, maybe not. Things didn't come as easy for him as for Medwick. Laabs played 11 years, eight for the Browns, and hit higher than .300 only once. He hit more than 17 home runs only once and never had as many as 100 RBIs.

But Chet Laabs was a survivor. He lasted more than a decade because he played with his heart and his head. He did the things that nobody who's never gotten his shirt dirty notices. I watched him more than Medwick because the Browns would let us Browns Brigade fan club members into Sunday games for free. By watching him, I soon discovered that this was my kind of player. Later on my kind of player was simply the one who wouldn't call me a son of a bitch in the dugout. But at the time I still had dreams.

And back then reaching my dreams could be as easy as grabbing them and running. One day while watching the Cardinals, I notice that outfielder Pepper Martin is walking from the dugout with a broken bat. Since my father can't afford to buy me a bat, I figure, Why not get this broken bat and tape it up? Surely, Pepper Martin didn't save his broken bats. So, with five other boys, I wait down at the left field line underneath the stands for Martin to walk past us to the clubhouse. Around the seventh inning here he comes, carrying that magical Don Gutteridge model with a crack down the middle.

"Hey, kids, you wanna bat?" he shouts. And before we can answer, he slides it on the walkway past a guard . . . right into my dirty little hands. I grab the bat and run and run and keep running until I'm outside the park and the bat is officially mine. And then I walk the mile home, but slowly, picking up acorns and swinging at them, swinging at the air when I can find no more acorns. I walk so slowly that afternoon turns into night.

Back home, as I later learned, my concerned parents were having something just short of a panic attack. Their son, who sneaks into games, usually showed up in time for dinner. At nearly 7 P.M. I come clunking through the door. Worried now that I might need the bat for protection against my father, I quickly explain my good fortune. And guess what? My parents don't kill me. My dad, in fact, helps me find a roll of tape and then fashions my damaged treasure into a regular bat again. When Martin later became a Brooklyn Dodgers instructor while I was one of their outfielders in the minor league camp, I finally thanked him for that bat. He just laughed, as if he really didn't understand. But I'll never forget how my parents understood.

• • •

In the same way I grabbed that Pepper Martin bat, I began grabbing at all of life's challenges. Soon, sneaking into baseball games wasn't enough. I began sneaking onto streetcars. You know how everyone in the comic strips seems to have an Aunt Minnie? Well, I actually had one, and she and a friend would come into the city on Sundays to spend the day with us. They'd come by streetcar and then give us their passes so that we could spend the day going all over St. Louis. I was maybe nine years old at the time, and Ellery was just 12, but Pop didn't care. The way he figured it, hell, it wouldn't hurt us to grow up faster.

And grow up we did one day when Aunt Minnie didn't bring her friend. That meant she had just one pass. So my brother would jump on the streetcar and then toss it down to me and hope the conductor didn't see us. It was so much fun that sometimes we even tried to sneak in when we each had a pass. My father was one kind of authority, but a streetcar conductor was a different kind, one to be tested. Sort of like, I guess, an umpire.

Ellery was always giving me a hand like that. He was always the better athlete, always bigger and stronger, and— most important in a kid's world—he could jump higher. This actually hurt him one day around the corner from our house, over on Shirley Place. He was trying to become the only kid on the block to touch the top of the laundry pole in a neighbor's backyard. After several tries, amid loud cheers from an impromptu gathering, he touched it. But on the top of that pole was a hook that tore right through the palm of his right hand. Since then he's never been able to fully close his hand or throw a baseball properly.

But I saw something in that injury. I saw a boy decide that if he couldn't do one thing, he'd learn to do another. While Ellery couldn't throw with that hand, he could certainly catch. And 10 years later, after a fine college career for Santa Clara, Ellery made sure that Dick Williams wouldn't be the only professional athlete in the family. Check the roster of the New York Giants for 1950. The guy who couldn't throw became a receiver. So what if, after making the only potential touchdown catch of his career, he hit the goalposts and fell backward onto the one-yard line? He gave much more than 100 percent of what he had, which later made me wonder how come able-bodied players had so much trouble with that.

Ellery's injury seemed to trigger, coincidentally, a series of changes in our lives. Soon thereafter, in a completely unrelated event, our next-door neighbor helped Pop hook up with Metropolitan Life Insurance Company as a debit collector. In other words, my dad was being paid to make weekly stops at various homes to take money out of cookie jars to keep people current on their insurance. This job kept him and his bad moods out of the house, which was fine with me, but soon it moved us all out of our house when he was given a bigger territory in an outer–St. Louis suburb called Ferguson. This meant, at age 12, a move from a little house on a tiny, secure city street to a rolling, two-story brick place in what seemed like a cornfield with stoplights.

Where our backyard used to be an alley, in Ferguson it was an overgrown pasture where Ellery set up rabbit traps that would sometimes furnish our Sunday meal. We would spend our days walking through the surrounding fields, Ellery with his rifle and me with my BB gun, stealing turnips out of farmers' fields for lunch and shooting at everything from birds to rodents. And it was in Ferguson—maybe in part because I now had a separate bed for the first time in my life—that I first developed my swagger.

Sports became my way of being cool. Shortly after we moved there, I entered an "athletic day" at Vogt Junior High, which I would be attending in the fall. How about that new kid? I won every event. I could hit a softball a mile. I could do somersaults and gyrate with the best of the tumbling team.

But the strange thing was that after it ended, I wasn't happy because I'd won a trophy but because I'd beaten everyone else. It was then I realized, knowing only that I didn't want to spend the rest of my life taking orders, that my goal was to rise above everyone else in any way I could. And that way, it was apparent, would be athletics. I was only 12, but I was already weary of my father being the authority. Starting then, I wanted to be the authority. Why else would I have taken a job at the local movie theater stoking the furnace and sweeping the aisles? Not just because I was allowed to see the movies free. Because in having a high visibility job at age 13, you felt like you had power.

Not that everybody was ready for me to be the authority. One day I mouthed off to a big, quiet kid, thinking that anybody who wouldn't defend himself verbally was incapable of physical retaliation. Good thinking. On the playground, in front of most of the school and what seemed like every pretty young girl I'd ever known, he beat the piss out of me. For at least the time it took me to limp home, I was humbled.

My father, meanwhile, was constantly being humbled in his weekly attempts to collect insurance. He had more territory now, but that only meant more cookie jars and more faces pleading with him to leave them alone. It was a tough way to make a living, a fact that became apparent one day, after just one year of living in Ferguson, when he came home and announced that we were moving. And not just to another St. Louis suburb but to southern California. Hollywood, to be exact.

No, we weren't becoming movie stars. We'd still need to

work at the movies to afford them. My mother's cousin, Anna Marie Bertea, had landed my father a job as office manager with Bertea Products, a manufacturer of airplane de-icers. My mother's cousin had pull because she was the wife of the founder, Alex Bertea. Sure, it was nepotism, but for the first time my father wouldn't have to hit the pavement every dawn and stay out there on his sore feet until nightfall.

So what if a cousin arranged it? Pop was such a proud man that he'd have done nearly anything to get this kind of a job and establish himself as the leader of the family—even if it meant loading us on a train for a three-day trip to a new life. And even if it meant cramming us into a house with the Berteas until we found a tiny apartment in Hollywood. And even that only lasted a couple of months. Shortly after we arrived, Bertea Products moved to nearby Pasadena, so we moved to a little stucco house in Altadena.

It was there that I finally approached manhood, in more ways than one. We lived on Grand Oaks Avenue, just two blocks from the mountains northeast of Los Angeles. At night there would be deer walking the wide streets. During the day we'd be up in those mountains, chasing those deer. I once even shot one in the butt with a bow and arrow, although I never caught it and wouldn't have known what to do with it if I had. I was just being a smartass, just being me. When we grew hot, we swam in the mountain streams. When we grew restless, we wandered the mountain paths, an exercise that ended when my brother once got lost up there overnight. My parents were frightened but didn't panic. And rightfully so: they'd taught us to think and scheme and ultimately swagger our way out of jams. So my brother came strolling home the next morning like nothing had ever happened. Pop nearly killed him.

I first enrolled in Elliott Junior High, which carried students through their sophomore year in high school. Then I "graduated" to Pasadena Junior College, which covered grades 11 and 12 plus your first two years of college. At those schools, as in the rest of that sunny part of the country, there was a big emphasis on sports. And I played all of them. I lettered in baseball, football, basketball, track, tennis, swimming, and even handball. Don't laugh—I won the city handball title. My school sweater looked like a trophy case, and it did the talking for me on those rare occasions when I chose not to speak for myself. Sports gave me more than just a healthy complexion; they gave me the right to strut through the middle of campus in Levi's, a white T-shirt, and army shoes. Sports gave me the right to have similar-looking friends, all of us popular, all of us in positions of adolescent authority, kings of the student union. Swaggering, I thought, suited me.

But—a problem that would recur throughout my life— sports also kept me ignorant of reality. I was so busy playing that I never noticed the important reality a teenager could face: the sickness of his father. Being tough had finally caught up with Pop. He worked too hard, he smoked too much, and shortly after we arrived in California, he underwent major gall bladder surgery. I left one of my junior high practices three days after the operation, climbed on my bike, and rode across town to the tiny hospital on Fair Oaks Boulevard to see him for the first time since surgery. Once there, I received the shock of my young life.

My father, seemingly overnight, had grown old. His skin was pale, his hair was messy and white, he talked old, he smelled old. His barber was there, trying to scrape the white stubble from white cheeks. It scared me. Not enough to grab him and wonder what life would be like without him. Just enough to get on my bike and tear the hell away from there.

After that surgery my father tried to slow down but couldn't. The doctor told him he could only have two cigarets a day. Pop said fine, but then he cut those two cigarets in half so he could smoke four. For 45 years I've had to keep remembering this: that his habits, mixed with the gall bladder surgery, gave him an incurably weak heart. Unless I keep believing this, I'll continue to blame myself for what happened on that Friday night in the fall of 1945.

It was just another Pasadena Junior College football game

in which I was one of the stars, the left halfback who lined up next to future Washington and L.A. Rams punter Hall Haynes. The previous week I'd scored three touchdowns in a scrimmage against El Monte, so I was on a roll as we visited Alhambra. On the third play of the game, in a move that surprised even me, I broke a couple of tackles and raced through the middle for a 40-yard run that seemed destined for a touchdown. But just inside the five-yard line I was chopped down by three flying tacklers, and I heard something pop. It was my left ankle. I sucked the dirt and couldn't get up. I rolled on the ground in pain, surrounded by players and coaches, until a stretcher arrived. As I was taken to the sidelines, I noticed an unusual sight that momentarily made me forget the pain. It was my father.

When I was hit, my father—my tough, sweet father— had been so scared that he ran down from the stands to the sidelines. Now he was standing next to the coaches, shouting at me, wondering if I was okay, waiting for me to be carried from the field so he could comfort me. The funny, horrible thing about it was that I ended up fine. And he didn't.

That night, as I lay in bed with my foot heavily wrapped, I heard my father in the next room moaning. Then the sound of an ambulance. Unfamiliar heavy footsteps. A slamming door. The next day I woke up to the coolness of my mother's hand. She was at my bedside, comforting me, asking about my foot. Before I could ask about my father, the phone rang. My mother ran out of the room to answer it.

She returned a few minutes later in tears. It was the hospital. My father was dead. Cause of death: a heart attack suffered while running out of the stands to check on his younger son's football injury.

It was my fault. That's the first and only thing that ran through my head. My fault. My fault. If I hadn't been playing football so hard, if I hadn't gotten hurt, he would still be with me.

He was 47. I was 16. I was devastated. While my mother

collapsed in the back bedroom from grief, my grandfather and I called all the relatives. We summoned Ellery home from his Illinois-based air force unit, which he'd joined after high school. When we walked into our house following his all-day flight, I was standing there on my borrowed crutches (I'd been too distraught to see a doctor about my foot). Before even saying hello, I said, "It was my fault. Ellery, it was all my fault." My mother heard me and screamed, "I don't ever want to hear you say that again!"

So I never said it again. But for the next year I felt it. In some ways, like when I see how much sports have affected my relationship with my family, I still feel it.

A day after the funeral I finally went to the hospital for my ankle. It was broken. I had hobbled around for four days on an untreated broken ankle. My father would have been proud of my fortitude, at least. But it was too late for that. I could only hope to carry on some of his tough traditions and spirit. Unfortunately for some weak-kneed, prima donna baseball players, I think that's what happened.

• • •

As soon as my ankle healed, I resumed my attempt to go through life at the head of the race, only now with more fury. Because suddenly I had no choice. My father could no longer take no for an answer. My mom went to work at a plastics plant across from Bertea, and I went to work on kicking the world in the ass.

I soon learned I could do this through baseball, more than any other sport, simply because I was damn good at it. And so I spent more and more time with the game, not because of any of this "national pastime" rot but because this was my ticket to becoming the authority my father had once been.

My existence became baseball: for the school team, for local semipro teams like the El Monte Cardinals and Crawford's Market, even for a Night Owl League team that didn't play with a baseball but a softball. Don't laugh—Jackie Robinson once played in that league. I was there under an assumed name so that my school coach, who hated softball, wouldn't find out. Looking back, maybe I should have chosen a more nondescript pseudonym. The coach took one look at the name, figured out it was me, and suspended me for a game. Never again will I call myself Peter Waver.

Although I'd never talk back to that coach—any coach—when he suspended me, I said to myself, Fine, if they don't think I'm playing by their rules, I'll make my own. I'll become an umpire. And I did. Imagine that. Besides all those games in the outfield, I began spending time behind the plate at $5 a game, and at $2 on the bases. I don't mind saying that I've spent time in the same profession as John McSherry. And although I wasn't as fat as McSherry, I *was* a better umpire. I certainly didn't let any old, wrinkled, mustached manager mess with me.

When my grandfather helped us become one of the first houses in the neighborhood to have a television set—about a year after they came out—I began watching baseball. Every week I invited all the kids over to gather around the old RCA and hoot and holler, asking only that they follow one special rule: Nobody sit in the old brown easy chair. Nobody even touch it. That chair, placed in front of the TV, smelling and feeling like something sacred, was reserved for my grandfather. About the only time I remember him leaving it was when he discovered that, during an earlier lawn-mowing session, he'd accidentally cut its new antenna wire in half.

He had sat in the chair so long that it had grown saggy and coarse. But it was his. In this way, his own quiet way, he taught me that when you remove all the trappings, about the only thing a man really needs in life is a place to sit. My grandfather had his chair, and many years later I had the end of the bench nearest home plate.

As a manager I rarely moved from that spot, for a simple reason—your regulars had to walk past you and make themselves available for your advice at least three times a game.

Because I stuck to one spot, a fan could often tell the mood of my club from where everybody else sat. Usually, in my first year managing a team, the players sat bunched up right next to me. By the second year they'd be spread out across the middle of the bench. Not that players thought I grew increasingly tough, but by my final year as a manager many of them would be hugging the other end of the dugout, some of them even sitting outside it. The space between us . . . I don't know if even my father could have swum it. It was a gap, all right: a credibility gap. The more the players realized they'd be held accountable for their actions, the farther away they moved. Not just from me but from many managers. But where other managers may have moved too, I never did. Not in my seat selection, not in anything. Sometimes I wonder how many more World Series victories I'd have now if we'd met each other halfway.

The more I played and followed baseball as a teenager, the better I became, which meant the more competitive I became. I challenged guys to jump in the school swimming pool with me to see who could hold his breath the longest. I held impulsive footraces down the street. My buddy Vic Riesau and I would scream at each other over, for pete's sake, a game of Ping-Pong. Ping-Pong. One day I challenged him to a game in which I would hold my paddle in the crook of my elbow. He laughingly accepted the challenge, and then, in front of the local YMCA crowd, I whipped him. His biggest problem was that, to him, it was just ping-pong. To me, it was one more sport in which you could challenge someone— even your buddy—and then beat him.

Of course, as I already had a tendency to do, I took the competition with Riesau too far. One day in 1946, when I'd just turned 17, we were standing on the steps of the school's student union slapping each other as if boxing. I was shouting that I could kick his butt, he was claiming that if this were a real fight, I'd be on my ass. Up came one of our baseball coaches, who had been watching this scene and had what he thought was a brilliant idea. I remember the words like a right hand to the jaw: "You guys want to fight each other so bad," he said, "why don't you enter the Golden Gloves?"

Gloves? A real fight in a real school tournament? A legal test of my toughness? At first I thought, Wait a minute. Riesau was 6-foot-3, I was still a scrawny 5-foot-11. Riesau was not just tough but cool. Not everybody had a father who worked across the street from the school, running a barbershop called Al's Tonsorial Parlor. And Riesau had a score to settle with me: once at the YMCA, just fooling around, I had decked him.

I was worried about the idea of a real fight. But as soon as the coach issued the challenge, it didn't matter what I thought. I had mouthed off for too long to back down now. And Vic couldn't have been more excited. "Can they guarantee that we'll fight each other?" he asked the coach. The coach said they would do their best, and that was enough for Riesau, so it had to be enough for me. We were two punks who suddenly became light heavyweights.

The city tournament shaped up like this: In the first match Riesau was fighting some stiff, I was fighting another stiff, and if we both won, we'd fight each other. Then the winner of our grudge match would fight for the Pasadena Junior College championship. It sounded too juicy to be true, and of course it was.

In the first match the stiff stuffed Riesau upside the head, knocking him on his butt and his pride, knocking him out. Me, I won easily, but as soon as Riesau lost, I didn't care. The only reason I'd entered this event was gone. I didn't really want to fight this guy who'd beaten my buddy. Among his other character flaws, he was an offensive lineman on the school's football team.

But I had no choice. Second round, me against the hog lineman. The match started strong and then continued strong—too strong. For two three-minute rounds he and I slugged each other until we could no longer stand. He won the first round, I won the second; it had been a fair and hard fight.

One problem. The matches were three rounds. To this day Ellery remembers falling six feet out of the stands laughing while he watched me and the hog lineman play pattycake with each other for the entire third round, afraid to throw a punch for fear of falling on our faces. What began as a fight was ending as a senior prom. With a minute left in the fight, just as we'd started whispering sweet things into each other's ears—"You bastard, if you don't quit soon, you're going to kill me"—he actually broke our clinch. In what seemed like a delirious fit, he spun away from me and headed toward a neutral corner. In what was definitely a delirious fit, I swung my fist after him and hit him in the back of the head. He was knocked dizzy. And I was ruled the winner. Yes, a hit in the back of the head is legal, as long as it's not with a fastball. I was one match from becoming Golden Gloves champion.

But this victory was not a good thing. In more ways than one, it was the second-worst thing that could have happened. Because now I had to face the school's quarterback in the finals. It could only have been worse if I'd been a few pounds lighter and had to fight in the middleweight division finals. That featured the school's best boxer, a tough son of a bitch whose ability was aided by the fact that he was a deaf-mute and couldn't hear the bell that ended each round. But that's another story.

This quarterback had really boxed in his previous matches, and that scared me. But the damnedest thing happened. Turns out he had seen me slug and scratch, and that apparently scared him. He had also just seen me clobber that guy in the back of the head, which also possibly scared him. Or maybe he was just shy and didn't want to be my dancing partner. Whatever the reason, as we prepared to leave the locker room and walk to the ring, my opponent stopped and ran back to a toilet. And there he stayed. Standing alone in front of his porcelain refuge, he started hacking out a smoker's cough and holding his stomach and claiming that he was ill.

Some thought it was food, others thought it was his constant smoking, but I knew better. I saw something in his eyes that I would see many years later, in many pitchers' eyes as they stood on the mound with opponents crowding the bases. It was nervousness. It was butterflies that had not just danced in his stomach but flown up his throat. Only poets think butterflies never do more than dance in your stomach. The quarterback finally admitted it too. He was too nervous to fight and was last seen with his head inside that toilet. I was the winner by default. The champion by a dry heave.

But then the promoters panicked. They asked me if I'd like to at least fight for the title. How would I like to fight the guy I'd fought the night before, the guy I'd fought literally cheek to cheek? I told them, in so many words, "You gotta be shitting me."

Then the brother of the guy I beat the night before comes running down from the stands, in blue jeans and a T-shirt, and challenges me. "What the hell is going on here?" I asked. "What does it take for a guy to win a fight by default?" I finally grabbed my trophy, jumped out of the ring, and ran as fast I could, occasionally glancing over my shoulder to make sure I wasn't being followed by some guy talking sign language.

Even with the default win—or maybe because of it—I became cockier than ever. My razzing of rivals was reaching professional standards, while my jeering at friends was nearly getting me killed. Talk to them today and they'll say I was just a confident young man. Ask them back then and they'd talk about hating me.

All of which led to my initiation into my older brother's Pasadena Junior College fraternity, Sigma Lambda Phi. My brother attended PJC like me before going off to Santa Clara. It was a normal fraternity in that they'd been kicked off campus long before I arrived. They were a lovely group of guys who couldn't wait to take a couple of strong paddles to my butt. Not all the time: only after I'd been sitting bare-assed on ice. And of course they liked to make me shine their shoes. But that wasn't the worst of it. The worst came when they blindfolded their pledge class and took us up five miles of winding canyon road into the mountains north of Los Angeles. In the back of the car were just my buddy Doug Gorrie and I. We were their only two pledges. We soon learned why.

On top of one of those mountains the frat rats stripped us down to our underwear, dumped oil and flour on us, covered us in lead paint, and then drove home. Without us. We were stranded, miles from decency and civilization. Using tremendous foresight, I'd taped a dollar bill to the inside of my thigh before we left Pasadena. A lot of good it did us, when the only way to make a phone call was with a dime. We were lost and embarrassed until I realized we couldn't stay up in the mountains all night and watch our tears freeze. It was then I faced the fact that if you've got a problem, you deal with it, no matter how you end up looking.

If you have to fight with Carl Yastrzemski to help the Boston Red Sox become winners, then you do it. And if you have to walk down the middle of a highway almost naked in order to get a ride home, you do that. So we hiked five miles down the mountain, found a highway, and stuck out our oily thumbs. The first driver who passed us felt such sympathy that he stopped. We had to spread newspapers over the backseat of the car before he let us sit down, and our teeth chattered the entire way home, but this guy took us all the way to my buddy's front door. A half hour later the frat rats arrived there from their hangout, and all Doug could do was laugh. Me, I was back at my house, in bed, sick. But were we hot shit or what?

We were so hot that our hangout had to be an ice cream store—Larry's. Unlike the fancy gourmet places of today, it looked just the way this sort of place is supposed to look. It had everything from a blue-and-white sign dangling out front to jukeboxes on every table to back booths where the cool guys like us could put up their sneakers. It was here we would plan such things as driving around town with a big water drum and a hose. My buddy would pump the drum and I would aim the hose. We'd drive down Colorado Boulevard and drench half the juvenile population of Pasadena and then speed off—only once into the waiting arms of the police. Even then, they only made us dump the water out. And we dumped it (accidentally, of course) on their shoes. What did the cops do? They cleaned off their shoes, of course. We thought we were damn near untouchable.

It was also in Larry's Ice Cream Store that we'd plan such things as sneaking into the Rose Bowl. Not just the stadium but the actual New Year's Day game. It would be an annual event with us, our own little crowning of the Rose Queen. Call it our rose badge of courage. One way in was to tear the ticket so that you were only giving the usher the stub. Once inside, you passed the rest of the ticket back out to your buddy, who walked right through. A better, more daring way was to jump in the middle of a group of people and walk through quickly while pointing to the guy a couple of yards behind you and shouting, "He's got me!" Then you ran like hell before the usher really got you.

• • •

I have an affinity for the Rose Bowl for other reasons. Later I would work there during the off-season, numbering seats and cleaning restrooms and even weeding the rose gardens. And the Rose Bowl was really where my professional baseball career started. After my second year at Pasadena Junior College, I went through high school graduation ceremonies there two days before my first pro game.

Yes, unbelievably, even with all my off-the-field bullshit I'd been noticed as a baseball prospect. A Brooklyn Dodgers scout named Tom Downey was the first to tell me that, so of course I just had to tell everybody else. And that is pretty much how I became a Dodger. Not because I wanted to play with Jackie Robinson. Not because I wanted to become a member of baseball's lovable Bums. No, I became a Dodger simply because I bragged so much about this first Dodgers scout that other scouts, notably one from the Boston Braves, thought I wouldn't talk to them. Some might look at this as destiny. I prefer to look at it as the first time my mouth cost me money.

Downey, who also signed Duke Snider, said that his first impressions of me were formed when I was too young to wear a uniform but would still show up to watch those El Monte Cardinals play in the semipro league. I got my big break that way when a fly ball smacked El Monte center fielder Dick Gorrie in the head and knocked him out. They needed an extra player, so out of the bleachers I ran, directly to left field, and played the rest of the game in my blue jeans. Soon I had my own uniform, which Downey, who worked for the St. Louis Cardinals at the time, supplied. When top baseball executive Branch Rickey left the Cardinals to join the Dodgers, Downey went with him, and the semipro team became the El Monte Dodgers. And I was on my way to being a Bum.

I learned one more of life's lessons just before joining the Dodgers. The schoolroom was in Mexico, while I was with a winter traveling team from Pasadena. The teacher, the master, was Jackie Price. Strange as it may sound, I never knew baseball was allowed to be funny until I met Price, whose big league career spanned just seven games, in 1946 for Cleveland. Talk about Al Schacht and Max Patkin all you like. Read books about Bob Uecker and Joe Garagiola all you want. But understand, Price was baseball's true clown. While touring with him that winter, we first figured something was unusual when, while he was playing shortstop, two snakes crawled out of his shirt. And that was just the start.

You've heard that cliché about a guy who could fall out of bed and get a base hit? Well, Price could probably do that literally. How can I make this claim? Because I saw Price get hits while hanging upside down from a bar, and upside down from the batting screen, and simply standing on his head. If you're trying to imagine it, don't—it'll just make you queasy. He didn't even need a pitcher to help him in his batting tricks. He could also throw two balls up and hit one on the ground and one up in the air at the same time. Shows you how smart I am—I learned that one from him.

Jackie Price was also an all-thrill fielder. While playing for Indianapolis, he once caught the final out of the triple-A World Series behind his back. He could catch balls in his shirt, provided any resident reptiles were in agreement. He'd get one of us to shoot a ball out of a small cannon from behind home plate, and then he'd catch the ball while driving a jeep across the outfield. A stick-shift jeep. And what an arm. He could throw three balls at once to three different players. He could put a ball in a sling and throw it 600 feet—which, unfortunately, he did one day that winter while standing at home plate in a tiny park in the border town of Mexicali. I say unfortunately, because 600 feet from home plate was the middle of an adjoining bullfight arena. When teammates asked me to chase the ball down, I told them they could go to hell, and I hired some kids instead.

Even with all his tricks, Price might have been a more readily accepted big league ballplayer except for those damn snakes. I had no problems with him wearing the snakes in his jersey—after all, it was his jersey. But when they kept popping out on ground balls . . . Actually, even the snakes wouldn't have been so bad if, when Price was asked for his autograph, he wouldn't sometimes pull the snakes out and hit fans on the ass with them.

They say the great ones' careers rarely fade gracefully on the field and usually end in tragedy or farce elsewhere. So it was with Price, who saw his career expire in farce on a train. While traveling with the Cleveland Indians from Los Angeles to San Diego, he let several snakes loose. If only he hadn't chosen a car filled with a group of people whose sense of humor mirrors that of your average Romanian general. I am speaking, of course, of women bowlers. A few screams later, just loud enough for Cleveland manager Lou Boudreau to hear, and Jackie Price's career was history. My memory of him, of course, was not. I learned this game could withstand a little levity—just a little, mind you—a policy that guys like George Thomas and Kurt Bevacqua could later be thankful I possessed.

The summer following our Mexico tour, in 1947, my aspiring outfield dreams and I signed our first Dodgers contract, for a cute little $1,200 bonus. Less than 24 hours after my 12th-grade graduation in the Rose Bowl, I packed all my clothes—two pairs of jeans and five T-shirts—into a tin suitcase. I packed all my baseball gear into a little black doctor's bag that had once belonged to my grandfather. And I jumped on a Greyhound bus bound for Santa Barbara, where I would play my first season for the Dodgers' Class C team there. It was one of 28 Dodgers minor league teams. I was one of 750 Dodgers players. I was making $125 a month. So for once I kept my mouth shut.

First thing I did when I arrived in Santa Barbara was pay 75 cents for an army cot and another 75 cents for an army blanket. And without even checking out the local housing situation, I moved into the Santa Barbara clubhouse. I padded the cot with cushions from the stands, moved the cot into the shower area underneath the hanging sweaty shirts, and then perfected the neatest move of my early career. Every morning I would jump out of bed and run outside before William Hitchcock, the club's general manager, showed up. He probably wouldn't have been crazy about having a teenager living in his bathroom. But it was worth it. Falling asleep to the dripping sound of that day's uniform, surrounded by the smell of that day's sweat, helps you remember what you're there for. Ballplayers, you may have noticed, don't live like that anymore.

I did little more than endure in the three months that

constituted my 1947 season. It was the following February (1948), in the first of 39 straight spring trainings I attended, that I really began to learn. And with good reason. I was among the first group of players to use the Dodgers' brand-new spring training facility in a little-known central Florida town. Perhaps you've heard of Vero Beach? And Dodgertown?

I walked in that spring about the same time the facility's doors opened after the club moved south from Pensacola. I walked into a Dodgertown barracks, dropped my tin suitcase and black doctor's bag, ran back outside, tugged at my short hair, and gasped. This couldn't be real. This had to be heaven. There were fields as far as the mind could dream. These barracks were right next to those fields—free barracks, with free beds, and not even under sweaty uniforms. There was class and comfort and, of course, real live Dodgers. Heaven.

Five minutes into camp I had a slight change of opinion: this, I astutely observed, was hell. First, I was surrounded by hundreds of idiots just like me. There were so many of us that we didn't just have different numbers that went way past 100, but also different-colored jerseys. There were so many of us that the instructors had no idea who was hurt, so players who were injured from the waist down just wore white sanitary socks instead of the blue stirrups. And those injured from the waist up wore a gray cap instead of a blue cap. Not that any of those distinctions mattered, because we were all treated the same—like we'd never played a day of baseball in our lives.

Dodgers boss Branch Rickey, using then-innovative methods, divided us into groups, and each group spent the day working its way around the six diamonds in 30-minute intervals. For your first session you might work on bunting. A whistle would blow and you'd run one lap around your field, and then you'd run to a different field, where, after coaches took roll call, you'd spend a half hour working on sliding. Another whistle, another lap, another new field, and now you were working on getting a proper leadoff from first base. Or how to break up a double play.

The first key to surviving this camp was, of course, realizing that fundamentals were the most valuable tools a player can possess, something few players today seem to understand. The second key was to avoid, at all costs, being in a group whose sliding drill was at 8 A.M.— because they used a sawdust sliding pit, and you'd walk around all day trying to shake the stuff off your uniform. The final key was to lose all fear of snakes. To reach Diamond Six, where they sent the lowest level of players, we had to walk through a vacant lot that contained snakes. And they weren't safely buttoned inside some guy's shirt. It was the fastest some of us ran all day.

By the time camp ended after six weeks, you had either quit or were so fundamentally sound that the majority of mistakes you made that year involved bad hops. As it turned out, the best thing for me about those training methods was that I stole them shamelessly when I became a manager. Every one.

Long after Branch Rickey died, his fundamentals lived with me while I managed such teams as the 1967 Boston Red Sox and the 1972–73 Oakland Athletics and the 1984 San Diego Padres. They became my emblem as I tried to teach the Dodgers way to scores of players who thought Branch Rickey was a brand of chewing tobacco. Bunt the ball into the ground. Hit the cutoff man. Take the extra base. Rickey's insistence on the tiny and fundamental things was an eccentricity that led to one of the most consistently strong teams in baseball history, the Dodgers of the late forties and early fifties. And it was an eccentricity that stuck to my teams, stuck hard, stayed with me even into the 1980s despite attempts by younger players and critics to strip it off with phrases like "old-fashioned" and claims like "The game has passed Dick Williams by." I won a lot of games playing the "old-fashioned" way. Many modern ballplayers fail to realize that playing without fundamentals is like eating without a knife and fork. Sure, you might get full. But you'll make a mess doing it. And sure as hell, the guy using the silverware will get full first. Sounds simple and dumb. Like fundamentals. If believing that and believing in Branch Rickey mean that the game has passed me by—well, wherever it's headed, I hope it has a nice trip.

Following that first Dodgertown spring we took an 18-hour flight from Vero Beach to the West Coast, where, after a short session of extended training at San Bernardino, I returned to Class C Santa Barbara for my first full season there. Talk about a long way from Ebbets Field. This time I wasn't so scared or shy or serious. Now I was a veteran—and dangerous. With the memories of all those prospects making my skin crawl, I knew I had to do something to stand out. So I did, with—big surprise here—my crazy temper.

Well, maybe I wasn't crazy that first full year. But what do you call charging in from center field to fight a guy at third base because he'd spiked my pal Bobby Duretto? And what do you call that game in Stockton when I took on one of the DiMaggio boys? Okay, so it wasn't Joe, but he still had fists. It was Vince DiMaggio, and early one game he'd made the mistake of dancing around one of my fly balls that got hung up in the wind before he caught it for the third out. Later in the game another fly ball of mine died in front of him, and he let it drop to earth, giving me a double. While I was on second base, I couldn't help but comment on his change of fortune. "Take that, you showboating son of a bitch!" I shouted. He dropped his glove and ran at me, and I left the base and ran at him, and only a couple of quick infielders separated us. Even then, as a silly kid player, I had my rules. And I'd decided to fight to enforce them. One rule was, and still is: if you're going to be a hot dog, fine . . . but you better make the catch.

The only thing that bothered me more than the opposition that first year was—another surprise coming—the umpires. Whenever they made a call that hurt my team, they became part of the opposition. We got so mad at one of them, a guy named Cecil Carlucci, that before one game we put a dead gopher in his shoe. He came running out of his dressing room, shouting, "Williams did this, Williams did this!" My career was only a couple of months old, and already I had a reputation. Good thing old Cecil only made it to triple-A.

I was a good ballplayer— I swung the bat well and hustled my ass off— but I always had to be something more. I had to be the intimidating ballplayer, the mean ballplayer, the guy who left no doubt about his intentions. Remember: the ultimate authority. This even extended outside the ballpark. Once I nearly got killed at a local carnival trying to expose the workers as cheaters. The game was, you drop three plates and cover a circle and you win a stuffed animal. Some teammates and I kept trying but never quite covered the circle. I hate to get beat, and I was getting slaughtered, so I casually walked around to the back of the booth. Turns out some worker kept bumping the circle so it was impossible for us to win. As soon as I discovered him, some other carnies discovered me. They chased us back to our cars, but we were able to outrace them off the grounds, which gave us the right to spend the rest of the evening driving around town and laughing our asses off. In those days, at least for one 18-year-old guy whose life could be shaped as easily as his hair, failure was so unheard of that it was funny.

In that summer of 1948, on the second floor of a creaky frame house belonging to Mrs. Massa, four of us lived in one little room: me, Bobby Duretto, Gus Stathos, and Sam Latino. Eight bucks per person per week. One room. Four beds. No closets, just hooks to hold our jeans. One adjoining bathroom. And an old lady waiting at the bottom of the stairs every week for her rent. Living in that cramped space brought us closer together but, typically for me, ended up making the other guys want to wring my neck. Like when I'd borrow

Duretto's car and stay out with it past curfew, then Duretto would get in trouble because the manager only saw the car.

Just as I tried too hard to impress off the field, I often tried too hard on the field. Time for my first failure. After being recalled to Class AA Fort Worth from Santa Barbara late in the 1948 season, I slumped badly while trying to make the huge adjustment. I ended the year batting .202, and then—if you can believe this—I needed something to boost my confidence. The following year, in 1949, under a Fort Worth summer sun that taught me to play with a headache, I found that something. In fact, I found two of them. In the course of that memorable year I had my butt kicked by Bobby Bragan and my cheek kissed by Norma Mussato. Combined, the two were enough to end my childhood and start my career. On the spot.

Norma Mussato first. She is always first. She was a sweet Italian girl from a strict family that lived a mile down the street in Fort Worth from me and my roommate, Joe Landrum. Fort Worth impressed me as gigantic and hot. Behind every clump of sagebrush either a fistfight or a new romance waited, and I wanted to live it all. Little did I know: a mile down the street was waiting the rest of my life.

Throughout most of the 1949 season Norma and I didn't know each other, and understandably so. She liked opera, I liked extra innings. She liked getting dressed up and going dancing, I liked driving around town while spitting into a cup. She was class, I was crass. We shared only one thing, but it was something more than a vision or a dream.

What we shared was a milkman. His name was R. B. Dill, from Vandervoort Dairy, and he serviced both Norma's house and the driveway outside our garage. R. B. Dill spent the entire summer telling Joe and me, and Norma and her sister, that we should meet each other—none of us listening until finally Joe and I became too lonely to fear something as silly as a blind date. So one morning we opened the garage door and asked R. B. if we could meet these girls. He immediately set it up, and our destiny was determined in as long as it takes your heart to leap. We met the girls after a ballgame. Our car, our treat. Joe jumped in the driver's seat, Norma walked around the car to get in the front passenger side, and then . . . something came over me. The only other time I had this feeling was when I'd try to score from second base on a single and see the catcher grab the throw just as I arrived at the plate. It was the feeling like something big is about to happen, if only I *make* it happen.

So I did. I lost my head and made what was probably the most important aggressive move of my life. I grabbed Norma before she could get into the front seat and casually shoved her into the back. With me.

Both Norma and her sister were beautiful, but something inside me told me Norma was the choice. For then and forever. Maybe it was the way she talked like she didn't give a damn that I was a baseball player. Or that I was anybody but Dick Williams. Once in the backseat next to me, like anybody who spent more than five minutes with me was prone to do, she suspected I was crazy. A couple of hours into the date, when we were well into our second barbecued beef sandwich at the Pig Stand, she was certain I was crazy. Maybe it was because I asked her to marry me. I was only half joking.

At the time I had to settle for spending the remaining two months of the season squiring her around in a 1931 black Model A with roll-down backseats (a fact that may not make this book if she reads it first). But five years later, in 1954, she did marry me. And she hasn't permanently left me since, which leaves no doubt as to which is really the crazy one. We've even managed to live happily ever after, me and Norma—and R. B., whom I honored by becoming a spokesman for Vandervoort milk.

I only wish I'd met Norma earlier in the 1949 season. That way, maybe, in my bliss I'd have been less inclined to kill the other person who greatly affected my life that season and later—the Fort Worth player/manager Bobby Bragan.

Bragan was a former big league catcher and infielder who had come to Fort Worth 10 days before I made my first appearance there in 1948. It was his first job as a manager. He later managed parts of seven big league seasons, with Pittsburgh, Cleveland, and the Braves of both Milwaukee and Atlanta. He only won 48 percent of his big league games as a manager and never managed a team higher than fifth place. But there should be a note under my records reading: SEE BOBBY BRAGAN. Because a bit of every one of my wins belongs to him.

Bragan was the first manager to discipline me one on one, and thus taught me *how* to discipline. In other words, he was the first to make me run with the pitchers because he thought I was fat, not to mention being the first to run me in 100-degree heat. Of course, in doing all this, he took a cocky loudmouth with no direction and steered him on a path straight to Brooklyn. You did it his way, the Dodgers way, or not at all—meaning you sat your butt on the bench. I don't know how much that tight fist helped other players, but it certainly saved my career. And I have to think that, by using his same methods many years later, I probably saved an aimless career or two as well. In the case of San Diego, some say I may even have saved an aimless franchise, although nobody who has even seen the inside of Joan Kroc's pocketbook would ever buy that.

Bragan was not so much a manager as an instructor, which I believe is what you need in the minor leagues. Nowadays all these bosses of minor league clubs are doing little more than trying to win and make a name for themselves. They've forgotten that they're only there for the players, and have instead become just like the players, all trying to make the show. This is why I feel organizations should pay all minor league managers the same, no matter what classification, and move them around every year to expose them to all the different players, and in general make them realize that they're there to teach. If you win, fine—but that's gravy. Teach in

the minor leagues, win in the big leagues. That's what winners do. While they're at it, these owners should pay minor
league managers more, just like society should pay its teach-
ers more. This inequity is particularly loud in baseball, where
guys making $25,000 a year are teaching guys to make
$3,000,000 a year.

So Bragan, age 32, stocky and slow with a dark-lined face,
speaking with a thick drawl that sharpened itself into words
resembling scratches, was a teacher. A great teacher. Like the
time he taught me I should never take for granted something that will keep me alive. He was talking about baseball,
of course, but the lesson was delivered through my insistence
on juggling. That's right, I had a habit of juggling three
baseballs before games, just to pass the time. He never said
anything until once when, in a train station during a trip, I
decided to juggle three apples from our box lunches. During
one routine a teammate, Preston Ward, threw a half-eaten
apple that hit me in the nose. I promptly began juggling the
core and threw a whole apple back at him. A mistake, because the apple hit the ground and rolled between the legs
of you-know-who. The next day I didn't play, because, as
Bragan said, you don't throw things you're supposed to eat.
Is it any wonder that, later in my managerial career, I despised the San Diego Chicken and tried to keep him off the
field? Chickens are for eating, not for making fun of the organization that pays your bills.

Bragan also taught me less subtle things. Like, it's okay
for a manager to show how much he hates losing. In fact, the
players respect that kind of manager more. Boy, did we respect him the time he got so mad in Shreveport that he hurled
a ball out of the park. When the umpires threw him out, he
did a blind man routine all the way to the clubhouse. Took
him 10 minutes, using his bat as a cane. Looking back, it was
a pretty insensitive routine. But it showed us that he cared.

Or how about the time in Oklahoma City he was so convinced an umpire had screwed our team out of an important

run that he came to the park the next day with a photo of our catcher blocking home plate and tagging the guy out. Before the umpires could gather at home for the pregame meeting, he pasted that photo on the plate. He was thrown out of the game before there *was* a game. How much have times changed? The manager who replaced me in San Diego many years later, Steve Boros, was once thrown out of a game for bringing a videotape of the previous night's bad call to home plate.

Bragan also taught me, while he was at it, that it's okay for a manager to do everything within the rules to win. Again, it only shows how much you care. Like the time he cared enough to send up eight pinch hitters for the same batter before he finally got the right matchup. Or like the times he'd order a left-handed pitcher to warm up in the bullpen before the game, leading the opposition to believe the left-hander would be starting, while the real starter was a right-hander who was throwing outside the fence. This trick is impossible to do in today's modern stadiums, but that doesn't mean you can't stock the bullpen mounds with decoys. Something that was impossible even back then was placing an extra infielder outside the first-base line, in foul territory, on a bunt play. But damned if he didn't try it.

One more thing Bragan taught me was the importance of running. If you think my world championship teams ran, you should have seen Fort Worth. We ran so much that once the St. Louis Cardinals' farm team in Houston soaked the field to nearly all mud before our visit. And then when our first hitter reached base, the Houston ground crew ran out and placed hurdles between first and second. After a while we won and didn't even need to run, because our opponents were too worried about that to concentrate on the little things like pitching and defense. That's really how speed kills.

Bobby Bragan, like Chet Laabs and Jackie Price, is a man forgotten by baseball history. But not by me. By the time I left Fort Worth following the 1949 season, as an All-Star outfielder who now knew the difference between cocky and smart, there was only one way Bragan failed to influence me. One day he called me to his office and told me to stop dating Norma. Told me it wasn't smart to be hanging around foreigners. This was Texas in the forties. And the warning was coming from a man I admired as much as I had ever admired anyone. But this was also me and my life. And this edict, as I quickly told him, was bullshit. "I like that foreigner very much," I told him. And then I walked out of the room before I did anything I'd have regretted. I stomped outside into the thick Texas air, took a breath so deep that it hurt, and decided that maybe what I'd just done was stupid and might cost me my young career. But maybe, after 20 years, I was finally growing up. Maybe I was learning which fights were worth fighting. Maybe my career had just taken its first step in the right . . .

Nah. Most likely, I was just in love. Which is entirely possible, even for a dog-beating, DiMaggio-fighting, running-like-hell-after-his-father's-memory wise guy.

REAL BUMS

It was a winter day in 1949, although the only way you knew
it was winter in southern California was that my old buddies
and I could be found leaning on a bar and peering through
the smoke at Jimmy's Playroom on the corner of Lake and
Washington in Pasadena. When we weren't playing golf, this
was our new adult hangout. We chose it over the other local
places serving beer mainly because of its historic location—
next door to Larry's Ice Cream Store.

We could walk past Larry's blue sign, laugh, and then
duck into the dark stench of Jimmy's, hands in our pockets
and smirks on our faces, because now we were men. Those
of us not legally old enough to be men could walk in the
front door of Larry's, back through his kitchen, out his back
door, then go up five paces and enter Jimmy's through his
back door.

Hangouts like Jimmy's gave this Texas League All-Star
outfielder a place to throw out his chest and slurp a few cold
ones. I was doing the chest bit one winter day at Jimmy's
when, between beers and eight ball, I was handed a local
newspaper that contained a story featuring my name and these

words: "Because of his fine season, Williams will be returning home next summer to play for the Dodgers' triple-A team in Hollywood."

I guess "surprise" isn't the right word. I nearly fell off the stool. Hollywood was one of the Dodgers' three triple-A teams. One of the last steps before Ebbets Field. A big promotion from double-A Fort Worth. A chance to change milkmen. And a move to someplace damn near my hometown. Knowing that my buddy Irv Noren, a left-handed hitting outfielder, had made that jump a year earlier, I spent the rest of the winter thinking it was going to be my turn.

I wasn't deterred when a contract arrived in the mail assigning me to Fort Worth. I wasn't deterred upon learning it was for only $500 a month, just a $150-a-month raise. I signed it, figuring I'd sign a new one when I arrived in Hollywood. I wasn't even deterred when, after a couple of weeks of training camp at Vero Beach in the spring of 1950, I found myself assigned to the Fort Worth group. I guessed they must just be keeping my ego in check until the final days of camp, when I would get assigned to my real team. I thought again of Irv Noren.

With a couple of weeks left in camp, when players began making living arrangements for the coming summer, it finally sank in. Like cleats into mud. I was still with the Fort Worth group. I was going to remain with the Fort Worth group. For the entire summer. Goodbye, Hollywood. I'd been a fool to believe otherwise. I'd been a fool to believe what I read in the newspapers—something I would never be accused of again. I'd been a fool to believe in my own arrogance. In my mature wisdom I concluded that my only recourse was to become a bigger fool: I asked for a meeting with Branch Rickey.

I walked into his small, carpeted office in Dodgertown— just a phone, a metal desk, pictures on the wall, and a disheveled man with eyebrows nearly as thick as his cigar. He peered at me from behind tiny wire-rimmed glasses and brushed some ashes off his guyabera shirt, never altering his gaze. I knew then this was no ordinary meeting with a baseball man. This was an audience.

I slowly stated my case. I'd had a good year in Fort Worth. I deserved to be promoted. If nothing else, I deserved more money. After I became a manager, this same spiel was sung to me by many young players over the course of many springs. If they ever wondered why I didn't throw them out of my office, why I even seemed sympathetic, this is the reason. I was once one of them.

While I talked, Rickey just stared. When I was finally finished, he said, just as slowly, "Why are you worrying about what kind of money you make in the minor leagues, or what minor league team you're on? None of it matters until you get to the majors. Nothing matters until you play your way to Brooklyn . . . and you can't play your way to Brooklyn by sitting on the bench in Hollywood. If you're any good, we'll find you in Fort Worth. We'll find you in Timbuktu."

I walked out of there not knowing whether to be flattered or flustered. Like Eddie Stanky once said of a conversation with Rickey: I'd gotten $100,000 worth of advice and no raise. But I had been humbled. And maybe that was more valuable than anything. That season at Fort Worth, realizing that nobody ever moped his way out of the minor leagues, I hit .300. Then guess what happened. Yes, my contract was purchased by the Dodgers. The following spring I would have at least some chance to make the big league team and go north to Brooklyn. So who needs Hollywood?

First, though, I had to make a slight detour. Actually, in keeping with my penchant to never do anything half-assed, it was one hell of a detour. It was the winter following the 1950 season; I was in Cuba playing for the Almendares Scorpions Club, one of four teams in the Havana Winter League, which was then open to Americans. Today only Cubans play baseball in Cuba, but then the country was like a modern-day Puerto Rico, with the people friendly and willing to do anything to help Americans. Even if it meant pitching batting practice to Americans. This much I learned one day when, to my shock, while I was standing in the batting cage before a game with Marianao, the pitching mound was overtaken by this tall, strong right-hander who had a uniform and locker but no place on the roster. He was a local student leader who, at the time, had all the national clout of a school punk. But as with other local punks who liked to pitch batting practice and act like a player, the team let him.

And this is how I came to hit off Fidel Castro. Don't worry. He laid it in there, and I kicked his ass.

Although I had no further contact with Castro, in Cuba I also took batting practice against another future dictator. This one was a short, paunchy guy. Name of Tommy Lasorda. The problem was, his "batting practice" would occur in real games. He was a Dodgers prospect like me, but pitching for Marianao, he could never seem to get me out. Finally, one day he glared at me and shouted, "I'm going to hit you, you son of a bitch!" I shouted back, "Go on, hit me, it's only fair, seeing how hard I've been hitting you!" So he hit me. Threw a curveball that followed me right out of the batter's box and plunked me in the back. From that day I've admired and respected the future Los Angeles Dodgers manager.

When I was managing San Diego, it would have been natural for Lasorda and me to have a rivalry, but it just wasn't there. We both remembered a time when baseball players really played, really cared, so much so that if all else failed, you hit your opponent in the back with a curveball. And you never, ever let him see you apologize. Tommy may claim he bleeds blue, but he bleeds to win just like I do, and how can I hate a man like that?

Tommy and I also saw each other socially in Cuba. His wife, Jo, would cook us steaks at their little apartment. And he and I would do local promotions for the team, although that quickly stopped the time a radio commentator, just before interviewing us, laid a pistol on the table! Turns out he had it there as protection against surprise attacks by political enemies, who could pop up anywhere during those shaky times. But I wasn't absolutely sure. Maybe he was concerned that one of us would mercilessly rip another player. For the first time in my career, I did not.

Life, in general, was pretty good to me down there. I lived with three buddies in a rented home near the beach. All the games were played in the same place, Gran Stadium, a one-deck bowl seating about 35,000 fairly well-behaved fans. When I returned six years later, after Batista had taken power, people would cross the outfield carrying protest banners, and one demonstrator was even killed behind the left field fence. But in the winter of 1950 my world was still calm. For all of a month.

In November, back home in Pasadena, my mom received a letter addressed to me from the United States Government. It should have been stamped DETOUR. This ballplayer known for his fighting was being summoned to do it for real. The Korean War wasn't going to wait for me to catch my dreams. My draft notice had arrived. Oh, shit.

It would be nicer to write about how patriotic I felt. It would be easier to write that I willingly took up arms in defense of our country's values. It would also be dead wrong. I hated hearing about the letter. So close to making the big leagues, I was suddenly so far. I hurried out of my house to the nearest beach and ran along the shore as fast as I could, hoping that amid my sweat and sore lungs this letter would somehow disappear. But all that happened was that I got sand in my shoes. Which is just what it feels like to get drafted when you're on the verge of reaching Ebbets Field. I won't bullshit you. I was crushed.

I know it sounds terrible—all of this will sound terrible—but I delayed induction as long as possible. One of the owners of the Cuban team allowed me to use his address in Miami as my permanent address. That meant the draft notice needed to be transferred, and all the red tape took about a month, buying me more time with the team. I took my preinduction physical in Miami and then played for another month while those papers were being processed back in California.

I was given brief hope, and more time, when doctors shook their heads looking at a left knee I'd hurt as a high school junior. The injury was inflicted in a football game by a buddy who later became an opposing major league manager— Houston's Bob Lillis. The injury was a torn cartilage that didn't seem so awful in high school but then seemed much worse— thank God— when doctors frowned at it and ordered X rays.

But when the reports came back, I had passed. I was a Class C profile, meaning I probably wouldn't have to go to the front lines. But I'd still passed. Damn. I was supposed to report to Uncle in Pasadena on February 7, 1951, at 7 A.M.

I had a week to show up, and the Cuban owners kept me to the last minute by flying my mom and her new husband, Edmund Hodel, to Havana for a weekend to cheer me on. But seeing them, and dragging out my days with the Scorpions, only made things worse. When I finally left the Cuban tropics for what was becoming a crowded southern California, my spirits were at an all-time low. It was such fun to fight through traffic that February 7 morning to sign away the next, oh, what seemed like a hundred years of my life. Not until I reached the steps on the induction center, where I sat with my head in my hands, did I receive my first bit of hope. There, running up to meet me with that silly grin on his face, was my buddy Vic Riesau. Hot damn! He too was being inducted. At least I knew I wouldn't have to go through this torture alone.

All the recruits took a bus up to Fort Ord in Monterey, spent 10 days being processed there, and just when I caught a bad cold from working in their meat house, we were bused to Camp Roberts near San Luis Obispo. It was in the middle of rolling hills and long flat fields, with not a telephone pole or nonbarracks rooftop in sight. The officers said we were there because the surroundings looked and felt like Korea. Swell. The almost deadly quiet at night haunted me as I thought of the flashy pachanga bands of Cuba. I'd gone from the big league's doorstep to nowhere. My only hope was that with my buddy Riesau at my side I could somehow decorate this place in my own colors.

It started with our drill sergeant. He was from the South, which is about as surprising as an opera star being from Italy. He had a hilarious accent, or at least a bunch of us found it so hilarious that we mocked him behind his back. For once I wasn't the only young asshole on the block—this place was loaded with them. Soon we mocked him just loud enough so that he'd turn around and yell, "Who said that?" After a couple times of this, he'd tell us all to run in a circle with our rifles until we dropped.

I also passed the time by competing with Riesau in a sort of basic training olympics, which was easy because "events" were held every day from morning till night. My favorite was the crawl-under-the-machine-gun-fire dash. This was done by getting on your belly with your ass down and scrambling over such fun things as logs while machine-gun bursts whizzed above your head. Stand up and you're dead. Looking back, I probably should have planned this better. I decided to race Riesau about 10 seconds before the sergeant gave us the order to move. From our positions on our bellies, I spat out a little dust and turned to him and said, "I'll kick your ass this time." He was stunned but said, "Wrong, I'll kick your ass," and off we went. It was so impulsive that we nearly crawled our belts off and finished 20 yards ahead of everyone else. The sergeant thought this was funny, so he made us do it again. Who won? I don't remember—which should give you the answer.

My view of basic training was this: they were trying to make a soldier out of a guy who didn't want to be one. They'd give me a hand grenade and I'd throw it like a baseball. They'd say no, you have to cup it in your hand and throw it differently. I'd tell them, if my ass is on the line, I'm throwing that thing like a guy is trying to score on me in the bottom of the ninth. My ass, my way.

Ultimately, the army did nothing but make me miss baseball more than even I thought possible. First thing every morning, I'd scrounge around Camp Roberts for a newspaper sports section to read about all the top young spring training stars and inspect their pictures. I'd think, This guy is a puss, this guy doesn't have shit, and so on. Mostly they were stories and photographs that could have featured me. It didn't help that, in that spring of 1951, one of those touted rookie prospects was Mickey Mantle, whom I never said a word about.

I know I should have looked at basic training like I was preparing myself for my country, but all I could think about was the Dodgers. All my life I'd had only one goal in my puny brain, and now that goal was being moved out of my grasp without a fight. I think that's what bothered me most: that the army had taken me, and for the first time in my life I couldn't fight back. Even later, when I was thrown out of many baseball games, I'd stand just out of view of the umpires and, with the tiniest of whispers, fight back. In the army I possessed no such options. Or so I thought. But then three months into my tour of duty, with two weeks left in basic training, I figured a way out. Or at least my body figured a way. I'm still not sure what my mind had to do with all this. You can't will an injury, can you? I hope not.

One day I left some ditch during our field exercises and rode back to base on a chow truck for a camp baseball game. I was on my company team, and I wanted to make the Camp Roberts base team and avoid more ditches, so during this game I was hustling. In a late inning I found myself chasing a fly ball in center field. It was a home run, a ball that would surely go over the clifflike dropoff that served as the center field fence. But for some reason I kept chasing it. I chased to the dropoff and jumped and—whomp—fell on my butt as the ball fell on the ground, and we both tumbled down the ravine. I lay there in pain, but it was an interesting sort of pain. Because the most pain was in my bum left knee. My Section C beauty.

I spent that night in the barracks because I wasn't due back in the field until the next day. But the next day I couldn't walk. I hobbled over to sick bay, where doctors were overloaded with young assholes who'd taken the wrong way on a hike and gone six miles farther than scheduled. Because I was the last person the doctor saw—when you have a last name that begins with *W,* you get used to this—I received a final full blast of built-up anger.

"Where are your blisters?" he asked gruffly. I told him I didn't have any blisters. Then I showed him my knee. It was puffy, and when I moved it, it chirped like a cricket. The doctor actually seemed pleased. "Congratulations," he said. "You're the first one with something wrong with you." He called in another doctor, a Colonel Morbitt, a man whose name I will never forget, for reasons you'll soon see. Morbitt squeezed the knee and sent me hobbling to another room. When I was called back in 20 minutes later, Morbitt was frowning, and suddenly I was scared. What, I'll need an operation! The leg needs to come off?

"Soldier, I've got some bad news for you," he said, pausing while I turned white. "We're going to end your army career. You can't serve with this knee."

Bad news! I almost shouted with joy. I nearly embraced Colonel Morbitt with the fervor of a guy who had just stolen home—which, in a sense, I had. Instead, I calmly spent the next three days filling out papers that usually took a week, and then I was going, going, gone. How eager was I to get back to Pasadena? I walked out in front of Camp Roberts and stuck out my thumb to hitchhike there. A guy drove me right to my front door. Three months, three weeks, and three days after joining the army, I was a civilian again.

Appropriately, I'd made more money in my escape than

in my time in uniform. The army paid for your return home
from the site of your physical exam. My physical was in Miami,
so I was given transportation fare from there to Pasadena at
three cents a mile. Considering I was able to hitch home by
just buying this guy gas, it turned out to be more money than
I'd made in my entire time in the service.

At the time I didn't analyze my getaway. Why should I?
All I knew was that as soon as I took those khakis off, my
knee felt better. The morning after I arrived home I called
Buzzie Bavasi, the new Brooklyn general manager, and he
told me that under a new rule I could demand 30 days in
the big leagues because I was an ex-serviceman who had been
on a major league roster when I was called to war. This was
the government's way of saying our careers would not be pe-
nalized. But, Bavasi advised, I should go to triple-A St. Paul
first because I'd missed spring training. I got on the first plane
there. At the time my concern was not the army but a return
to my normal life.

But looking back, as I often do now, I wonder what really
happened that afternoon at the rocky, isolated army ballfield.
I wonder if I really needed to chase that fly ball over that
ravine. Surely, I didn't try to get hurt on purpose. My knee
was already injured, right? I've always gone after fly balls hard,
right? I believe that, and I can sleep with it. But sometimes,
when I'm feeling bad about never having served my country,
about never having really tried, I wonder if I still don't owe
somebody something. For a man who likes no debt, that kind
of wondering can make your skin peel. My war effort wasn't
the first time I cared about baseball more than reality, and it
wouldn't be the last time I suffered for it.

Of course, I wasn't thinking about this stuff back then. I
was too busy cramming a missed spring training into one
afternoon workout in St. Paul during an off-day immediately
after I arrived. I took a few swings, the knee felt good, the
timing wasn't too far gone, I was ready to begin my long-
overdue triple-A career. But after that first workout St. Paul

manager Clay Hopper said that owner Mel Jones wanted to see me in his office. "Dick," Jones said when I arrived, "you can't play here." My jaw grew tight and my face red. "Okay, so I missed spring training," I replied. "But I've played a couple of good years at Fort Worth and I played this winter and I can get back in shape quickly . . . "

"Dick," he interrupted, "we aren't sending you down. We're sending you to Brooklyn. Two other teams claimed you off wartime waivers, which means you've got to play one full year in Brooklyn or else the Dodgers have to give you up."

I was stunned. The Brooklyn Dodgers? Duke Snider? Jackie Robinson? So quickly? This was the first I'd heard of that waiver rule. I was stunned, then scared. I'd never been to Brooklyn, not even New York City. I'd never been on a subway. My palms grew wet just thinking about subways. How could I be ready for Charlie Dressen's teams when I wasn't even ready for the A-train? How could I be one of the Bums?

Well, I couldn't be. And I never was. My first indication was that instead of flying me to Brooklyn, they sent for me by slow train. A couple of days later I was on the streets of New York City with my tin suitcase and my doctor's bag and knees that knocked. I had a room at the St. George Hotel in Brooklyn—a subway ride from Penn Station, which I didn't dare try. Instead, I paid a then-huge sum of 15 bucks for a cab.

After spending the night in this hotel, I found my way to the front door the next morning and prepared to find Ebbets Field. But it was a frightening subway ride away, and I couldn't afford any more cabs. I might've stood at the curb all morning if pitcher Bud Podbielan hadn't shown up at my side and asked if I wanted to join him on the subway. Did I ever! With me nearly clinging to his jacket, we got off the train at the Prospect Park exit and walked two blocks, past a bowling alley and a couple of stores, and there it was. Ebbets Field. The first big league stadium I had seen other than Sportsman's Park. The date was June 3, 1951. I'll never forget what I saw, or, more important, how I saw it.

Ebbets Field was an aging stone structure that looked like a palace, stretching for what seemed like miles around four city blocks. I went through a gate, turned right, and headed down to the clubhouse with just my timid face and my doctor's bag. I ducked through the clubhouse door and was promptly blinded. Swaggering around the rubber mats that covered the hardwood floor in this tiny room, in various stages of undress even, were future Hall of Famers Jackie Robinson, Roy Campanella, Pee Wee Reese, and Duke Snider, among others. Big league swaggers. I dressed quietly, speaking to no one, and then hurried up the dirt runway and leaped over the four steps to the field.

And damn. First thing I thought was, What field? All I could see were stands, row upon row of stands, two decks that rose to the sky, interrupted only by a roof. As my eyes lowered, I caught sight of the most amazing sign in right field: HIT THIS SIGN AND WIN A SUIT. Goodness, I thought, I could hit that sign. I'd do anything for a new suit. Then I finally focused on the grass. This was absolutely the greenest place on earth. Later that night I was consumed by a glow cast from the giant light standards on the roof. It was like daytime, only it was night.

While staring at the field that first afternoon, my trance was broken by a quick, sharp voice. "Long way from home, huh?" Jackie Robinson said, smiling. "Nice to see you." Robinson remembered me as a friend of his brother Mack, another Pasadena local hero. He also remembered me from my first and only encounter with movie stardom. In 1949 I did well enough in Pasadena auditions to play a bit part in *The Jackie Robinson Story*. Watch the movie closely and you'll see me perform one of baseball's greatest feats. For one of Robinson's home runs, I'm the Jersey City Giants pitcher who gives it up; and then, as Robinson is rounding the bases, I'm the second baseman. A very low budget production.

Robinson, a big-hearted production, remembered. And from the moment he saw me standing speechless in the clubhouse that June day, he took this 22-year-old baby under his wing. He would show me where to go and what to do, something I needed to learn with every new city. He would constantly remind me to watch my mouth and my wallet. On those dark days when I realized that I'd never be accepted into the Dodgers clique of stars, he would sit beside me in the clubhouse and remind me that I was still a Dodger.

Jackie's behavior was so special because most of those lovable Bums and Boys of Summer lived in a special off-the-field world to which neither I nor later Norma was invited. Guys like Pee Wee and Snider and Gil Hodges and Carl Furillo and Carl Erskine would insulate themselves with their popularity and turn their backs on the team's younger players, the ones like me who were dying for their leadership. They'd drive to work together, play bridge together, and never much care if anyone else on the team was alive. From the moment I arrived there the other reserves told me, "You'll never get close to those guys, so don't even try."

Jackie was different, probably because he really knew what it was like to arrive from the outside. He had broken baseball's color barrier in 1947, and four years later he was still fighting society's barrier, one that would keep him out of certain restaurants and hotels. At the end of every spring we would embark on a barnstorming tour that was more like a march of shame. We would leave St. Petersburg by train and, en route to Brooklyn, stop and play at places like Jacksonville, Mobile, New Orleans, Nashville, Chattanooga, and Richmond. Ten days, 10 towns, and in every place somebody would shit on Jackie. He could eat here but couldn't sit there. He could drink here but couldn't piss there. He was tough. Rickey knew he was tough, or he wouldn't have picked him to be the first black.

But that forced toughness wore on Jackie's face, in his voice, and all over his smile. After one of the many times Jackie had his life threatened in one of these podunk hells, Pee Wee stood up in the clubhouse before the game and made an announcement: "I want everyone on the team to go back there in the bathroom and put on blackface, and then tape on the number 42 to your jerseys. Then we'll all walk outside and they won't know who the hell to shoot at." From the back of the clubhouse Jackie laughed hard, like a jackhammer. Even in northern cities, despite my invitations to eat where we could both eat, he would eat only in his room. The one thing we could do together was see movies in the afternoons. Jackie always loved movie theaters, mostly because he could have fun and nobody would know who he was.

I needed Robinson more than he or the Dodgers needed me. I learned this on my first road trip, when I jumped in the bottom bunk of a sleeper car I was assigned to share with Hodges. I knew I was supposed to be in the top bunk, but Hodges was in a different car playing bridge with Pee Wee and Billy Cox and Preacher Roe. So I figured I'd lie there a minute and read a magazine. But no sooner did I focus my attention on a story than I felt two strong hands on my side. It was Hodges, and he was picking me up. Then he was dropping me on the upper bunk. "That's where you sleep, rookie," he said gruffly.

He said it in a way that made me realize I wasn't just any rookie but the one who had skipped most of the 28 Dodgers minor league teams to be there. I was the rookie who had made the team only because he'd been drafted into the service and then discharged with a disability. I was a rookie who didn't even count as part of their regular 25-man roster — I was their 26th man. If it wasn't for the war, I wouldn't even be there.

It took me about three days to figure this out and about three minutes to call a meeting with manager Charlie Dressen and general manager Buzzie Bavasi. They knew what I wanted, so they let me speak with Commissioner Happy Chandler. My request was odd but simple: "Get me out of here," I told Chandler, who enforced the waiver rule. "They don't want me, because I'm their 26th man. They all think I need more seasoning in the minor leagues, so let me get it. I will not go through an entire year as an outcast."

"Yeah, you might be over your head here," Chandler said,

agreeing with something that I'd hoped he would deny. "But the rules are the rules, and we have to stick by them. Don't worry. By next May 29th you'll probably be sent back out." Then Dressen added something that seemed innocent at the time but was to help form the way I approach the game. "In the meantime," he said begrudgingly, "I'll let you know how you can help."

And so he did. While it didn't have much to do with actual baseball, eventually it did have much to do with the way I managed. Although in the box scores I contributed little to the greatness that would give the Brooklyn Dodgers three pennants and one postseason playoff during the parts of five years I was with them, I will go down in history as playing a role in their success. Dressen made me the Dodgers' DSA: designated smartass.

First because of inexperience and later because of a career-killing shoulder injury that stole my starting job, it was my duty to sit the bench and scream at the opponent. From Dressen I learned more about sarcasm and needling than hitting and fielding. I learned it wasn't enough to just want to beat your opponent. He had to know how badly you wanted it. A good way to do that was through sarcasm and needling. Relentless sarcasm and needling.

• • •

It was in Brooklyn that I began professionally ragging people. After I worked on it, few in baseball had a bigger or more effective mouth. Officially, I was ranked third on baseball's list of loudmouths, behind only Leo Durocher and Eddie Stanky.

I was a verbal hit man. For example, Dressen and Giants manager Durocher had disliked each other since the time when Dressen was a coach for the Yankees and Durocher, then a utility infielder, stole Babe Ruth's pocket watch. Dressen didn't like any young punk who didn't respect an authority like the Babe. So every time we played the Giants in a big game—

which was often, considering we fought them for the pennant every year in the early fifties—Dressen ordered me to scream at Durocher about the watch. The dugouts were near each other at Ebbets Field, so I could shout from one end of our bench and Durocher could hear me loud and clear. "What time is it, Leo?" I'd yell to him. "How's Ruth's watch running? Still working? Bringing you good luck? Lee-ooo. Oh Leee-ooo!" Dressen would be laughing like hell, while a flustered Durocher wanted to kill me. I knew this because every time I batted against the Giants I got knocked on my butt, presumably on Leo's orders. Since most other teams reacted to my catcalls the same way, I got more playing time on my ass than my feet. At least I never let one hit me in the head, which was fortunate, considering that at that time our batting helmet was nothing more than a plastic insert in our cap.

Not that I shouldn't have been at least maimed. You could field a couple of teams' worth of guys who had reason to hurt me. The Chicago Cubs were one. I helped hassle their manager Frankie Frisch so much that one year he was thrown out of the first 11 games the Cubs played in Ebbets. He'd scream at us, then scream at the umpires for not controlling us, then scream at them just for looking at him cross-eyed, and then he'd be gone. Then there was Philadelphia manager Steve O'Neill. He was 5-foot-10, about 300 pounds, and every time he'd walk back to the bench and sit down, I was under orders to shout, "Oooooooo-omph," with the last syllable coming as his big butt hit the bench.

Soon I became such a hit man that I'd be called in from the bullpen thinking that I would get into the game, when in fact Dressen just wanted me to sit next to him and yell at somebody. Like catcher Smoky Burgess. When he batted for Philadelphia, I became a vocalist, breaking into my worst rendition of "On top of Old Smoky . . ." Or how about outfielder Wally Westlake. I'm not certain what team he was playing for when I'd make him mad—it could have been Pittsburgh, St. Louis, or Cincinnati, three of Wally's five big league teams—but I do know that he had the league's strongest ears and shortest set of nerves. When Westlake came to the plate, Dressen would call me over and say, "There he is, go get him." So, with our Ebbets Field dugouts nearly on top of home plate anyway, I would crawl into his mind: "Hey, Wally, this is a fastball coming, a fastball, a fastball . . . no, no, it's a curveball, a curveball . . . watch out, watch out." I probably had nothing to do with Wally's failure to become any more of a big star than I was. That wasn't my purpose. My job was not to hurt anybody but to make Brooklyn a better team. The players understood that then, just as I understood it when their pitchers tried to put a hole in my head. They were just trying to help their teams by getting my mouth out of the game.

Today, of course, nobody understands. As a manager, I wished my players would be needlers, but few wanted any part of it. Modern-day players seem to have formed friendship societies with agreements never to yell at one another. Most of them are all working together, with very few willing to make anybody mad enough to jeopardize their ass for the sake of winning. That's why some of my players hated me: because I didn't give a damn about their corporations and I'd needle their buddies anyway. The players on all teams want to work together now so nobody loses. Which means somebody does lose—the fans.

There is a rule banning pregame fraternization between opposing players, which would help cut down on this comrade bullshit, but umpires never enforce the rule. So players in different-colored uniforms talking along the same foul line during batting practice have become a common sight—while hard slides and red faces are now rarities.

About the only thing that hasn't changed since my Dodgers days is the umpires' bad attitude toward my needling. In Brooklyn they hated me so much that I'd get not just myself but the whole team thrown out. Once, first-base umpire Bill Stewart—he of the bulldog face with jowls down to his ankles—looked into the dugout and shouted for me to shut up. So I shut up. But Don Newcombe shouted, "Fuck you and the mule you rode in on!" Yes, even the Boys of Summer cursed. Stewart was so angry he cleared the bench. Now, he didn't throw us all out of the game, just out of the dugout. Those of us who weren't in the lineup had to go to the clubhouse and wait until we were called to replace somebody.

Amazingly, this wasn't the first time our entire bench had been tossed from the dugout. Such maneuvers were particularly embarrassing at the Polo Grounds, and not only because all of the Giants were laughing. Since our clubhouse was behind the center field wall, we had to walk single file through the field to leave the game and then run back through the field when it was our turn to bat. A Polo Grounds dugout ejection carried special risks as well—like another ejection. Once, after outfielder Cal Abrams was summoned out of the clubhouse after an ejection to pinch-hit, he walked so slowly around the field that by the time he reached home plate, he was ejected again. This reminds me that dugout clearings were nearly as bad in Boston, where we had to walk through the Braves' dugout to leave the field. Once we were so mad about a Boston ejection that Preacher Roe kicked a hole in the umpires' door. The press got hold of the story and blamed it on Jackie.

Only once do I remember us getting even with the umpires. It was the time one umpire—whose name, thankfully, escapes me—shouted into the dugout, "One more word out of Williams and he's gone!" Dressen immediately sent me to the bullpen and then ordered another guy in the dugout to imitate me yelling my usual abuse. The umpire turned to the dugout and shouted, "That's it, Williams is gone!" Dressen shouted back, "How can you throw him out? He's not even here!" And then Dressen gleefully pointed to the bullpen, where I stood up and waved. "He's still gone!" shouted the angry umpire.

My role as captain of the Dodgers debate team may have

helped us win, but it hurt me in the clubhouse. I became increasingly alienated from players who didn't understand the art of heckling and just thought I had a big mouth. I'll never forget Pee Wee Reese ripping my ass after I got sent down to triple-A St. Paul one year. "Those jokes will go over good in St. Paul," he said. Years later, in *The Boys of Summer*, author Roger Kahn gave me another rip. He called me "deadwood," implying that I was taking up a spot on the roster. He was obviously forgetting two things: First, my heckling was used as much by Dressen as other players' bats were. And second, as their wartime rule player, I was a 26th man who didn't count as a roster spot anyway. Of course, I probably wouldn't even have been in the book if I hadn't later become a manager: I think Kahn was just looking for a current name to help the thing sell.

I'm not the first Dodger, incidentally, to question Kahn's accuracy and judgment in his so-called great work. At least a couple of other Dodgers have said that the book is bull. Kahn's suspect credibility finally caught up with him when his book about Pete Rose didn't include that he gambled on baseball, which is like writing a book about former President Reagan and leaving out the word "Iran." Kahn said Rose never told him about baseball gambling. Maybe he never asked.

My Dodgers heckling didn't keep me from improving my play. In fact, not playing gave me more time to work on playing. Before games I was always one of the first to arrive at Ebbets Field—which was easy when nobody would ride to the park with you, not even in your fancy $2,800 Pontiac, something I'd splurged on in a moment of insane confidence in my future. Lonely but determined, I would take extra swings, extra ground balls, do extra running. By the time the game started, I was already in need of a shower. But after a couple of innings of sitting, my sweat had dried and the only thing sore was my throat, from screaming.

This hard work began paying off on June 11, 1951. In the first game of a doubleheader with Pittsburgh, in my first

major league plate appearance, I pinch-hit for Gene Her-
manski late in a close game with two out and no one on. With
a full count, I hit a little chopper back to pitcher Bill Werle
for the third out. Thirty minutes later, imagine my surprise
when I saw that for the second game I was starting in left
field and batting leadoff. I was badly in need of making a
good first impression, so I did what I've since told my own
players to do: I manufactured that first impression. I beat
out a bunt for a hit. I beat out a blooper to left field for a
hit. I tripled down the right field line for a hit. I went four
for five. In my first big league start.

Fame lasted one sundown. With Furillo in right, Snider
in center, and Andy Pafko in left, Dressen didn't need me.
Besides, the Dodgers were involved in one of baseball's
weirdest pennant races, one that would not end until Bobby
Thomson hit his "shot heard 'round the world." I played in
only 23 games that year, batting just 60 times for a crappy
little .200 average, so I really wasn't part of those incredible
fall happenings. But I was on the bench and in the clubhouse, and I saw and heard and felt everything. And, oh,
how it taught me. How it changed me. Forever.

In mid-August the Dodgers had a 13½-game lead over
the hated Giants. It was then that Dressen, who had instructed me so well in voice control, spoke too loud. "The
Giants is dead," he proclaimed. Until then I'd never believed
it, but there is such a thing in baseball as talking too much.
By saying that, Dressen was talking too much, I knew it right
away. And not because it angered the Giants but because it
turned our team positively giddy.

I'll never forget Jackie Robinson yelling in the Ebbets Field
shower room after one August win, yelling through the wall
that separated his shower from Giants manager Durocher's
shower in the other clubhouse, yelling above the steam and
the spray, "Leo, eat your heart out! Leo, eat your heart out!"

It was an interesting choice of words. Because that is just
what happened to the Dodgers over the final month and a

half of the season. Our hearts were eaten out. The Giants won 37 of their final 44 games, and for us to even force a playoff with them, we needed a comeback 14-inning win over Philadelphia on the final day of the season. That set up a three-game showdown, of which only one pitch needs to be remembered.

Thomson's two-run homer off Ralph Branca won the first game—you forgot that little irony, didn't you?—and then we pounded them 10–0 in the second game. It came down to one game for the National League pennant. And that game came down to us needing just three more outs for a victory, leading 4–1 in the bottom of the ninth.

But we were in trouble. Hunched up in the corner of the dugout—no way was my mouth getting involved in this game—I could see and feel that trouble with every late inning move. All of the players could. Around the middle of the game, Dressen had begun running up and down the dugout like a college basketball coach. He kept shaking his head and alternately shouting instructions and swearing. It made us quietly wonder if, in trying to keep us calm, he wasn't losing his mind.

And the guys on the bench weren't the only ones bothered. The effect of Dressen's behavior was punctuated when Robinson ran in from the infield with a disgusted look on his face after the bottom of the eighth, after starter Don Newcombe had struck out the side. Robinson glared at Dressen and shouted, "Will somebody please tell Charlie to sit down and relax? All this running around is making us nervous." I looked at Robinson and realized that it was too late. Dressen had already blown it. By losing control of himself, the manager had lost control of his team.

Newcombe started the ninth by allowing a single to Alvin Dark—a future manager who would cross my path later, in a less innocent way. Then Newcombe gave up a squib single to Don Mueller between first and second base that was just out of reach of first baseman Gil Hodges, who was holding

Dark on the bag. History won't record this as a particularly important single, but most of us in the dugout will remember it as a crucial hit. Why? Because it could have been prevented. There was no preventing Thomson's historic homer, but tell me, with Mueller batting, why the hell wasn't Hodges playing behind the runner, where he could have made the ball into a possible double play grounder, or at least one easy out? Why hold Dark on first base when your team is leading by three runs? It was a grade school error of big league proportions. And don't call me a second-guesser, because we were first-guessing it over in the dugout. What the hell was Dressen thinking? As long as I can still see Hodges futilely attempting to catch that grounder, don't ever tell me that Ralph Branca cost us that game with his pitch to Thomson. Don't even try.

One out later, Whitey Lockman doubled home Dark for one run, placing the tying runs on base and bringing Thomson to the plate. It was time for another strategic error, although this one was understandable. Dressen, realizing Newcombe was through, had to decide between Carl Erskine and Branca as his relief pitcher. Just as bullpen coach Clyde Sukeforth was talking to Charlie on the phone from the bullpen, telling him that both pitchers were ready, Erskine threw a 50-foot curveball, bouncing it to the catcher. It turned out to be the most important curveball of his life, because Dressen saw it and winced. I remember the wince, like he'd just swallowed a piece of his tobacco. He immediately asked for Branca. It was a hunch, and I can't blame a guy for a hunch. Except I shortly learned that if you get burned in a big game, it had better be because of more than a hunch. You'd better be able to back up your decision with something that will hold up under years of baseball history's scrutiny. Making a move because a guy throws one bad curveball in the bullpen—that reasoning doesn't last, as Dressen spent the rest of his life understanding.

Branca's first pitch to Thomson was a fastball right down

the pipe. He didn't swing. Strike one. Thomson stomped around the batter's box, kicking up dust. That one pitch apparently made him wake up. Of course, I never dreamed just how awake. Nobody could've dreamed what would happen next, on a high pitch we thought he'd take for ball one. At the last moment he reached up and chopped at it. Some chop. The ball went over Andy Pafko's head in left field with such force that Pafko thought it would bounce off the fence, so he turned to catch the rebound. Line drives that hard don't go for homers, do they? This one did. It was hit so hard it went into the lower seats of the Polo Grounds lower deck on a line drive. The Giants had won the pennant . . . the Giants had won the pennant. And on a Dodgers bench that had spent most of the summer talking itself blue in the face, now there was silence. Absolute silence. It was like someone had just died.

I have since seen probably the second-greatest hit in baseball: Pete Rose's 4,192nd career knock, which moved him past Ty Cobb as the all-time hit leader, was a single against San Diego when I managed there. But that hit was a celebration for everyone, or at least everyone but Eric Show, who sat down on the mound after allowing it. The Thomson hit, at least for 30 guys wearing Dodgers uniforms, was devastation.

We had blown a 13½-game lead and then a 4–1 lead in the bottom of the ninth, and finally, officially, we'd blown the pennant. After the homer we had to do something nearly as unthinkable—walk 500 feet across the field from our dugout to the clubhouse behind center field. In a silence punctuated only by sobs, we passed Eddie Stanky riding the back of Leo Durocher, we passed New Yorkers who appeared drunk and immortal with joy, leaping off 18-foot retaining walls and falling to the field uninjured. They danced and jumped in the dirt and acted like we were invisible. We wished we were, particularly when the remaining fans in the bleachers spat on us.

The personal tragedy shook Branca with such force that

he didn't even try to be invisible. He sleepwalked into the clubhouse and dropped his 6-foot-3 frame across the five steps that separated the two levels. As we reserves had to walk to our lockers in the upper level, we had to step around him, none of us looking down, but none of us able to ignore his sobs and cries of "Why me, why me?"

Dressen summoned us together—he didn't need to ask for quiet—and made another famous yet inane statement. "Wait until next year," he said, becoming the first baseball manager to be quoted thus. It may not have been such a bad thing to say, considering this was a Dodgers team just four years away from winning a world championship. But at the time it sounded stupid. Since then, knowing how insulted I felt when I heard the reality of our defeat glossed over in promises of the future, I've reacted to season-ending losses by telling people, "Next year, my ass." And I mean it.

I don't think I fully realized the impact of such a loss until that winter back in Pasadena, in Jimmy's Playroom, when I felt such a pain in my stomach that I couldn't finish my beer. This greatly alarmed my buddies. Not my pain, my half-empty beer. They rushed me home without ever asking about my stomach. Later my stepfather found me curled up in agony on the bathroom floor and took me to Huntington Hospital, where my father had died. Just as I became certain it was my time to join him, I learned that I just had a kidney stone. I'm sure it was caused by the Dodgers trauma. Once again baseball had barged into reality.

I passed the stone and left the hospital three days later, only to encounter another sort of pain. Dressen, who lived in nearby Bel Air, came out in the newspapers and said that next season, 1952, the Dodgers would be stuck with two players who "ain't major league." Because of the ex-serviceman's clause, they were stuck with me until at least May 29, when I would have had one calendar year with the big league team. So I knew he thought I was one of those ain't-major-league players.

Not that I believed it. I'd finished the previous year working hard, and I was adjusting better both on and off the field. This meant I was learning both the curveball and the best way to hide women from Dressen during bed check.

You see, I had developed a reputation on the Dodgers for being not just a loudmouth but a womanizer. At the time I was just dating Norma off and on, with Fort Worth rarely crossing my mind. So I could play the field, and if you believe *The Boys of Summer*, you believe that in one week in 1952 I slept with five women of different nationalities. Once again, that's wrong. Took me at least two weeks.

But the important thing here was that I managed to keep my act away from Dressen. That was no small accomplishment, considering the legendary bed checks he ran. First he'd send in the clubhouse attendant we called Senator Griffin, a very unusual man. Senator Griffin was a heavyset chap who collected hats and funny costumes, but when doing bed checks he was serious. He wouldn't just make sure you were in bed. Oh, no—the honorable Senator also had to make sure you were alone. He'd check under the bed, in the closet, behind the shower curtain, anywhere his weird fantasies might picture someone. If there wasn't anyone in the room besides you, great. But if *nobody* was there, then you were in real trouble. Dressen would give a baseball and a pen to the hotel elevator operator and tell him to get the autograph of everyone who arrived after midnight. Every late arriver would sign it, thinking they were doing the guy a favor. It wasn't until the next day they realized they'd done Charlie the favor.

I kept my ears open and learned the timing of these bed checks, and then I just timed my fun around them. Only when I was feeling invincible would I get into trouble, like that night late in my Dodgers career when I experienced 24 of the worst hours of my life.

It started, like all my late night partying, with the Senator's bed check. After a teammate and I bid him goodnight, we ran downstairs and headed for a back alley bar, where two girls were waiting for us. To avoid seeing the Senator again in the lobby, we sneaked out the hotel's back door through the kitchen. An alarm went off, and through the pots and pans we ran, right into the waiting black gloves of the police. They questioned us and, realizing we were guilty of nothing more than stupidity, released us. We walked out to the alley, turned right, and headed for the bar . . . and here were some more cops, wanting to know what the hell we were doing in the alley at this late hour. We explained ourselves to them, we were released again, we finally found the bar. But it was closed. And the girls were gone. They couldn't wait for us one measly hour. We went back to our rooms and hit the rack.

The next morning I missed my wakeup call. I arrived late for a morning workout, and everybody was pissed at me. I stepped into the cage all bleary-eyed and lined a ball off Ralph Branca's injured elbow. Put him out of action for an extra week. Now everyone was really pissed at me. That night, unbelievably, I was in the lineup. I went zero for four, and a fly ball landed in front of me. Is it any wonder I didn't have many Dodger friends?

And is it any wonder that I only ran bed checks my first three years as a manager, in 1967–69 with the Boston Red Sox? And even then I never went into anybody's shower. And I always brought along a coach for protection. I finally abandoned the practice when I realized its only benefit was seeing many good-looking women while opening doors on many surprised players. This was particularly true in Anaheim, although Margo Adams was still in diapers then.

I care more about what the players do at 7:35 P.M. than who they're with at 1 A.M. It's not, and shouldn't be, a manager's reponsibility to make sure his players care enough to get a good night's sleep. That caring stuff always has to come from within. It did with me, and it should have with my players. Emphasis on the words "should have."

I began the spring of 1952 intent on showing that I could

do more than just heckle opponents and fake a clean living. I arrived in camp in great shape and worked so hard that soon I was even allowed to play before the ninth inning of hopelessly lost games. But that dreaded May 29 date was approaching like midnight, and all I could do was hope Dressen didn't think I was totally outclassed. So I pulled one gutsy play that may have saved my major league career. I can call it gutsy because it involved virtually no athletic ability, only smarts.

I was playing left field, with a runner on first and second and nobody out, when the batter laid down a bunt. The only play we had was to first base, and Gil Hodges took the throw for the one out, with the runners moving to second and third. The guy rounding second took several more steps after crossing the bag—common on such bunt plays because the second baseman is over near first base and the runner can get a good jump if there's an error. Seeing this, I sneaked in from left field until I was nearly on top of second. Hodges saw me, the runner didn't, and Hodges made a quick throw that I caught just in time to tag the runner diving back. That's the kind of play I love. Luckily, that day I wasn't the only one. Dressen told me soon afterward that I wouldn't be sent down when my year-long lease was up. Finally I was a Dodger for real. Finally I'd be counted on to make a contribution to these guys who treated me like a batboy. Finally I was one of the contributing Bums . . .

. . . for all of three months. What happened next was perhaps repayment for my good fortune in getting out of the army early. Maybe it was because I'd spent some of my life being a smartass. Whatever the reason, after finally moving past Andy Pafko as the starting left fielder, after actually starting for two straight days, on a hot August afternoon in St. Louis—the city of my birth—my world as a player came to a virtual end.

It was just a routine sinking fly ball, the kind that always falls in for a single. Why I didn't just let it happen like that,

I don't know. Well, I do know. Three games into becoming a star, I wasn't about to let anything drop harmlessly in front of me. Not a baseball, and not my career. When the Cardinals' Vern Benson hit it, I charged it. Shortstop Pee Wee Reese and third baseman Billy Cox drifted back and then gave up on it, but I kept charging. They stopped and prepared to take my relay throw after the ball had hit the ground, but I kept charging. And charging. Then I dove. And I heard a crack. It wasn't the ball hitting my glove. It was my right shoulder hitting the ground.

There was immense pain, followed by something even scarier—numbness. I could barely move the arm, just enough to lob the ball back to the infield. Then I collapsed. The next thing I heard is something that rings in my ears even today. It was Dressen shouting, "Get him up and get him out of here!" What class. As bad as some players say I treated them, I never, ever kicked a truly injured player when he was down. In fact, at the time of injury I've often been known to pamper. I run out and stand with the guy and pat his back and do all kinds of un-Williams-like things. This is why.

If it wasn't for Cardinals manager Eddie Stanky, I might never have gotten to my feet. He helped me up and off the field—another thing about that day I've never forgotten. Many years later, when my son Rick was looking for a place to pitch college baseball, I told him there was only one: the University of South Alabama, for coach Eddie Stanky.

When I reached a clubhouse bench that sorry afternoon, all I could think of was that I was never going to play again. Maybe it would've been better that way. As it happened, I did play again, but I was never the same. The shoulder injury was diagnosed as a three-way separation, which today could have been easily fixed. Back then all they could do was stick in a couple of pins and hope nature would save me.

Nature didn't. I went from being a hard-nosed outfielder to one who could barely throw the ball to second base. I went from a proud major leaguer to one who, every time he threw the ball in from left field, would hear people shout, "Infield fly, infield fly!" I wasn't throwing baseballs, I was throwing balloons. Later in my career I was allowed to play third base as long as I didn't try to throw the ball to first base on the fly. While playing for Baltimore, I was ordered by manager Paul Richards to skip it. Well, at least my ineptness there gave somebody a chance. Maybe you've heard of the Oriole who replaced me at third. First name of Brooks.

It was some injury. In an irony that haunted me until I retired as a player 12 years and four teams later, this "tough guy" had been stripped of his fists. And to think I had finally become a starter Dodgers outfielder. "This balls everything up," Dressen said at the time. And how.

Before that injury I'd spent six years with the same organization, all in one position. In the 11 years following that injury I was traded six times, spent time with five different organizations, and played four different positions. I was forced to forget about being a star, about being able to cockily play my way out of any jam, about being anybody's hero. My dreams—finished. My life to this point—a waste.

But there's a funny thing about injuries. They often force you to do things in a different way, your career takes a different direction, sometimes to a far better place than you ever would've reached if you'd stayed healthy. That's what I've told my seriously injured players, because that's what happened to me.

My injury forced me to watch, to listen, to learn every tiny detail about this game that once I could play in my sleep. Because if I ever wanted to play it again, I could no longer be faster or stronger than anyone. Now I had to be smarter.

I would sit on my butt in the dugout for nine innings and watch both the game and its players like I'd never watched them before. I studied opposing pitchers. I studied strategy. More than anything, I studied human nature.

And through it all, Dick Williams the player slowly became something else. He became someone who thought before he acted. Someone who took nothing on the field for granted. Someone who wanted to leave nothing on the field to chance. Slowly, painstakingly, in a process that took 12 years that began from the seat of his pants, he became Dick Williams the manager.

Not that everybody wanted me to watch at first. Although disabled, I sat on the bench for the 1952 World Series with the New York Yankees only after I promised the league office to keep my mouth shut. But while they could shut my mouth, they couldn't close my mind. And beginning with that World Series, during my many years on benches I saw more baseball than I'd ever seen as a full-time player.

From a vantage point that no other manager would ever have, I saw what it might take to manage a baseball team. It was then, sometime during the mid-fifties, that I decided that's what I wanted to do. To take my competitive fire, mix it with my knowledge from the dark side of the bench, and turn a team from a loser to my kind of winner . . . what could be more satisfying? At least, that was the plan.

While I was learning all this, I was still happy playing, bouncing from Brooklyn to Baltimore to Cleveland to Baltimore to Kansas City to Baltimore again and finally to Boston. During that time, having set my sights on a future job, I was now ready for a future partner.

This is where Norma Mussato comes in. Or should I say, where she returns to the picture. Since meeting her through the milkman in 1949, I'd flown through Fort Worth and dated her off and on until 1952, when I finally decided I couldn't see her enough to make it worth seeing her anymore. Brooklyn was just too far from central Texas.

So I continued on my reckless way, dating other women and even proposing to one. But what does Norma do? She becomes a flight attendant for Braniff Airlines and follows my career through her travels. I didn't know this, because during that time she wouldn't make the first move and call me. So even though she knew almost everything about me, from the time of our breakup in 1952 until 1954, not once did she let me even know she still existed.

Then one day in early 1954 a buddy of mine saw her and, out of the clear blue, hit her with the big one. He told her I was marrying a girl from St. Louis. What happened next is what I love about Norma. Her brain clicked. She ran out and bought new clothes. She arranged to accompany other flight attendants on a promotional trip to Chicago, where I was in town with the Dodgers. Once there, Norma and the other attendants phoned nearly every large hotel until she discovered where I was staying. She then called my room from the lobby and left word for me to call her. Remember, this is a woman I hadn't spoken to in two years.

First thing I said when I reached her was "What the hell are you doing here?" Next, I asked her out for a drink. Why? I was overcome by her knowing what she wanted and then working like hell to get it. What she wanted, crazy as it sounds, was me. I knew this after meeting her in the bar, because I spilled my drink all over her new dress and she said nothing. After spending three days with this feisty Italian who obviously would stop at nothing to open my eyes and claim victory over my heart, I knew what I wanted was her.

This was later proven to me just before our wedding, on an island in a lake near Fort Worth. We began discussing whether it was possible for a woman to be legally raped if she didn't put up a fight. Remember, this is back when society still didn't quite understand those things. Norma, of course, believed that no woman in her right mind would not put up a fight. And then she ordered me to go behind a sand dune and come charging out like an attacker. She said she'd show me what a real fight was like.

Stupidly I followed her orders. I went behind a sand dune, waited several minutes for her to get scared, and then came charging out behind her. She was scared, all right—so scared she spun around, kicked me in the head, and knocked me out. Right then I confirmed that I really did want her in my corner.

I couldn't ask her to stick around with me immediately following those impromptu three days in Chicago. After all, I was still engaged to this St. Louis girl, and the Dodgers' next stop was St. Louis, which would have made things a little sweaty. So I weaseled out of a commitment by simply asking Norma if she ever flew into New York and if she'd like to stop by Brooklyn and see me sometime. "We'll see," she said.

That was good enough for me. The next day, in St. Louis, I broke off my engagement with the girl, and a couple of days later I was in the midst of spending a week with Norma in New York and in love, although we still stayed in different parts of town. We were so much in love that later that summer, after I was sent down to triple-A St. Paul, she changed her schedule so she could fly to St. Paul. Sometimes she'd fly to other cities to see me, particularly Kansas City. This was a true sign of love because the only thing open really late after a game was a burlesque show, which she attended with me despite her constant blush.

After the 1954 season we were married. The wedding would have gone smoother if I hadn't forgotten the marriage license. But then, Norma always was the one person in my life who could make my knees quiver. Today, three children and some terrible Dick Williams temper tantrums later, we're still married. To endure living with me, she gives the marriage more than 100 percent, which is more than I'd ask of anyone. Where 35 years ago she acted like she was the lucky one, today I am certain that it's me.

How about the time, one of my favorite times, when Norma decided to celebrate our fifth anniversary by bronzing my old cleats? She went into the Kansas City clubhouse one morning, found the clubhouse man, and asked him for the shoes. While he was pulling them out of my locker, she spied one of my old-looking gloves and decided to have it bronzed too. Problem was, that was my game glove. I discovered this later in the day and, much to my outrage, had to break in a new glove. When I learned what had happened, I had to laugh to keep Norma from crying. She's so sweet. So unlike me. What the hell. Everybody always said I played like I had a bronze glove.

Not that anybody, particularly Norma's mother, believed that this big league ballplayer was intent on staying married. In fact, that winter, just before our wedding, I left my car in Fort Worth during a trip to California, just so her mother would believe I was coming back. "Don't worry, he's coming back," her mother, Josie, would say. "But just in case he doesn't, at least you have the Pontiac."

That first year was easy for us both. I requested to go to Fort Worth, as the Dodgers obviously had no plans for me and my sore arm. If I had to go to the minors, I'd just suck it up and go past triple-A down to double-A, only because it meant Norma and I could start our first year out right. You see, I'm not always such a bad guy.

It paid off for me that year, as our Fort Worth team was a collection of baseball brains that should probably make history as the most aggressive second-guessing collection of athletes ever. That Cats team contained *six* future big league managers or coaches: Danny Ozark, Sparky Anderson, Norm Sherry, Joe Pignatano, Maury Wills, and me.

And in having fun, this was also where I had my last great year in organized baseball. I hit .317 with 24 homers and played left field every day. This was when, in the second game of a doubleheader on the last day of the season, I played every position in one game, including pitching in the eighth inning and catching in the ninth. Didn't do too badly as a pitcher either. Struck out two and walked one. But 60 feet was easy. It was throwing from 200 feet that hurt.

The Dodgers were impressed with my season and raised my hopes by putting me on their defending world championship roster for 1956. So much for the fun. Norma, toting our baby daughter Kathi while sick and pregnant with our first son, Rick, moved to Brooklyn and learned firsthand what I'd been telling her for years. Although we lived in the Bay Ridge suburb like many other veteran Dodgers, they'd still have nothing to do with me. Worse, their wives would have nothing to do with Norma. When I'd go on the road and my wife needed support with the baby and her pregnancy, she had none. No other wives called. None offered help. Norma asked another young player's wife for advice about the cold shoulder and was told, "You just don't hang around with the special little cliques. You stick to your class." And except for help from some wonderful downstairs neighbors we still correspond with, the Maravells, Norma bore her burden alone. The Dodgers, indeed, could be bums.

By the middle of the 1956 season, after playing just seven big league games, I was finally traded to Baltimore, a team that would trade for me twice more. It hurt to be leaving such a successful place as Brooklyn. But it felt good to go where we were wanted, and where working men like myself were the majority.

The years between 1956 and my final playing stop in Boston in 1964 are a blur, and rightfully so. Only once, in 1961 with Baltimore, did I play for a winning team. And that year I hit .206. In general, during that time I never hit more than .288 as a regular. I never had more than 16 homers. Never more than 75 RBIs. In other words, on today's market I'd have been worth a couple of million a year, plus a no-trade clause.

But back then—well, I was known for a couple of things:

- In Baltimore I used to adjust my jock strap and cup so much on the field that other wives told Norma to ask me to please stop.
- When I was traded from Baltimore to Cleveland in 1957, it happened so fast Norma didn't hear about it until she tuned in to a Baltimore-Cleveland game on television. When she saw me run onto the field in a Cleveland uniform, according to neighbors within five blocks, she screamed.
- In Kansas City in 1959 I hit four homers in four days.

That being such a supernatural feat for me, I didn't wash one stitch of my uniform during the streak—afraid I might wash out the magic. Also, because I drank one beer in the afternoon before my first homer, I drank another beer in the afternoon before my second night game . . . and then another before the third game, and then another in the afternoon before the fourth game. During the fifth game, hitting that fifth straight homer proved to be the toughest thing I've ever tried. This is because it was a day game. Okay, so maybe *you* like a beer for breakfast.

I can only conclude that beer really did help my performance. Another time, on a hot day in Baltimore, I walked through the clubhouse in the 10th inning when I saw veteran Hank Bauer, who was already out of the game and in his underwear, having a beer and a cigaret. "Oh, man, that beer looks good," I said. Bauer put down his cigaret and motioned to me with the bottle. "Here," he said, "have a swig." And so I took one—a nice, long, cold one. It was so good and I was so hot that I felt like sitting down for a few more. But worry not. I went back into the game and homered to win it.

• I made such good money during this time that I was forced each winter to take a variety of fun jobs. Like unloading marble off freight cars. Or working as a carpenter's assistant in West Palm Beach, Florida, during the day while selling pari-mutuel tickets for jai alai games at night. Or selling men's clothes at Ray Strutt's in Pasadena. Or riding my bicycle to the Santa Anita racetrack to place bets for neighbors. I'd weave through the traffic and chain up that bike in valet parking.

My favorite off-season memory was of the winter Irv Noren and I spent stripping wallpaper. Halfway through our first job, at the home of some nice old ladies, while we stripped the paper as if blindfolded, Irv bragged to them that he wished we had a dime for every wall we'd treated. "Yeah," I said, as the ladies turned white. "Then we'd have 20 cents."

• I even converted to Catholicism. It was in Fort Worth

in the winter of 1956, and the priest was Father Sullivan, who I forced into a vow of secrecy. This was going to be my little surprise for my Catholic wife and Catholic kids. I knew they were tired of me accompanying them to church on Sunday and just sitting there. I was finally getting to where I wanted us to be a family in all ways.

So—quietly—this German Lutheran ballplayer studied and studied his Roman Catholic religion books, and one day I invited my family to church on a Sunday afternoon. And then I shocked the bejesus out of them by getting baptized. What surprised them more was that for the next three weeks I was the holiest person on earth. "Don't worry," Father Sullivan told a very worried Norma. "It will wear off." There's a wise guy in every pulpit.

• • •

In the meantime my arm had gotten so bad that during one of my stays in Baltimore, I became the first and perhaps only player in history to platoon with himself. With a left-handed hitter batting, I'd be moved to left field, where there was little chance of the ball being hit to me. When a right-hander came to the plate, I'd be moved to right field for the same reason. Not only was it embarrassing, it was damn tiring.

Thank goodness I made my final stop in Boston. This was a team ripe for a player who would be their manager. When I arrived as a 34-year-old veteran finishing out his career, this was a team that didn't have a career. They were coming off a 76–84 record in 1962. The year before that they'd also won just 76 games. The year before that, just 65. And so on. They hadn't won a title of any sort since 1946, when they were defeated in the World Series by St. Louis. Before that their last postseason appearance had been in 1918.

So entering 1963, they'd won only one pennant in 45 years. I soon saw why. Even though they had a new manager in Johnny Pesky and a new hitting star in Carl Yastrzemski, they had the same old problems. The place was a country club.

Players showed up when they felt like it and took extra work only when it didn't interfere with a card game.

I endeared myself to the team when, after winning a couple of hundred bucks from a guy in a gin rummy game during a rain delay, I announced that if I ever became a manager, I'd fine anybody who lost that much in a clubhouse game. A couple of hundred bucks is a huge distraction. It could make a guy play pissed off. They all laughed when I said this, but a couple of years later, while I was managing many of them, no money was allowed on the table of clubhouse card games. Let them play with matchsticks and figure out their losses *after* our ballgame.

Poor Pesky was constantly being dumped on, by both general manager Mike Higgins and the players. Guys like Dick Stuart. Stuart, who often ran around the clubhouse backstabbing Pesky to promote his own interests, was best known for his poor fielding—writers called him "Dr. Strangeglove" and claimed he'd bought his glove from the Portland Cement Company. He was so bad that he once received a standing ovation for leaning over at first base and deftly picking up a windblown hot dog wrapper.

But Stuart should also be known for his bad head. He was the poorest excuse for a caring baseball player I've ever seen. Once in Boston, with the bases loaded, Stuart got hit in the arm with a pitch. That would have sent him to first and scored a run, except he wanted a chance at more than just one RBI. So he complained to the umpire that the ball hadn't hit him—with a welt growing on his arm as he spoke. The umpire, who couldn't believe a guy would intentionally cost his team a run on a bluff, changed his call and let the selfish wonder stay at the plate. I shouldn't need to tell you, Stuart eventually struck out. I don't care if he did hit 75 homers in two years with the Red Sox. He tried to hit nothing but home runs, and those players are no good for anybody. The Red Sox won a lot of games when he was there, didn't they?

As I sat the Red Sox bench in both 1963 and 1964, with

73 of my 205 at-bats coming as a pinch hitter, I saw plenty. Even when I wasn't on the bench, I saw plenty. I was ordered to room with young Tony Conigliaro, to provide him with veteran influence. The setup lasted just two months, because during that time I never saw him. Not late at night, not first thing in the morning, never. I was providing veteran influence to a suitcase. I told management they were wasting their time, and I began rooming with Russ Nixon. Conigliaro was later accused of breaking curfew and fined $1,000. He promptly, and wrongfully, accused me of being a snitch. Things between us afterward, as you shall see, were never the same.

But sure, I bitched about a lot of things. Players who didn't understand why had no idea how much it should hurt to lose, and how damning it should be to not care. Maybe those players never felt like they had to prove themselves to somebody. Well, I did, I still did, even though this was nearly 20 years after my father's death. I wanted to prove that I wasn't a loser. I bitched because I didn't want to be associated with losers, and that's the best way to describe the entire Red Sox state of mind in the early sixties. Losers.

I bitched so much that in the spring of 1964 I was given our "blue" rookie team to manage during an intrasquad game. It was like: Here, see what you can do when you're the boss. I bitched so much that minor league director Neal Mahoney wondered out loud whether I would ever like to manage for real. "Would I?" I exclaimed. "Would I like to be able to do something about everything in baseball that bothers me? Would I like to be able to teach people how to win, and maybe mold winners out of losers? What do you think?"

Mahoney then let me know what he thought. Following the 1964 season, at the same time I was being given my expected release, I was offered a job as a player/coach for the club's triple-A farm team in Seattle. I was also told that since the Red Sox might move the Seattle farm club to Toronto and Seattle manager Edo Vani would not be going with it, I could actually be managing before I knew it. I jumped at the opportunity. Without inquiring about the particulars, Norma and I moved from Fort Worth to California so we could be closer to Seattle. A new phase of our life was just beginning.

Then one day that winter I heard a piece of news out of the winter meetings in Houston: the Seattle franchise was moving to Toronto. My heart leaped. This could be my shot. And so I waited for the Red Sox to call. And waited. And waited. Finally, a couple of days later, when I was just about distraught, Norma told me to forget protocol and call Mahoney. I did . . . and he said he was just preparing to call me. Does anybody ever believe that line? I did, particularly since, on the spot, he offered me the job of managing the Toronto Maple Leafs.

Suddenly it was too real. My end of the phone went silent. Me, with no previous experience, suddenly a full-fledged manager at baseball's highest minor league level? One part of me thought, What a brash, headstrong thing to do. But then another part of me realized it was the perfect Dick Williams type of move—brash and headstrong. Even if I would be making a much smaller salary (by nearly half) than the $18,500 I made in my final year as a player.

"Well," I said into the phone, looking at pregnant Norma and our young children Kathi and Rick, looking at the cheap furnished apartment we had rented just to be closer to Seattle. "I guess it's time I back up my mouth."

"Yes," Mahoney said, "I guess it is."

IMPOSSIBLE DREAMS

His name was Mickey Sinks. He was a mediocre pitcher for my triple-A Toronto club who weighed in at 210 pounds—all of it on his fanny, not his fastball. He was generally a pretty meek fellow, but on that late night in summer 1966 something strange got into him, something terrible. Me.

With Toronto headed for its second straight International League playoff appearance, my players would likely be needed for about 15 days after the regular season. But Sinks walks in my office late one night and says he can't pitch for me during that time until I answer one question: "Will I be brought up to the major league roster at the end of the year? Because if I'm not, I'm not staying for the 15 extra days. I've got a teaching job lined up. I've got to make some money."

An innocent question. And I gave an innocent answer: "I have no idea who's going to be placed on the roster. That won't be decided until this winter."

But the answer wasn't good enough. Sinks, still in uniform, glares at me and my 170 pounds tucked inside a $49.95 seersucker suit. "Okay, then you give me your opinion," he says. "If you had your choice, would you put me on the major league roster?"

A tough question. But the tougher they were, the more honest I was. Already, in just my second year of managing, I'd learned that was the only way to keep your head above the shit. Honesty he wanted, honesty he was handed. "Mickey," I say, "if it was my decision, you wouldn't be put on the roster."

I say it while looking him right in the eye. That's my first mistake, because I never see his fist. Boom! He flies across the desk and punches me in the face. Luckily, I fall forward instead of back. Then I surprise him by wrapping him in a bear hug, pulling him to the ground, and then sitting on him until the trainer, who had heard us scuffling, arrives. "Take this son of a bitch away!" I shout as my guy drags the poor right-hander out the door and out of organized baseball.

As I straighten myself up, I'm feeling pretty good. My first fight with a player, and except for the makings of a shiner on my left eye and a cut underneath, I'm okay. He's gone and I'm still here. Then I smell something funny. I look down. Oh, shit. Literally—oh, shit. Apparently, I'd strained so much while bear-hugging Mickey Sinks that I'd shit my pants. Ruined that $49.95 seersucker suit. Smelled like an outhouse. I put my head in my hands and thought, What have I done? What will I do? Turns out, how I answered those questions set my career on the successful and stubborn course it would follow for the next 20 years.

Unsure what I would say about the incident to my team, I decided not to say anything. I decided to show them. I called a clubhouse meeting the next day and brought out the pants. Let them see where I strained. Let them smell the stench. I told them: You mess with me, I'll shit all over you. Then when they finished laughing, I added: If this is what it takes to win, everybody in this room will be wearing diapers. They didn't laugh then. They went out and eventually won me a second straight International League Governors' Cup championship.

And this is how Dick Williams became a manager.

I had accepted the Red Sox offer to boss Toronto in 1965 even though Norma and I were unsure whether we could learn to live on the low salary. Turns out that was no big deal. My problem was learning to live with something far more painful: the losing. Plus learning how to accept defeat without shitting on yourself.

Soon after taking over the best Red Sox prospects, I recognized a vast difference between being a bench jockey and a bench boss. When you're the player with the big mouth, the only thing you're accountable for is you. Your strikeouts, your hits, your errors. But as a manager you are suddenly judged by an entire team, and your important statistics are whittled down to two. Wins and losses. Your wins. Your losses. And only yours.

That sounds simple. But for one who wasn't used to being judged by the actions (read: screwups) of others, this was a concept made in hell. Beginning in Toronto, my competitive fire, kindled in me during those days of learning to swim upstream in a Missouri river, became a continuous rolling explosion. If we lost and we'd done everything right, I'd try to understand. It would be painful, but I'd try. But if we lost because one person had made a mental mistake, I'd blow up. Sometimes right on the spot, even before the game was won or lost. So fearful was I of these mistakes that I wanted to eliminate, then and there, any chance of the mistake happening again in that same game. My wins, my losses, and my explosions. If I thought somebody didn't care as much as I did, I'd damn near kill him. That's how I felt. Losses, dressed up in mistakes and nonchalance, made me a deadly weapon.

Take Joe Foy. Along with Mike Andrews and Reggie Smith, he was one of several future Boston stars who played for me in Toronto. After one particular screwup in 1965, his life—not to mention his career—almost came to an early, tragic end. One uneventful night he had made a mistake in the field, and as he entered the dugout after the inning was over, I reminded him of it. Like I said, I think players should know of their problems on the spot. Well, Foy didn't want to know about it. In the middle of what I thought was a helpful lecture, he turned and started walking to the other end of the dugout. As quick as it takes to turn red, I realized this wasn't just another angry player. This bordered on insubordination. It took every bit of my knowledge of lawsuits to keep me from following him. Only my mouth did.

"You don't like what I'm saying, pal, you just keep walking," I shouted. He stopped in his tracks with a startled shake. I kept at it. "You just go right up to that clubhouse and take your fucking uniform off and get the hell out of here."

He stayed. And so did his frightened expression, accompanied by his teammates' open fear. The next day the expressions were gone, but the team was playing better. And Foy, who was probably ripping my ass under his tobacco breath, was playing harder. Not because of me but in spite of me.

And I thought, That's fine. If that's what it takes to win, I'll do it. No matter what some great baseball philosophers who have never worn a uniform say, players give you 100 percent not because they want something but because they hate something. Me, I gave 100 percent because I hated losing. Others hated failure. For the ones who treated losing and failure lightly, I figured I'd give them something even better to hate. Me. I tried to make some players win just to show me up.

And it worked. History will confirm that Foy played so well after our little chat that he was named the International League's Most Valuable Player before being called to the major leagues in 1966 and enjoying a solid six-year career, including a World Series appearance. As for his teammates—well, they couldn't have made my managerial debut more fun. Two championships in the first two seasons. And for once I wasn't being paid to be the outfielder I never was after my injury. I was being paid to be myself.

Not that it made me feel my personal life was worth anything. Because, despite my wins and moments of self-realization, it wasn't. I often wonder if I managed so desperately in those first two years partly because the rest of my world was so horseshit. Remember, I'd accepted darn near a 50 percent pay cut to trade in my Red Sox uniform and take this job. We'd always been poor, but now we were dirt-poor. Already Norma and I had two children: Kathi (age 10) and Rick (9). Then on March 20, 1965, in my first spring as a pro manager, Norma gave birth to our second son.

Having a new baby was wonderful. The bad part was that Norma gave birth in a hospital near our apartment in Arcadia, California, while I was at the Sox minor league spring training site in De Land, Florida. If it wasn't for the care of Art and Addie Zullo, the apartment house's resident managers who helped Norma with the kids while she was running from the doctor's office to the grocery store and back, I don't know how she'd have made it. One consequence of our geographical separation was that at our training site I announced that the baby boy's name was Joel. Imagine my wife's surprise when she heard about the announcement while cradling our new son, *Marc*. Nice communication. I could have sworn we'd agreed upon . . . well, it didn't matter. As you might have already guessed, she was the boss, not to mention the one closest to the birth certificate. So Marc it was. I explained it to everyone in De Land by saying we had a baby to be named later.

Because of the new arrival, Norma couldn't join me until the first week of May in Toronto, at which point I finally laid eyes on Marc. Then I saw too much of him. If you think your newborn had a bad bout with colic, well, consider this: Marc had it so bad that the doctors finally put him in a hospital so Norma and I could get a few nights' sleep.

My second season in Toronto was quieter, but only because we were too poor for the five of us to spend the summer together. We were so poor around that time that driving through Fort Worth the previous winter we'd had to float the guy in the toll booth a check. For a quarter.

After I was settled in Toronto for that 1966 season, Norma

sent Rick up to keep me company. I figured, How much trouble can a 10-year-old be? Well, he wasn't trouble in a conventional sort of way. But Rick, unlike his daddy, was the kind who made friends easily. And soon, before games, he was inviting what seemed like every child in a 12-square-block area to our motel for lunch. In order for me to afford this, everyone could eat but me. And so I didn't. I spent most of the summer munching on ballpark snacks only and dropped 25 pounds, down to my Mickey Sinks fighting weight. I must admit that sometimes, beneath my self-imposed shell, I let this soft heart get the best of me.

But after that second season it appeared my hunger was going to pay off. A year earlier the Red Sox had promoted their business manager to the rank of general manager. His name was Dick O'Connell, and from the start being around him was a blessing. He loved kids, and seeing as he showed up unannounced to watch a three-game series in Columbus that year and talked only to me, I assumed he was also interested in kid managers. Shortly before the end of the Red Sox' 1966 season, another horrible one in which they made fools of themselves, he fired veteran manager Billy Herman without naming a permanent replacement. Then he had the gall to hold up the annual organizational meetings in the fall of 1966 until after I'd led my Toronto team to another championship and could join them. Usually such things aren't done for a triple-A manager. I knew something was up.

When I arrived in Boston, rumors about me replacing Herman were running through town like the autumn wind. I thought, I should know better. I remembered the boy who once thought he was going straight from Fort Worth to Hollywood, only to have his hopes shattered by Old Man Rickey. I knew all about believing rumors. So what did I do? I believed them. Every whisper. I prepared to be tapped on the shoulder at any moment and anointed Red Sox king. It didn't calm me when, shortly after my arrival, interim manager Pete Runnels ushered me into the tiny Red Sox clubhouse beneath Fenway Park, threw open the door to a cozy cubbyhole with his name on the desk inside, and said, "Let me show you your new office." I laughed uneasily.

For the first three days of the meetings nothing happened. I was starting to sweat. I was starting to wonder what the hell I'd told my friends back in Toronto. Then we had our final dinner together with all the front office people at Jimmy's Harborside. After that dinner O'Connell motioned for me and Eddie Popowski, who had already been named a coach for the 1967 season, to jump into his car. Just driving us back to the hotel, O'Connell said. But then he went around a corner, pulled up to a curb, and without even shutting the car off, turned to me and stuck out his hand. "I want to shake the hand of the next manager of the Boston Red Sox," he said.

There. Just like that. Thank God. "Thank you very much," I calmly told O'Connell. But inside me that fire was building up again, starting to burn through my spirit. And inside I was thinking, Mr. O'Connell, you made one hell of a choice. Maybe that sounds cocky. But I wonder—what are a person's chances if he takes a job and doesn't say that to himself?

We drove to O'Connell's house, and he laid out the rules. They were simple. A one-year contract for $25,000. No other guarantees. No other breaks. No extra hopes. He made it clear he was taking a chance on me, so I would just have to accept what he offered. By the time I left Boston two days later, the truly generous O'Connell had upped my salary first to $30,000, then to $35,000. I had been manager two days, and the rules were changing already.

Knowing the craziness that awaited me the following spring, that winter in California I decided there was only one way to prepare for it. I went on a television game show—*Hollywood Squares*, with Paul Lynde and Charlie Weaver and all those people. I won my first three rounds and then lost when I said that the plural of "cello" is "cellos." The show's experts claimed it was "celli." A couple of days later those experts called me and told me they were wrong. "Cellos" was acceptable. Boy, did I feel bad. You know how much I hate to beat somebody at his own game. I was asked back on the show and became the first person ever to survive for five straight days. I promptly won $2,700 and a Honda motorcycle and a trip to Paris for one, which Norma didn't allow me to take.

The game show was no big deal, but it made me think. Was this going to be my lucky year? A couple of days into my first spring training I discovered the answer to that question: a resounding no. The youngest manager in the league (age 37) had gratefully accepted a black eye. The previous season, the Red Sox had lost more games than all but one other team in the league. They finished 72–90, in ninth place out of 10 teams. Note: nobody in the history of baseball had ever gone from ninth to first in one year. They also had the worst pitching staff (3.92 ERA) and worst fielding average (.975) of anyone in the league. Note: the two things I cared about most were pitching and defense.

The one good thing about this sick situation was that I knew it would respond well to my particular method of treatment, because it required you to do anything and everything to win, because it demanded a blind loyalty to winning. Period. And I knew my method worked best with terrible teams. With teams whose weak nature had backed them into a corner. With teams that had tried the conventional motivation methods (I'm okay, you're okay) and the new motivational methods (I'm a superstar, you're a superstar) and still failed. With teams that had run out of choices. The 1967 Red Sox were such a team. When you think about it, I had them right where I wanted them.

I made my first move a private one. If I was going to place my team on edge, I wanted to put myself on edge. Despite the tenuousness of my one-year contract, I arranged for a three-year lease on an apartment in the North Shore Gardens complex in the Boston suburb of Peabody. And then I bought furniture that I arranged to pay off in three years. There. Now I would definitely be managing every game like it was the World Series. One bad year and they'd repossess my sofa. Norma thought I was crazy. She was right. I was crazy. But that was good, because soon I would be asking a young baseball team to be crazy with me.

After setting guidelines for myself, I arrived for my first spring training as a big league manager bearing many rules for the players, most of whom had either played with me or under me. Meaning, they knew I knew all their bullshit.

Among the first rules I imposed was that this team would have no captain. It had become a cruise ship overrun with people thinking they were captains. It was sinking with captains. I told the players that the cruise was over. They didn't need a captain anymore. They had a new boss now—on the field, in the clubhouse. Me.

No problem. Well, one problem. The official captain was popular outfielder Carl Yastrzemski. Everyone wanted to know how I would break the news to owner Tom Yawkey's favorite player. What would I tell the legend? Hey, I didn't tell him squat. I recognized no captains, so I had no reason to speak to him as a captain. I told O'Connell there would be no captains, and that was that.

Maybe I could have done it more gracefully. Maybe Yaz and I could have gotten off to a better start if I'd called him into my office and asked him to resign as captain. Yeah, and maybe I should have asked everyone on the team how many games they wanted to play. And maybe I would have lasted in Boston about six months. And had my goddamn living room repossessed. The hell with grace. I wanted wins. Isn't that what the fans wanted? My ass was on the line on a one-year contract, and during that time this team was going to do everything Dick Williams's way, not Millie Putz's way, nor Yaz's way. Eliminating the club captaincy was just my first way of passing that message along. Okay, so Yaz lost the $500 fee paid a club captain. I wonder how much he made after we finally stopped playing more than six months later, in the middle of October, in the World Series.

Besides, Yaz didn't seem to take the news too hard. At least, not at first. He came to my office early in spring training, closed the door, and told me he'd do anything I needed. Said he'd help me in any way he could. I could tell he was trying to clear himself of any responsibility for problems with previous managers. I responded, "Yaz, I don't blame you one bit for the bad atmosphere around here. We're all starting new, and everybody has a clean slate. So let's make it work." I emphasized the word "let's." Yaz didn't have the outgoing and enthusiastic makeup to be a chief anyway, but he could be one hell of an Indian. And I needed that Indian.

Not that all the meetings in the world could've made me give him one ounce of special treatment. Everyone was watching my reaction that first spring when Yaz's wife left their Winter Haven apartment and made her annual return to Boston to care for their children. The team policy had always been that players who are alone stay in the team hotel. Yaz was now alone, but nobody before had ever asked him to move out of his apartment. Would I ask? No, I would not. I ordered. And whether he liked it or not, Yaz complied. It wasn't a personal thing, it was a team thing. In other words, I wonder how many substitutes and "no-name" guys later played hard for me because of it.

Another rule: everybody show up on time. Everybody knew this, but not everybody believed it until pitchers Bob Sadowski and Dennis Bennett arrived 30 minutes late for one of my first workouts. They had the nerve to blame it on the hotel. Said they didn't get their wakeup calls. First I publicly chewed their ass. Since their lateness was a sign of disrespect for the rest of the team, I wanted the rest of the team to see them paying for it. Then I took it one step further. This first spring I would take everything one step further. I ordered the hotel to give 7 A.M. wakeup calls to every player, every day, regardless.

And I made a personal note to myself—no more trusting Bennett and Sadowski. Maybe this is why neither was with the Red Sox by June. If you're going to be late for a workout and lie about it, you'd better be a great pitcher. Neither Bennett nor Sadowski was. Bennett later threatened to sue me for saying he was a bad influence on the younger players. But the suit was never filed. Must have realized that truth is an unbeatable defense.

I administered several other rules, most of them based on two principles that have guided my career: give 100 percent, and don't make mental mistakes. Having gotten my team's attention with all this, I got down to the business of baseball. At my first full squad workout, I gathered the Red Sox around the on-deck circle and told them we were going to relearn the game, inch by inch, base by base. Any resemblance between this and the old Dodgers training methods was not coincidental. The procedure took two hard working days, but by the end there was little doubt as to my love for fundamentals and detail. The players learned what I loved. And they learned to respect what I loved.

Soon camp was working smoothly, with nobody standing around, not even the pitchers who weren't pitching. The reason for this was volleyball. Sounds weird, but I ordered them to play daily games. It was good for their coordination and conditioning, and even their competitiveness, as the winning team had to do only half of their postworkout sprints. No, this is not how most managers occupy their pitchers. Traditionally, between workouts pitchers shag batting-practice fly balls. But having been a player, I knew better. During those shagging times they usually stand in circles and talk about who's screwing who, who's mad, and whatever. Fly balls are the last thing on their minds. Go watch your favorite team take batting practice—you'll see. In comparison, I figured, how much internal trouble can a little volleyball game cause?

Well, two days into the volleyball games I had problems. Ted Williams–size problems. The legendary Williams, probably the greatest hitter in baseball history, was kind enough to join my first camp to work with the outfielders. Except that the former Boston star preferred to spend most of his time with our pitchers. I don't know why, but I think he didn't want them playing volleyball. Apparently, Williams thought volleyball time was like vacation time, so he would interrupt the games by lecturing them on hitting the slider, or handling the curveball, or whatever. My impressionable pitchers wouldn't dare ignore him, and I didn't blame them. So I blamed Williams.

Several times I told him, "These pitchers have work to do. Can you go talk to our outfielders instead?" He'd never say anything, just sort of walk away like a hurt puppy while muttering that pitchers could get injured playing volleyball. It went on like that for a couple of days, and then all of a sudden Williams was gone. He'd packed his bags and left camp without saying one word to me. And for the next three springs, while I was still the manager, he never returned to camp. Somebody had heard him say, "Volleyball! What is this game coming to?" But he never said a word to me. That is, until the following October, at the World Series. He was full of congratulations then. Funny thing, not once did he mention volleyball.

What the hell. As my pitchers soon learned, they didn't need Ted Williams to tell them about the rotation of the ball. Their weird manager even took care of that. Several times I jumped behind home plate and put on a mask and umpired intrasquad games so I could help them. I must have been a hell of an umpire—nobody argued with me.

But it turned out to be the only time that spring nobody argued with me. After six weeks in Winter Haven, when spring training finally came to an end, I thought, When is this supposed to get fun? I had pissed off an entire team, alienated its greatest star ever, and—oh, people in Las Vegas were saying we were 100-to-1 shots to win a pennant.

I was thrilled when the 1967 regular season finally started, because by then what else could go wrong? How about, on the third day of the season, a manager blowing his rookie pitcher's chance for immortality? It happened at Yankee Stadium. I sent a kid to the mound who was making his first major league appearance. Surely you remember Billy Rohr. Previously his claim to fame had been that he was part Cherokee. But with two out in the bottom of the ninth inning in that game, he was on the verge of something else: a no-hitter. Incredible as it may sound, he had walked five but allowed no Yankee hits. Even more incredible was that Russ Gibson, making his first major league start, was the catcher. It almost goes without saying that a pitcher on his way to a no-hitter needs an experienced man behind the plate. Gibson was working nothing short of miracles.

Then up stepped Elston Howard for, conceivably, the game's final out. Watching Howard stalk to the plate, I remembered how my buddy Joe Landrum was once throwing a no-hitter for Fort Worth with two out in the ninth when Bobby Bragan went out to calm him down. All Bragan did was make him more nervous, and Landrum quickly allowed a hit. Even knowing this, I foolishly went out to talk to Rohr just before his first pitch to Howard. Blind loyalty. Good enough for Bragan, good enough for me. What do they say about those who ignore history? That they're doomed to repeat it? After I returned from my little visit—during which I tried to tell Rohr how to pitch to Howard, but he was too excited to listen—I watched the kid work the count full. Then he laid in a curve, Howard plunked a ball over Mike Andrews's head at second base, and the no-hitter was lost.

At the time I thought, Oh well, we still won the game 3–0. But as time has passed, I've beaten myself over the head about that trip to the mound. You see, Rohr made just seven more starts in his big league career. Within two years of that great start, he was finished, ending up with a career record of 3–3 and a 5.64 ERA. In other words, he had one shot at fame, and my meddling may have helped blow it for him. And it may have sent him quickly on his downhill slide. It was then that I began learning something I've repeated many times when praised: a manager can't win a pennant, only players can. A good manager gives all the credit to his players and counts his lucky stars for being allowed to sit in the dugout. A manager can't throw a no-hitter. He can just mess one up.

Not that I gave a shit back then. I immediately had other worries. Two days after Rohr's start we were in the process of losing a game to the Yankees by blowing 13 chances at knocking in runners who were in scoring position. Meanwhile, relief pitcher Bill Landis was pitching for us like he had no brain—meaning he was walking people. I guess he'd forgotten that the first step to building a winning baseball team is taken when pitchers stop walking people. Just throw the fucking ball over the plate. How hard is that? After Landis had walked three batters, I strolled to the mound, carefully, because he had shit all over himself, and I didn't want to step in it. I told him if he didn't straighten up, his next pitches would be from the back of my doghouse. No sooner did I return to the dugout than he walked another guy. Needless to say, I didn't pitch him for another 28 days. He was in my doghouse. Everybody got the picture.

Those first couple of months I wasn't so much managing a team as making a point. And not just with my players. I showed them I would fight to make not only them but everyone else in the league care more about the Red Sox.

Like the umpires. Once early that season I argued with umpires at first, second, third, and home plate during one game. Believe me, hitting for the cycle is easy compared to arguing for the cycle. I also began trying something that won't win me any good sport awards but maybe won me a few pennants: arguing with the umpires even though I agreed with their calls. Not that I hated the umpires; I was only trying to inspire my team, and arguing with the umpires was the easiest means to that end. The umpires knew my scam, which didn't make them sleuths or anything, because I would tell them. I'd run out and start screaming about an obviously correct call and then pause and say, "Hey, I know you're right, but I've got to do this to help my team." Usually, they'd chuckle for an instant and then we'd continue to argue until I either ran out of breath or was thrown from the game.

Bottom line, I wanted everyone, including the umpires, to know that the Red Sox were trying to win. I wanted everyone to pay us some attention—serious attention, because from such attention springs fear. This need for attention is also what got me in trouble with the American League office that first year. In the late innings of a game attended by league president Joe Cronin and umpire supervisor Cal Hubbard, I noticed that Cronin had left and Hubbard was socializing with friends around him. After the game I was harping to the media about a questionable late inning call by umpire Red Flaherty that I had protested until handed my first big league ejection. Flaherty, you might remember, was a war hero and a bad umpire. I told reporters, "Can you believe they would make that call with his supervisor in the stands? Of course, Cal Hubbard was asleep by then. Then again, at least he was still here. Cronin had been gone since the fifth inning."

Nice mouth. Cost me $100. Add the league president to the growing list of people who thought Dick Williams was ready to flame out. But in becoming the first Sox manager thrown out of a game at Fenway Park since 1964, I was winning fans. And I remained sane because we were winning baseball games. Not a ton, but three months into the season, on July 13, we were 42–40, in fifth place but just six games behind the first-place Chicago White Sox. I mention that date because that is when the impossible team became the Impossible Dream.

It started with Yaz, who was having what may be the best year of any player ever. Certainly, it was the best year of any player I had ever been associated with, and I played on some pretty good Brooklyn teams. Yaz wound up leading the league in the three most important hitting categories, with a .326

average, 44 homers, and 121 RBIs. That accomplishment, baseball's Triple Crown, is so rare that it hasn't been done since. Yaz also led in hits and runs scored and total bases and slugging average. I don't think anyone will ever have a year like this, for one simple, largely ignored reason: players capable of having such great years are rarely signed to just one-year contracts, like Yaz was. You know, the kind of contract that gives a player instant adrenalin.

Behind Yaz, the rest of this formerly disjointed team had worked themselves into a good chorus. My rookies from Toronto, Reggie Smith and Mike Andrews, were playing like hardened veterans. Brash Tony Conigliaro was playing like he'd forgotten all about that $1,000 fine. Or maybe like he hadn't forgotten. And there was veteran pitcher John Wyatt in the bullpen, throwing like a kid again.

Come to think of it, Wyatt was doing everything like a kid again. I remember one game when he had somehow reached third base, turned the corner, and promptly got caught in a rundown. While scurrying back and forth, some things dropped out of his jacket pocket. No big deal. Just some cigarets and matches, his car keys . . . and a tube of Vaseline. Before he was able to pick up the tube and hide it, judging from his expression, it looked like Landis would no longer be the only one on the Red Sox who had shit himself.

Wyatt's little tube of Vaseline really didn't bother me, though. I never encouraged a guy to throw a spitball, probably because it's so hard to throw one right. But if he did throw it right, then I looked the other way. As long as he was getting batters out, he could pitch it out of his ass. And as long as he didn't embarrass the club, like the time in 1967 when rookie Gary Waslewski tried to throw a spitter and wound up with a gob of Vaseline hanging off his head. Right there on the mound. Looked like somebody blew his nose on him. Waslewski is eternally thankful that, as you shall see, he's more famous for something else.

The one character who could—and almost did—drive me around the bend was my third baseman Joe Foy. He spent our reunion season once again setting the tone for players who play in spite of me. We would go through these cycles where I'd bench him for a couple of days, he'd call me a "two-faced sneak," he'd return to the lineup and hit a couple of home runs in a doubleheader, I'd bench him a week later for being so fat he couldn't bend over for a ground ball (I was actually quoted on that), he'd drop the weight and return to hit a couple more homers in a three-game series somewhere, and then we'd cuss each other out. Ah, the romance of baseball.

Then there was pitcher Jim Lonborg, who entered the 1967 season with a career record of 19–27 and departed it a changed man. He'd suddenly gotten tough. No longer were pussy .200 hitters beating him. No longer was he beating himself. He proved all of this to us on June 21 in Yankee Stadium. We were leading 4–0 in the second inning when up stepped Foy, who had hit a grand slam off the Yankees the night before. The Yankee pitcher Thad Tillotson, in an obviously horseshit attempt at retribution, threw a ball off the top of Foy's batting helmet. For once I was thankful Foy's skull was so thick. As he trotted to first base, I said, to no one in particular, "We know what we've got to do."

Lonborg, that day's starter, knew. And in the bottom of the second inning he did it, hitting Tillotson on the shoulder. A brawl ensued, maybe the most amazing brawl in baseball history because, despite Reggie Smith's flying tackle of Tillotson, and Rico Petrocelli's left hook that knocked Joe Pepitone from the game, nobody was ejected. And with my new tough guy Lonborg still pitching, that wasn't the end of it. In the top of the third Tillotson hit Lonborg and the benches cleared again. Then in the bottom of the third, without even a suggestion from me, Lonborg retaliated by brushing back Charlie Smith and then hitting pinch hitter Dick Howser in the back. The benches cleared a third time, and Yankee manager Ralph Houk and I were threatened with suspension. Whoa, I said.

For Lonborg, the season of his life was just getting started.

In that one incident he had proved to me and to the rest of the league that he wasn't going to be just another frightened kid with talent. He was going to be a scary kid with talent. All by not being afraid to pitch inside.

Thanks to Lonborg and others, beginning on July 14 the 1967 Red Sox season actually became fun. On that day we defeated Baltimore 11–5, with good pitching from Lonborg and a homer from Conigliaro that disappeared over Fenway Park's wonderfully large green left field fence and didn't land until the Massachusetts Turnpike. Some people thought the homer might mean we'd soon be playing out of this world. They were right. For 10 straight games we didn't lose once. It was a winning streak as strange and wonderful as an open parking spot in downtown Boston. So strange, in fact, that it didn't reach its peak on the field but in an airport, after we returned home from Cleveland following our 10th straight win on July 23. We had moved into second place, one-half game behind the White Sox.

On the airplane we received word that there were "a few" people waiting for us at Logan Airport. We laughed about it, joked about how maybe our little group of wives and kids had grown. But then we tried to land. "A few" people turned out to be 10,000, swarming the tarmac and forcing us to change our incoming flight pattern and land on a different runway. We got off the plane, climbed on a bus, and drove over to the crowd of people, who couldn't have been more wide-eyed than we were. This was more people than the Red Sox had averaged in attendance in the last 10 years. These were people who, judging by their cheers and chants and banners, were actually glad to see us.

When the bus stopped, Yaz stood up and asked the obvious question: "Does anybody know if they're hostile?" We pushed my son Rick, who was our batboy and sometimes traveled with me, out the door first. Just to check. He was cheered and slapped on the back. The rest of us followed, and the responses grew louder with each player. It was even more heartening than amazing. Today Boston is considered perhaps America's top baseball town. The fans fill Fenway even when their team is lousy and losing. Baseball talk fills the radio and television airwaves even in the dead of winter. I like to think back to that midsummer reception, when we weren't even in first place yet and couldn't see out of our bus for all the fans' faces pressed against the windows, and wonder if it didn't all start there. Put it this way. When I arrived, they hadn't drawn 1,000,000 since 1960. In my three years not once did they draw less than 1,700,000, and it's been pretty much that way ever since.

Our hot streak was certainly fueled by those fans. We were never more than three games out of first place the rest of the season. Some of the guys played mad at me, others played inspired because of me, but all of them played. Even my buddy George Scott.

Scott and I spent the year engaging in—how should I put this?—guerrilla warfare. In his second season as the Sox' regular first baseman he'd come straight to the big leagues from double-A Pittsfield, so I'd never managed him in the minor leagues. Good thing, because we'd have killed each other. Scott was a likable guy with a weight problem—in both his belly and his head. I once said, "Talking to him is like talking to a block of cement." Everybody thought I was joking, and even Yaz told somebody it was a rather cruel joke. But it was no joke. I meant it.

Our problems started in spring training when I played him sporadically in right field to give a guy named Tony Horton some time at first base. George, of course, bitched and bitched. He didn't realize that I'd play him at first throughout the year, that Horton couldn't carry his jock and would later be traded. He didn't understand that I was just trying to give Horton a chance before turning him loose. That's what spring training is for, isn't it? Giving somebody a chance?

But no, George wouldn't listen. It was because of Scott that I first adopted a policy that should be followed by managers and fans alike: when you read about a player bitching in spring training, ignore him. In the spring, when he can't be held accountable by statistics, a player will complain if he doesn't play enough, and then complain if he plays too much. As was the case with Scott, most complaints have nothing to do with reality, which even most bitchers realize. In spring training you should consider the players as just dogs trying to mark their turf for the upcoming season.

I spent half the season trying to figure out just what Scott's turf was. It was a difficult task because I don't think Scott himself knew. Not only wouldn't he listen, he wouldn't understand. Like one road game, in the top of the fifth inning, we were leading but it was raining, so we needed to finish this inning to get an official game. I ordered my guys to swing at the first pitch, a common ploy among teams trying to speed up a possible rain-shortened victory. Just like managers who are trailing in the rain will order their guys to bunt the ball foul and run way past first base and walk, walk, walk all the way back to the plate, only to bunt it foul again. Or managers who will order their team, while throwing the ball around the infield before an inning, to "accidentally" toss the ball down into foul territory and then walk down to get it. I'd seen all of those tricks and had never seen a player not understand them. Until Scott. When I told him to make an out, you'd think I'd told him he had to be seen in public in a tight T-shirt. His face went blank. "Make an out?" he asked. "Christ, it's hard enough to make a hit!" Sadly, about the only thing that Scott understood was money. So naturally, being the concerned manager that I was, I immediately offered him cash bonuses for hitting the ball to the opposite field (right field, in his case). For every hit he got from shortstop to the right field foul line, I'd pay him $20. Only one catch. For every hit down the left field line, where he always hit them, he'd have to pay me $5. It was highly illegal, but what the hell. I've never seen any famous hitting coach change a guy's swing any faster.

Just as Scott and I got our spring problem fixed—our fight ended when I put his name in the opening day lineup at first base, as planned—another problem arose. I realized that this 6-foot-2, 210-pounder had a striking ability to gain as much as 10 pounds a day. I'm still not sure what he ate, or how much of it he ate, but some afternoons he'd walk into the clubhouse and could barely squeeze into his pants. Once when we were playing the California Angels in Anaheim, he borrowed 20 bucks from then errand boy, now Sox co-owner Haywood Sullivan. He used the money to take a cab to Los Angeles. I didn't realize that you could sightsee in grocery stores, but when Scott returned several hours later, he'd gained seven pounds.

As one of the first teams to use a video camera in baseball, we taped the fatted Scott's sluggish swing and showed it to him. You know what he said? "That ain't me, that's somebody else." Brilliant. He obviously wasn't going to listen, and our daily weight discussions were becoming a distraction. So in the August heat of the pennant race, in another three-game series in California, I did what you might guess I'd do. I made it more of a distraction. I benched him for all three games. He could have played if he'd made my required weight of 211, but seeing as he was about 220 pounds at the time, I knew he had no chance.

Before every game of that August 11–13 series, with my players gathered around, we put Scott on a scale. And he was always miserably over the limit. So he didn't start—this man who would eventually, that year, hit 19 homers with 82 RBIs. And we lost all three games, scoring a combined total of only three runs.

Everyone was in an uproar. Even the Angels' shortstop Jim Fregosi spoke out in defense of Scott, saying, "We have nine managers in this league and one dietitian." Of course, he never said it to my face. Scott griped, but somehow, by the third day, I think he understood. By the time we returned home from California to play at Fenway two days later, he had made his weight. And he later helped make our season, playing like a man plays when he knows he's just a couple of steps from the bench. The first game following his embarrassing weekend he homered in a 4−0 win over Detroit. The next day he hit two homers to help us to an 8−3 win.

Many years later I read a newspaper interview with Scott, who was then managing in Mexico. He said he finally understood what I'd gone through and why I'd had to treat him like I did. And then he thanked me for helping make him a winner. You'd be surprised to learn how many former players tell me that. But not that they wait until about 10 years after they've quit to tell me. I guess it takes that long for them to stop being mad at me. By the way, after the 1967 season I sent the Angels' Fregosi a note. It read, "I guess the dietitian won."

• • •

A week after the Scott incident, just as everyone was working together and focused on the pennant race, something else happened that made this dream seem even more impossible. On August 18 at Fenway Park, in the fourth inning against the California Angels, we were startled out of our seats by the loud pop of a baseball hitting flesh and the sickening sight of a strong young outfielder crumpling to the ground. The outfielder was Tony Conigliaro. The sound was a fastball from California pitcher Jack Hamilton making contact with his left cheek.

My heart nearly stopped. I raced to the plate and saw a man lying motionless, with blood rushing from his nose and a left eye already beginning to blacken and swell as we watched. In a few minutes he started flipping his legs around in agony, and we could no longer watch. While all of us stood around looking at something else, anything else, a stretcher was finally brought out and Conigliaro was carried off. Tony and I had our disagreements, but at this moment I actually prayed.

Oddly enough, it wasn't so much Jack Hamilton as Conigliaro's own aggressiveness that did him in. At the time, as our starting right fielder, he had 20 homers and 67 RBIs in just 95 games. You don't hit that way by being timid; he loved to crowd the plate and force the pitcher to give him something good to hit. Hamilton, it turns out, wouldn't be forced. He threw the ball where it wouldn't have touched most hitters. But Conigliaro was planted smack in the ball's deadly path.

We were all very upset by the beaning and tried almost immediately to visit Conigliaro in the hospital. But team owner Tom Yawkey said no. And not just in the beginning. Every time I tried to visit Conigliaro, Yawkey said no. He allowed only himself that privilege. Conigliaro later said he resented me for not showing up. I wish he'd asked me about it first.

When Yawkey wasn't visiting Tony, he was in our clubhouse. It was his daily presence there that convinced me we really did have a chance at the pennant. Because the only time I ever saw Yawkey was when we won. If somebody told me I saw Yawkey five times during the period I played for the Red Sox (1964–65), it was four times more than I remember. Maybe if I got to the park early we'd catch him showering in our clubhouse. He liked to play pepper with the batboys, although he needed to wear shin guards because he was diabetic and couldn't chance the bleeding caused by an injury.

During my first three months as a manager I saw Yawkey even less, and not because he forgot the number of my office phone. I was the first manager in several years who wasn't his drinking buddy or bobo, and this made him uncomfortable. Even though I played for the Red Sox, I wasn't considered a member of his business "family," because I wasn't in his social club. Yawkey tolerated my presence only because his new general manager, Dick O'Connell, wanted me. And that was fine. As long as I won, I figured, Yawkey wouldn't touch me.

Because I did win, though, suddenly I couldn't get him out of my face. In the second half of the 1967 season you'd have thought he was one of the damn players. He was in the clubhouse, around the batting cage, on the field until the last possible minute, chatting and kibitzing and being about as fake as an owner could be. I'd pass him in the clubhouse before the game as he sat bothering the players in front of their lockers, and I didn't have much to say. Why should I? Where had he been whenever we got our asses kicked earlier in the season? And didn't he know that being friendly with players would soon make them think they were in good with the owner and didn't have to listen to Williams? Didn't he understand how players worked? His presence in our domain late in 1967 wasn't just a distraction, it was an insult.

Yawkey's bullshit even wafted over to Norma through his wife, Jean. With a houseful of kids and an ornery manager to take care of, Norma didn't attend many games. It wasn't her idea of a good time to cook about 10 different meals at 10 different times during the day, pack everybody off to a game, then arrive home at midnight and get ready to start the cycle again. So Norma wasn't out there much. I know, because Jean Yawkey kept track of each time from her seat in an upstairs box. When Norma would show up, Jean would always find her and say, "Where have you been? I haven't seen you in a while." As if all Norma had to do was cheer for a team. I'm lucky she never spoke her mind to Jean, because I might have been fired on the spot by Yawkey in retaliation.

In the final stretch of the pennant race, all of that anger and ill-will was replaced by happy, crazy, catch-your-breath feelings. As the season entered its final week, we were tied for first with Minnesota, while Chicago was one-half game behind and Detroit was one and a half games out. Then we lost two straight to lowly Cleveland, getting outscored 12−3 and blowing our tie for the lead. Here's where the fun started. On Thursday, one of two straight off-days, we were tied with Detroit for second place, one game behind Minnesota and one-half game ahead of Chicago. But we had one advantage. Our final two games of the season would be in Fenway Park against first-place Minnesota. We would get to play the best to become the best. I couldn't wait.

Because I couldn't wait, on Thursday I did probably the craziest thing of the year. The White Sox were playing a doubleheader with Kansas City, and I could only pick up distant reports of the game on the car radio. So I took a six-pack of Miller beer—they weren't making Miller Lite back then—and I climbed in the front seat of my car in the parking lot of my apartment building. There I sat through the evening and into the night, hoping and wishing and trying to will the White Sox to lose both games before I went nuts or my car battery died. And they did—they lost both games, and then lost their last three to Washington to put them out of it.

After a rare Friday off-day, on Saturday we welcomed the Twins to a Fenway Park that, for September, was crowded and steamy and splendid. We trailed the Twins by one game. Unless the other second-place team, the Tigers, won three out of four games in a weekend set of doubleheaders with the Angels, the winner of this Twins–Red Sox duel would win the pennant. To me, it was almost like the World Series come early. For the first game, I went with Jose Santiago to keep with the regular rotation, giving Lonborg the start in Sunday's final. True, if we didn't win Saturday, there wouldn't be a Sunday. But if you play like you aren't going to win, often you don't.

And not changing strategies worked. Once again, under-managing triumphed over overmanaging. Santiago allowed just two hits over seven innings. On offense Carl Yastrzemski continued a streak that cemented my feeling that his season was baseball's best ever. In this biggest of games he went three for four with a three-run homer and four RBIs. Overall, in his final 13 at-bats of 1967, all pressure appearances, Yaz had 10 hits. In that situation, with a pennant on the line, I challenge any of today's players to top that. (And remember, their agents' mouths can't bat for them.)

George Scott added another homer in that Saturday game as we won 6−4 to pull into a tie with the Twins for first place. Afterward we received even better news—the Tigers had only split that doubleheader with California after blowing a 6−2 lead in Game Two. They would need to sweep a doubleheader Sunday in order to tie the winner of our Sunday game for the pennant. For the first time I thought, Maybe we are a team of destiny.

But—not for the first time—I was feeling funny about a relationship with a player. In the ninth inning of that Saturday game, with the Twins trailing 6−2 but with a runner on second and two out and Harmon Killebrew batting, you'd think I would order an intentional walk. No. I wanted to win this game now, so I ran out and told Gary Bell, "Whatever you do, let him hit it." We could afford the risk that the son of a bitch might hit it nine miles. Two runs didn't matter. Guess what happened. The son of a bitch did hit it nine miles for his 44th homer, tying him for the league lead that Yaz had just taken with a homer two innings earlier. And a day later their seasons ended in that tie. So while Yaz still won the triple crown, he didn't win all three categories outright. All because of me. I went to a red-faced Yaz afterward and apologized for trying to win a game. It was one of the first, and last, times I have ever done that. Just the sound of it makes me sick.

Now everybody started saying we were a team of destiny. Funny thing, destiny. It doesn't come from the heavens but from a will to do absolutely anything to win. Our final regular season game proved to me that if I didn't give these players any other bit of wisdom, I gave them that. On Sunday afternoon we were trailing the Twins and their starting pitcher Dean Chance, 2−0, when my starter Lonborg came to bat to start the bottom of the sixth inning. Some thought I might send up a pinch hitter for him. But he had become one of my toughest and smartest players, and if anyone could figure out how to pull our ass out of the sling . . . well, he could and he did. He came through with the most important hit of the season. And, not coincidentally, one of the shortest.

With all the world expecting a strikeout or groundout, Lonborg never even took a full swing. On the first pitch from Chance he bunted. Not a sacrifice bunt, because there was nobody on base, but an honest-to-goodness Rickey Henderson–type bunt. All 20 feet worth. Surprised the hell out of me. Shocked the living shit out of the Twins. Their third baseman, Cesar Tovar, was so stunned that he bobbled the ball, and Lonborg was safe on first. And old Fenway Park, with 36,000 fans crammed into every creaky corner, was literally shaking. So was I.

Singles by Jerry Adair and Dalton Jones loaded the bases, still with none out, when Yaz came up to bat. You should know what happened next. He singled up the middle to drive in two runs and tie the score. I knew then this team had done its part. It had found that way to win. Destiny, take over. Sure enough, we scored three more runs that inning without a ball leaving the infield. Ken Harrelson's grounder was thrown late to home plate by shortstop Zoilo Versalles, scoring Dalton Jones. New pitcher Al Worthington threw a couple of wild pitches to score Yaz. A ball off the knee of first baseman Killebrew scored the fifth run.

Which was all we needed. The Twins would score just once more off the fabulous Lonborg. When Rich Rollins's pop fly was caught by shortstop Rico Petrocelli with two out in the ninth, that was it. We had clinched at least a tie for the pennant. The stands erupted in a burst of screaming from frantic people who surrounded Lonborg and carried him around the field. He appeared in the clubhouse much later, his uniform torn to pieces. By that time his teammates had covered themselves in beer and shaving cream and were laughing like kids.

Me, I was worried. I tried to reach the mound immediately after the game to congratulate Lonborg, but I couldn't get there, so I retreated to my office to think. Hey, we hadn't won anything yet. Detroit had won their first game against California, and if they won their second game, there would be a playoff for this pennant. I thought about who would start the playoff game, and then I walked out in the middle of the celebration and grabbed him. It was Lee Stange, who had already had a couple of beers. "Careful," I told him. "You're starting tomorrow."

Why couldn't I have let it loose right away? Why couldn't I have enjoyed this moment when we had the pennant almost in our grasp? Wasn't this an occasion for celebrating, no matter what happened next? Why did I have to wait until the end of some other game to be happy? Looking back, I wish I had partied, celebrated everything in my life that was even close to giving me reason to celebrate. But I couldn't celebrate anything but absolute victory, which is the only reason I compete. And so while my team went bonkers in our tiny clubhouse, I walked up to Yawkey's office to monitor the rest of the Tigers game with O'Connell, the coaches, and our wives. My competitive edge, which had helped this team reach the threshold of success, had also—ironically, painfully—kept me from celebrating any part of that journey. I could celebrate only the end result.

It turned out, thankfully, that my stay in Yawkey's office didn't last long. The Angels took a 4–3 lead over Detroit in the third inning of their second game, and then, as I learned from the clubhouse radio, they made quick work of an 8–5 win. I went downstairs to join my team for the final innings. When the Tigers finally made the last out on yet another miracle—Dick McAuliffe hit into a double play for only the second time all season—we had finally won it, and I finally lost it. We had formally, officially, won the American League pennant. A 100-to-1 shot was going to the World Series. A loudmouth reserve outfielder had led a team to baseball's biggest game of all.

It was Impossible. It was a Dream. And I finally allowed myself to jump through the clubhouse, screaming and shouting, "It's over, it's over, it's over!" If those more closely resemble the words of a relieved man than a happy man, so be it. For me, relief is happiness. And for at least a few moments on that October day in Boston, I drowned myself in it. The best and funniest thing about that celebration came from the lips of Tom Yawkey. He hadn't drunk in several years but actually raised his glass of champagne and said, "I will drink to you." Then he started to cry.

"Mr. Yawkey," I said in a rare moment of open compassion, "I'd love to have that tear." Then I turned to my son and said, "Ricky, remember this minute the rest of your life."

And then I looked across the clubhouse at Lonborg and—oh, shit. I became me again. I started thinking about the World Series against the powerful St. Louis Cardinals. Didn't anyone else know that this exciting finish had cursed us? That since we had to use Lonborg in Sunday's season finale, he couldn't reasonably pitch again until Thursday's Game Two of the Series? Didn't anyone else see that in just three days we had more challenges to meet? I did. I began to ease out of my partying mood. I was thinking, Let's see—Jose Santiago will start Game One, and . . .

For many, our Impossible Dream lasted all winter and was to carry them through many colder winters. For me, it lasted that half hour. Winning has its price, and mine was always that I could win but couldn't enjoy it as long as there was more winning to be done. As cops on horseback escorted us out of the Fenway Park area at midnight following our afternoon clinching, with the streets still filled with drunken joy, all I could think was, How are we going to hit Bob Gibson?

The Series was more exciting than most thought it would be. It appropriately mirrored our season as we were knocked down, got back up, got knocked down again, climbed up again, and so forth. But unfortunately, in this shorter drama, without enough time for any destiny, we ended up on our ass. The memories are not good.

We lost Game One in Boston to the heavily favored Cardinals and were beaten worse than the 2−1 score suggests, as Santiago was racked for 10 hits in just seven innings while Gibson threw a six-hitter. That was one of the best parts of the series, watching Gibson protect the mound like it was his own home, throwing inside and hard and keeping each of our hitters worried about becoming another Tony Conigliaro.

We came back in Game Two with Jim Lonborg, our version of Gibson. He didn't allow a hit until two out in the eighth, when Julian Javier knocked a ball into the left field gap for a double. Yaz couldn't chase it down, but he more than redeemed himself with two homers that gave Lonborg a one-hit, 5−0 win.

As we headed to St. Louis for Game Three, I realized that this World Series was missing something. It wasn't like the Brooklyn Dodgers against the New York Yankees. There wasn't any fire. There wasn't any hate. It wasn't like a 12-round heavyweight fight, it was like a two-week party. Somebody needed to stir things up. About 10 pitches into Game Three, I finally got my chance. Cardinals pitcher Nelson Briles hit Yaz in the leg with a fast one that wasn't even close to the plate. It was an obvious retaliation for Yaz's two homers the previous day. And it sucked. I went nuts on the bench, and I would have thrown at Briles if this wasn't the World Series and we were hanging on by our cuticles. But after we'd lost 5−2—partly because Yaz went zero for three—I said my piece: "The St. Louis Cardinals are as bush as the name of the beer company that owns them." There. Now this series had been placed on edge. My ballplayers do better when feeling that edge. I hoped the Cardinals didn't.

I didn't make many friends with that statement, and may have even lost a few, as St. Louis was still my old stomping ground. My time away from the stadium during the three Series games there was spent at giant parties and family reunions in the hotel. It was at these affairs that I met my Series MVPs—Most Valuable Partiers. They were two guys who showed up in my suite the first night. And the second. And the third. They were pleasant fellows, got along well with everyone, drank and danced and ate their share. When they called me before we left town to see if there was any more partying to be done, I told them no, but added that it had been good to see them. Then I started wondering. Just who were they? Turns out nobody in my family knew them. None of my friends knew them. Maybe they were spies for the Cardinals. Or maybe they were just, well, two guys looking for a good time. Whoever they are, I hope they had fun, mostly because it sounds like something a young St. Louisan named Dick Williams might have done.

My little remark about the Cardinals after Game Three didn't do us any good in Game Four. A pitcher like Gibson has a habit of neutralizing such things. He threw a five-hit shutout while Santiago suffered an elbow injury and didn't make it out of the first inning, leading to a 6−0 loss that put us in a deep hole, three games to one. Once again we were one loss away from the end of our season. And with Santiago hurt, our pitching rotation was screwed. It's funny, but I wasn't worried about the next game, simply because we still had Lonborg. At that late stage of the season, when a guy is throwing well, a good outing becomes a foregone conclusion. Look at the Dodgers' Orel Hershiser in 1988 or Oakland's Dave Stewart in 1989. A pitcher who ends the season hot rarely blows up in the postseason. Hitters are a different story—October brings some great ones to their knees. But with pitchers who have reached a great stride, it seems like that stride becomes unbreakable.

And so it was with Lonborg, who threw a three-hitter in a 3−1 win. He set the record for fewest allowed hits in two consecutive Series games—four. And more important to me, in those two games he walked only one batter. After celebrating Lonborg's win for about five seconds, I became worried again. Who was going to start Game Six back in Boston? Then I thought back to a promise I'd made when it didn't look like there would be a Game Six. It was a promise to rookie Gary Waslewski, who had appeared in just 12 games for us during the regular season while going back and forth between Boston and triple-A Toronto. After the kid had thrown three scoreless relief innings in Game Three, I told him he'd earned the right to start in Game Six. Little did I know that there'd be a spot available and he could hold me to that promise.

Well, he didn't have to hold me to anything. I was going to keep the promise and let him start. If there's anything more important than winning, it's my word. So we flew back to Boston, and as I was fretting over putting this kid in a tough situation, something happened that made me relax and realize that this World Series was actually fun. Back in my neighborhood of Peabody I was made to feel like a little boy again. The locals threw me a parade.

That's right. Even though the World Series had not ended, and even though it was cold and drizzly, the town lined the streets for a parade. In my honor. I was so surprised and genuinely delighted that I couldn't tell them no. As Norma and I were driven through the crowded streets, waving to masses of umbrellas and slickers, I noticed my next-door neighbor Brenda Halper and her children huddled up in the town square watching and waving like everybody else.

Norma shouted down to her, "What are you doing here?"

She shouted back, "What else? We came to see you."

Norma replied, "You can walk out the door in the morning and see me. Why would you come down here in the rain?"

She shouted, "You and Dick had a heck of a year, didn't you?"

It finally sank in then: yes, no matter what happened in this World Series, we *did* have a heck of a year.

The next day, in Game Six, the kid Waslewski allowed just two runs in five innings and helped us to an 8–4 win, making me feel even warmer. But I knew, and I think everybody else at least suspected, that Game Seven could be the most lopsided tiebreaker in Series history. They were going with Bob Gibson, who had three days' rest. With no Santiago, I had no choice but to pitch Lonborg on an almost unheard-of two days' rest. Twice before that season he'd pitched with that short a break, winning one and losing one, but in a big game we'd need every inch of him.

No matter. I'll be damned if I lose a Game Seven with anybody but my ace. I was praying for one last miracle. I didn't get it. Gibson threw a three-hitter, while Lonborg allowed more than three times that many hits in his first six innings, leading to a 7−2 Cardinals victory. As we watched the better team celebrate on the field, I forgot for a moment how incredible it was that this 100-to-1 shot got within one game of the world championship. I was too depressed. I didn't look at how far we had come, only at how close we'd gotten. Once again, close was not enough. Only Dick Williams could walk out of a World Series clubhouse feeling like a complete loser.

Several days after the series I drove to Fenway Park to talk to Mr. Yawkey about a new contract. Oh, well, I thought, next year we'll do even better. You're asking how much better one overachieving team can do? I don't know. I definitely should have thought of that. First thing, Yawkey didn't want to give me the three-year contract that both O'Connell and I were asking him for. He said he didn't want to give me any more than a two-year deal, even though he had to figure, like everyone, that in a couple of weeks I'd be named baseball's Manager of the Year. Maybe he knew about the final payment date on my furniture loans. Or maybe, more likely, he'd decided on another steambath buddy for the job.

I think Haywood Sullivan, still just an office flunkie at the time, was also pushing Yawkey to withhold the security I felt I had earned. But finally, reluctantly, and with plenty of sourness, Yawkey gave me a three-year contract. I walked outside the office and glanced down at the Fenway Park field where a worker was cutting away the left field sod. A little investigation showed that the sod was going to be laid in Carl Yastrzemski's front yard, sort of as a reward for his season. How about that. Yawkey didn't want to give me a piece of his lousy bank account, but he was giving Yaz a big piece of his heart. I was so confused that coach Bobby Doerr and I left the park that day without my son Ricky, who was helping clean up the clubhouse. It wasn't until we got across the Mystic River Bridge that we remembered him.

That was appropriate, because over the next two years I would forget just about everything. Not only my son but my wife and the rest of my family. I would forget my manners, my common sense, sometimes even that I was a human being. The very determination and drive that I'd instilled in the miracle Red Sox would turn on me. What I had once made good had to be better. Where once a pennant was enough, now nothing short of a World Series win would do. That being damn near impossible, I became damn near impossible.

In the middle of 1968, when my problems with the pressure had reached a peak, I'll never forget Norma asking, "Why did you have to build the Red Sox so fast? Why did it have to happen in one year? Why couldn't it have taken longer? Don't you know that after where you've been, the only direction you can travel is down?"

I didn't know that then. I know it now.

The two-year nightmare began shortly after the Series with a phone call from our front office. There had been a skiing accident in Vail, Colorado. Jim Lonborg had torn his knee apart and would not return to the team until after a couple of months of the 1968 season. As his 6–10 record and 4.29 ERA that year indicates, he never really returned at all.

So I showed up in Winter Haven for my second spring training without my Cy Young Award winner. I took one look at a fat and sloppy George Scott and realized I would also probably be without my first baseman, who looked as though he'd celebrated that winter by eating a Christmas dinner every night of the week. (Indeed, he went from 19 homers and a .303 average in 1967 to three homers and a .171 average in 1968.) Then I looked at the rest of a relaxed team and wondered if any of them cared as much as I did . . . if any of them realized we were still one step short of becoming true champions. Players being human, they didn't. Me being me, I didn't accept that. So I pounded on them harder than ever, accepting nothing less than their best effort at all times, privately despairing when I didn't get it. There was never enough time to teach, never enough time to make them understand. So in the spring of 1968 I began to take my work home.

I would storm into our Winter Haven apartment and yell at Norma for not having everything neat. Or scold her for not cooking everything perfectly. I'd be sarcastic and nasty and an absolute pain in the ass. I never hit Norma, never touched my children. But my words and expressions hurt just as much as if I had hit them.

During that time a newspaper did a story on my son Ricky because he was a batboy. Ricky told the reporter, "My father is the boss at our house. Everybody does what he says." When I read that quote, I knew something was wrong. I didn't want to be a boss. I wanted to be a father. Suddenly I seemed to be failing at that. Also at being a husband. And I had the nerve to be cocky about it. A couple of times when Norma said, "I think we should talk about getting separated," I'd just look at her and say, "Where are you going?" It wasn't until she shot back with "*I'm* not going anywhere" that I realized my tough wife was serious. Looking back, if it wasn't for the sake of our children, she probably would have left me before I left the Red Sox. Left me for good.

Not that she didn't try it once. It happened one day late in the spring, when I finally pushed too much. She'd been crying every day over my horseshit treatment of her and the kids when she finally decided, Enough. I came storming home following another lackadaisical spring game and told Norma she was a bad mother. Then I turned and stormed out, headed for what was increasingly becoming my best friend: a bottle of scotch. When I returned, Norma was gone. My quiet saint can take only so much, and then she bolts. This time she packed up all of her things and the kids and drove three hours to our winter home in Riviera Beach, Florida. Sitting in my empty apartment, I thought, She's gone for good.

Did I chase her? What do you think? There were fundamentals to be learned, discipline to instill. So I ignored the fundamental laws of marriage and forgot about self-discipline, and I stayed in Winter Haven. I did not chase. I would not chase. The next day I went back to work, like always. And the next day. And the next day.

When I phoned her, she was still furious with me, so I stayed away. Only after a week did I realize that perhaps I'd forced her to run from me. Maybe I was someone to be avoided. Maybe Norma was smart to leave. And maybe I damn sure better get her back. So after one game I drove to Riviera Beach and walked in just as she was cooking dinner on the backyard grill. "Have you got an extra hamburger?" I asked quietly. And then I apologized, and she returned.

That should have been the end of it. God, how I wanted it to be the end of it. But for the manager with the curse, it was just the start. For the next two years not only did I fight with Norma, but for the first time in my life I fought with my drinking. Not beer, I was always okay with beer. Scotch was my problem. That's what got me. Smooth and sweet and explosive. Scotch turned my jokes to insults, my serious comments to sarcasm. I drank to relax. I drank because, under the heat of 1967's instant success, I couldn't provide an encore alone. I needed help to stay sane, and the bottle, I foolishly thought, gave me that help.

No, I wasn't an alcoholic—at least, not that I could figure, and Lord, how I tried to figure. I was just a very tense guy who frequently needed a few shots of scotch to relax, to settle down, even if that scotch inevitably made me hateful.

I'd gather with my coaches in Yawkey's upstairs bar at Fenway and have a pop or two or three before leaving the park after home games. And maybe a pop or two or three in the hotel bar after certain road games. I might get to feeling a little good, find somebody nearby and say something a little mean, and then find my bed and forget about it. In the morning nobody would say anything, because I was the manager.

And when I was a drunken son of a bitch, I didn't release my anger on baseball people only. At a private party in my own home I might get drunk and hammer on some poor soul for asking an innocent baseball question. The next day, when Norma and I were speaking again, she'd tell me: This is it, no more scotch. Okay, I would say; but there was always another game, always another loss to forget or another win to celebrate. On a few occasions I would even drink before dinner, during dinner, and after dinner. Let me tell you, anybody who has a mixed drink after dinner is headed for trouble. Our marriage could have used counseling, but Norma couldn't even approach me with the idea. Hell, she couldn't even approach me with hello. I was Mr. Manager, and I could damn well manage on my own. I didn't need hello, thank you.

Not that I didn't actually have plenty to contend with as Mr. Manager during those last two years in Boston. I was the one who had to put up with things like Conigliaro's comeback from his eye trouble. Yes, it was a brave and impressive effort he made, but Conigliaro soured everyone by expecting all of us to treat him like a superstar. In the spring of 1968, his first attempt to play since the awful beaning, he claimed that I wouldn't give him enough swings. Hell, I gave him too many. I probably coddled him. In the beginning I basically let him come and go as he pleased, telling him to stop whenever he felt uncomfortable at the plate.

Soon he said he felt good enough to play regularly, even though it was obvious he wasn't seeing the ball. The guy loved to play. But he also loved to go catting around at night, which continued to make me worry that he was hampering his comeback. After seeing him at bars more often than batting cages, I finally decided, He plays like one of the boys, he'll be treated like one of the boys. Before one spring game he asked to sit out with a sore throat. I told him no, he needed the work, and made him play. He went zero for four and apparently was so stressed that he couldn't see the pitches. The next day, from his apartment, he called our trainer to say he was sick again. According to Tony, he heard me in the background shouting, "If he spent less time in the bar, he'd be fine." I don't remember saying that—shit, if *I'd* spent less time in the bar, I'd also have felt better—but apparently, Conigliaro was so mad that he wanted to come to the park and fight me, except that our trainer drove to his apartment and persuaded him not to.

As you might have guessed, Conigliaro wasn't healthy enough to play that year. He finally returned the next and had a couple of damn good seasons for the Sox after I left, actually hitting a career high of 36 homers with 116 RBIs in 1970. In the end he did come back, and I was very happy for him, just as I was deeply troubled by his heart attack several years ago and his death in early 1990. Say what you will, the guy was a fighter. Between the lines there was nobody who played harder, as his great comeback years witness. He was a fighter and so am I, and that's probably why we got into so many verbal scrapes. I'm never sure who got the better of who, but I know that by having Tony Conigliaro in there fighting every day, the game of baseball was the winner.

Did I ever have trouble in 1968. After losing Lonborg and Conigliaro, we lost Jose Santiago with his recurring arm problem after just 18 starts. Then Mike Andrews was out for several weeks with an injury. And important backup out-fielder George Thomas got hurt and missed all but 12 games of the season. We ultimately lost our heart and wound up 86–76, in fourth place, 17 games behind first-place Detroit. This record wasn't as bad as it sounds, considering we had won just six fewer games than in 1967. But the Red Sox front office was upset, and I was devastated.

Nineteen sixty-nine would be better—I promised it to myself and my team and the public. And 1969 *was* better. That team ended up winning one more game than in 1968, going 87–75 for a third-place finish behind Baltimore in the newly formed American League East Division. Considering it was only the second time the team had won that many games since 1951, I'd call it a damn good finish. Too bad I wasn't around to revel in it. Because on September 22 at 4 P.M., with nine games left in the season, I was fired. Canned. Axed. Shit on. The first time. In anything. Ever. And stunned by it.

What happened? How could a Manager of the Year get so dumb in less than two seasons? I hear some people in New England are still asking themselves that. So am I. This wasn't just my first job, it was like my first love. It wasn't just a firing, it was more like a shooting. More than 20 years later, talking about it still makes me snarl, thinking about it still makes me hurt.

What happened? First, I think Tom Yawkey had been looking for an excuse ever since I was hired. When he saw how I didn't appreciate his front-running attitude, and how I'd give neither him nor his favorite players (e.g. Yaz) special clubhouse treatment, he decided I wasn't right for his team. Mr. Yawkey didn't want a professional baseball man, he wanted a politician. And you know me.

So he was looking for an excuse. And much to his delight, he found two. The first occurred in July 1969, in a newspaper story, when he publicly graded me just "good" on a scale that went from fair to good to excellent to outstanding. Just good? After all I'd been through with this once-terrible team? Just good? During an injury-filled year that still gave the club its second-best record in 18 seasons?

I was in Yawkey's office at 9:40 the next morning. I didn't kiss his ass, and couldn't if I'd wanted to. I would have had to move Haywood Sullivan, once a flunkie and now a head rat, out of the way. Sullivan, who now is a co-owner of the club, began his push to the top by constantly ripping me to Mrs. Yawkey. I know, because Norma would walk in the front office and overhear him. Sure, Mr. Yawkey eventually pulled the trigger on me. But it was Haywood Sullivan, perhaps feeling I was getting too much recognition for a lousy manager, who loaded the gun.

Hey, Haywood, if you're reading this: I never wanted your power. I never wanted your office. I only wanted to win with your baseball team. I only wish you could have gotten off Mr. Yawkey's lap long enough to see that.

So no, when I walked in that morning, I didn't beg Mr. Yawkey to change his mind about my grade. That wouldn't have been fair to me or the fans of New England, who, judging by their sudden fanaticism, felt I was doing a good job. I just told Mr. Yawkey that I was extremely sorry he felt that way but I was doing the best I could. And if winning a pennant wasn't good enough, then I was very, very sorry indeed.

I don't think I yelled. Well, maybe a little bit, but just so the older man could hear me. All he said was "I just don't think you are doing good enough." Said it over and over until I walked out.

A month later Yawkey found his other excuse in mounting complaints about how I treated my players. Complaints from the players who weren't playing. Complaints from the ones hitting a buck ninety, from the ones who were always in my doghouse. Interestingly enough, in 1967 my so-called doghouse had become a source of humor. The players understood it as an attempt to keep them motivated enough to win, and the public appreciated it because it kept the players honest. One group of people actually sent me a wooden board shaped like a doghouse and little pegs of wood with the names of all the Red Sox on them and hooks to hang the pegs on. It was cute, and so what if it came from the prisoners at the Walpole, Massachusetts, penitentiary?

But as the team lost, that doghouse ceased to be a joke to

the players. My methods of motivation that had once worked so well suddenly flamed out, ignited by the players' tender egos. I'd helped them become champions, so now they wanted to be treated like champions. All of a sudden people were saying that I no longer had an open door policy. Hell, for these players, a truly open door would've had to be taken off its hinges. Every manager I know was praised for having an open door policy when he took over a team and then criticized for not having an open door when he was fired. Face it, every manager can't change that much. In most cases, it's the players who change: after they win and celebrate once, they become unsure whether another celebration is worth the high physical and mental price.

Finally, one August night in Oakland, the consensus was that I had finally pushed a player too far. It was here, apparently, that Mr. Yawkey found his last straw. With two out and a Boston runner on third, our batter hit a grounder deep to the third baseman. Our runner on third, thinking that the third baseman would throw to first to end the inning, idly trotted down the line to home plate. Little did he know that the Oakland third baseman had caught the ball too deep, so a throw to first was impossible. If our runner had been hustling, he'd have scored. Instead, the Oakland third baseman saw him lollygagging and threw to home plate for the easy tag and third out.

Our runner had made a mental, physical, and just plain inexcusable mistake, and I had to bench and fine him for it. One problem. The runner was Carl Yastrzemski.

As Yaz approached the dugout bench, seemingly oblivious to his error, I asked him if he had a bad leg. I sounded sarcastic, perhaps, but I was serious. He wasn't. "Evidently, I do have a bad leg," he replied.

"Well," I said, sarcastically now, "evidently you do. You can't run, you can't play. You're out of the game and it will cost you $500."

You should have seen the cold stares from the bench. Or worse yet, felt them. Yaz shot me a nasty look and stalked off to the clubhouse. The rest of the team, stunned, fell silent and eventually blew a lead and the game. After the game, while Yaz said nothing, Oakland's Reggie Jackson said he could understand why I'd fined my star but not why I'd taken him out of the game. But Reggie didn't get it. I'd taken both actions precisely because Yaz was the star. If I'd let that slide, then nobody would be running to home plate.

I was still fairly ignorant of any front office harm done to me—of course, I'm ignorant of just about everything that happens off the field during the season. Thus, when we returned from a trip in late September, I thought nothing of making my usual stop the following morning in Dick O'Connell's office. O'Connell is the dearest boss I've ever played for, and I used to love just talking ball with him. On this morning we talked a little about the team, and then I talked about a coach I'd been pushing O'Connell to hire, a famed hitting instructor named Charlie Lau from Baltimore. I asked O'Connell if he had approval to hire him yet, and O'Connell said no. Then I made a little joke: "Well, have you gotten approval to hire my other coaches back?" Just a joke. But O'Connell wasn't laughing.

"No, Dick," he said. "Nobody's coming back next year. Not even you. The old man left word for me to make a change. And now I'm making it."

He was extremely apologetic about it, even though this was obviously not his decision. So I couldn't get mad. Not at first. Maybe I was too stunned. Maybe it was because I didn't hear it from Yawkey, who had gone to his vacation place in South Carolina to avoid dirtying his hands. The first thing I told O'Connell was "You want me to manage the rest of the season?" Now he really looked funny. "Uh, sure," he said.

Of course, I didn't last that long. Soon after we beat the Yankees 4 – 3 that night, the news leaked. The next morning I was being called by reporters, and that was it. O'Connell confirmed the announcement shortly after noon on September 23. I was no longer the Boston Red Sox manager.

That's when it finally sunk in. When I finally heard the

words made public. Fired from the Boston Red Sox, number 23, on November 23, after 23 years in the game. Sick, sick coincidence. I felt a sudden rush of anger at the absentee Yawkey, who had forced O'Connell to do something we both hated. I was even madder at Yawkey's bobo, Sullivan. And I was furious at anybody who thought that just two years after bringing this team its most miraculous pennant, I had become an idiot. That's a pretty short time to lose so much baseball sense.

One person I wasn't mad at, despite wide reports, was Yaz. He didn't cost me my job. No matter what he might have said to his buddy Yawkey about me, Yawkey's mind had probably already been made up. One newspaper printed quotes from Norma about Yaz stabbing me, but those quotes were false. Norma, who talked to the reporter at our apartment during a firing-day wake, never said anything about Yaz. The hack inferred and implied and screwed up her quotes to make it look like she was ripping him. When she read it in the newspaper—which I had futilely tried to hide from her—she nearly ripped apart her breakfast.

I blame Yaz for nothing. In fact, today I consider him a friend. After all, he only won my team a pennant. He was a great player. And a smart one, probably smart enough to use my firing to avoid paying that $500 fine.

The Fenway Park fans and local media didn't feel the same way about Yaz. On the night after my firing he was booed at Fenway even though he had two homers in an 8–3 win. And the next morning a newspaper ran a drawing of me hanging from Yaz's bat. Funny picture. Today it still hangs in my den.

It's interesting to me, and sad for the fans, that since the time I left the Red Sox they still haven't won a post-1918 World Series, despite two more tries. Whatever Yawkey's actual reasons for firing me, I couldn't have been too stupid.

At least in leaving Boston and taking a no-pressure coaching job with Gene Mauch in Montreal the following year, I was able to settle down. Settle down in my drinking, in my treatment of loved ones. No, I still can't have more than a shot of scotch in one night. But at least I understand that now, along with most of my other vices. Why do you think I later embraced the idea of becoming a representative for Miller beer? Because I've always been able to handle beer. Being a Miller man has been my private revenge against my memories of scotch.

Time is funny. Overall, bad as it seemed then, I'll always remember Boston like you remember an old sweater: in the end it was uncomfortable and didn't fit, but most of the time it kept you warm.

I like to recall the first time I realized how I'd helped the importance of Red Sox baseball stretch beyond a field or a game. In the fall of 1967, in the middle of our miracle, a local woman called me with a request for her own miracle. Her son, Bobby Broderick, was dying of cancer and wanted to see me. It was at the end of an important home stand, but of course I went. I don't remember much about the boy, only that he was about nine years old and frail and clinging to the hope that the Sox might finally win the pennant. Even cocky Dick Williams didn't have the guts to promise him that we would, only that we'd try; and then, walking away from him down the hospital corridor, I *swore* that yes, we would try.

Bobby Broderick died 36 hours later. His mother informed us of this in a letter, written carefully and neatly on thin blue stationery. I still have it in one of my scrapbooks. Part of it goes like this: "There is no letter that can adequately describe the measure of happiness you gave Bobby Broderick and the people around him when you came to visit . . . A very special friend of ours who is a priest says Bobby is an angel or saint. He said, 'Don't pray for him, pray to him.' So, Mr. Williams, whether you want it or not, you have a real good 'in' in heaven."

The letter still makes me shiver. And that bit about me having an "in"—well, I needed it. Two years later I went to work for Charlie Finley.

OH, CHARLIE

With apologies to Reggie and Rollie and Catfish and Charlie and his lovely mule, any explanation of my Oakland Athletics experience must begin with a 16-year-old girl. Her name was Debbie Sivyer, and for a few hours each night at the Oakland Coliseum she would wear this green uniform and chase balls. Just like the rest of us.

She was just a kid then, just another ball girl. So, as was expected, when she attended the 1972 American League Championship Series in Detroit, she had to be chaperoned by Norma and the other wives. And, as might be expected, Debbie still managed to do her share of teenage partying.

What was not expected was what happened to this girl several years later. Ever had a Mrs. Fields cookie? That's Debbie.

And that basically describes what happened to all of us from 1971 through 1973, during three insane, strange, sometimes incoherent years, which also happened to be the best three years of my life. The Oakland A's and I began together in 1971 as innocents. Things soon turned bizarre. We began doing things none of us had ever dreamed. A nation turned its head to look, not because we were beautiful but because we were making such a damn racket. Now, nearly 20 years later, that same nation talks about us like we were famous. Like we're Mrs. Fields or something.

The wonderful thing about it was that those swinging, fighting, whatever-adjective-you-choose A's were not looking for headlines. We were just looking for ourselves. In finding that, we happened to become what may be baseball's last true dynasty. We also became baseball's last team that didn't hate having Dick Williams as a manager. Equally remarkable feats.

We got along so well for two reasons. Number one, this team was basically 25 versions of me, 25 guys who didn't give a shit about anything but winning. They didn't care about their appearance (we looked like damn hippies) or their deportment (we fought like sailors) or their safety (we led the league in Games Played with Death Threats Hanging Over the Players' Heads). The score after nine innings was their only interest, the rest of their world was like recess. So when I looked at them, it was like looking in a mirror.

Number two, this team was 25 guys who hated their owner, Finley. How did this help me? Well, it's impossible for even baseball players to truly hate two of their bosses at once. Okay, so I was the one who lucked out.

This ungodly period in my life began, appropriately, at the ungodly hour of 6 A.M. on the final day of the 1970 season. I was tucked into my hotel room bed in Philadelphia, sleeping better than I'd slept in several Septembers, peaceful in the knowledge that, as a plain old third-base coach for the Montreal Expos, this was one September when nobody was going to fire me. You may have noticed, owners almost never fire third-base coaches. They fire managers, after which third-base coaches quietly take their leave. With Gene Mauch secure as my boss, and myself secure as his lackey, that September phone call took several rings to rouse me.

"Yeah," I mumbled into the phone, and then I heard three words I would constantly hear for the next three years.

"Williams?" barked the voice on the other end. "You awake?"

My mind raced. It sounded like . . . no, it couldn't be . . . well, yes, I guess it was, that guy who'd left a message with the front desk yesterday, promising to call today at 6 A.M. That guy had actually called!

"Hello, Mr. Finley," I said, spitting the grit from my mouth.

"Dick, how're you doing, I promised I'd call and . . ." The man was talking so fast that I lost him after the first sentence.

And that was how Charles Oscar Finley and I got started. Before breakfast. With a furiousness in his voice and shit in mine. Come to think of it, even though we had some great times together, that's how we parted three years later.

But how was I to know that then? More appropriately, why would I have cared? Finley, who minces no words, immediately told me that he wanted me to replace John McNamara as manager of his Oakland A's. It was as if he knew what I thought only my heart knew: that I was dying to return to the game as a manager. Although the 1970 season had calmed my nerves and given me a great education under Mauch, it had also toyed with my mind. Here I was, a guy who had managed for three seasons, going to the World Series in one of those seasons, having winning records the other two, yet I was no longer a manager. Instead of sitting on a bench, I was in a coaching box. Instead of giving orders, I was hitting fungoes. Can a manager really be washed up at 41? Despite my outward happiness, that's what I'd been asking myself throughout 1970 until Charlie called, acting like he had heard the question.

And there was no doubt how I'd answer. I felt I was better prepared than ever to manage again. Working with Mauch from the third-base box for the Expos, I had refined my skills under a master. I'd learned how to work two or three innings ahead. I'd learned how to somehow work a bullpen so everybody stays ready. I'd learned so many little things, like how your entire team should be sitting on the bench in the early innings so they work on picking up the opponents' signs. If there was a clinic run by all managers, Mauch would be the head instructor.

All of the above will explain why my response to Charlie took, oh, three minutes. At dawn on October 1, 1970, with me in my boxer shorts and my dreams back in their proper place, I became manager of the Oakland A's. After phoning Norma, I phoned Mauch, who quelled my excitement in typical Mauch style, with a simple but suffocating sentence: "I hope you know what you're doing."

What could I tell him? I was taking this job even though I did know. I was playing for the Kansas City A's after Charlie had entered baseball upon purchasing the team in the winter following the 1960 season. By spring training we only knew one thing about this white-haired, soft-spoken man: he could be generous to a fault. He gave us each a clock radio as a spring training gift and several times treated groups of players to meals at the finest restaurants. I was traded to Baltimore before the end of that 1961 camp, so I didn't learn any more. But the remaining A's learned the other thing about Charlie: he cared about the game to a fault.

He fired his first manager, Joe Gordon, just three months into that 1961 season because, from what I heard, Charlie thought he wasn't playing the right lineup. Then, in revealing the first flashes of his showmanship, he made a production out of giving the manager's job to a hardworking Kansas City outfielder named Hank Bauer. He hijacked the public address system at Municipal Stadium and announced, while Bauer was in the outfield, "Hank Bauer, your playing days are over. You have been named manager of the Kansas City A's."

Not that Bauer lasted with Charlie past the next season. Finley would do anything to win, so he fired his managers often, making nine managerial changes in the 10 years before my arrival. I don't like getting fired, but I respect people who aren't afraid to make changes in answer to their heart. So I respected Charlie, who before the 1968 season had made the ultimate change, moving the franchise from Kansas City to Oakland. A couple of years and managers later is where I came in. And in listening to Charlie make his offer, I was satisfied with what I thought were the only two things that affected me: the club's ability and Charlie's motives. Since coming to Oakland, the club had put together three straight winning seasons, including one, under the recently fired John McNamara, in which they'd won 89 games and finished in second place. The outstanding scouts for the A's had put together what was not just a good club but a still-young one, with a chance to win at least 89 games for at least a couple more years.

And about Charlie's motives. Through all his wild rhetoric, I saw a guy who was crazy, all right—crazy about winning. Crazy about having guys do what they're being paid to do. Crazy about making things better. Crazy like a fox. This 53-year-old man with gray hair reminded me of somebody. Me.

And so we began a three-year marriage that got damn close to the death-do-us-part part. Fittingly, it got off to an unusual start from the moment I put on my first A's uniform. I noticed that my cap and my coaches' caps were white, while the players' caps were green. I thought some of us had just been given the wrong uniforms, when I realized this was another of Charlie's innovations. He wanted the coaching staff to be able to spot each other easily during workouts on the field and in the dugouts during games. And I understood that, perhaps a little better than I understood the styrofoam surfboards on my feet, which were another of Charlie's inventions—white shoes.

All of this came at a time when I felt baseball could have used a different look: no managers' uniforms at all. I still feel this way. Baseball is the only sport where the field boss wears a uniform, and thus the only sport where some field bosses look like beer barrels. If baseball would just let managers wear a pair of slacks and a golf shirt—they each own at least five dozen golf shirts, all given to them free of charge—I'm sure it would be easier for them to maintain their dignity in public. For those who still agree with baseball's current fashion statement, I refer you to San Diego Padres manager Jack McKeon. At least he has the decency to send somebody else to the mound to change the pitchers.

Only one thing helped me stomach that first A's uniform: my players looked great in it. But even in less stylish uniforms these guys would have been a beautiful sight. Already in place, waiting for me like an uncashed paycheck, were Bert Campaneris, Sal Bando, Reggie Jackson, Joe Rudi, Catfish Hunter, Blue Moon Odom, Vida Blue, and Rollie Fingers. Compared to what I'd walked into when I took over Boston, this was paradise. People talk about how I helped build the Oakland A's. I tell them: Hell no. From the moment I laid eyes on the A's I realized I'd be nothing more than a caretaker. Not that such a job is especially easy. Just ask the caretaker at your local zoo.

The clubhouse had three leaders: Reggie, Bando, and Catfish. Reggie was the guy with the lungs, the vocal one. His constant talking gave his teammates something to both laugh at and rally behind, and the best thing about it was that it was an act. I knew, because I used to be that kind of actor myself. Reggie was really just a talented but very sensitive and insecure person. In other words, get through his bull and you found a guy who'd play his ass off for you. And Reggie equated me with hard play. He still remembered having the greatest weekend of his life against my Boston team in 1969, with four homers, a triple, two doubles, two singles, and 15 RBIs. He remembered how I'd grumbled about him in the newspaper. And right away, believe it or not, he liked me.

Bando was the quiet leader, the leader by example. Particularly the example of having cocktails with me to discuss the game. He's the only player I've ever socialized with. I'd invite him to my hotel suite after games or during an off-day, and we'd just talk baseball. The rest of the team saw this and figured I must be all right. And from those first moments Bando became my clubhouse emissary.

The third leader was Catfish Hunter, who led with a different sort of form, the practical joke. Although he and his wife, Helen, later became great friends with Norma and me, he had an early problem with me by trying to establish his turf too soon. I'll let players lead themselves, particularly veterans like Catfish, as long as they first recognize and respect the ultimate authority. Me. This is where he made his first mistake, in a blunder that, typically, got us started toward our first American League pennant.

We had opened that first A's season by losing four of our first six games, a stretch topped off by a lousy 10−5 loss to Kansas City, after which we embarked on our first extended road trip. I was a little worried about a pitching staff that had allowed 40 runs in those five games. Then I became markedly more worried after Charlie called me and pitching coach Bill Posedel to his apartment and asked what the hell I was going to do about it. At the time, of course, I didn't realize that Charlie would be questioning me virtually every day, asking me what the hell I was going to do about everything.

By the time our plane landed in Milwaukee to begin the trip, I had advanced from worried to angry. We got off the plane and boarded a bus that would take us to our hotel. Then from my front row seat I saw this flight attendant coming toward us, clacking her heels across the runway. She jumped on the bus, breathless.

"Somebody on this team stole a megaphone from the plane," she told me. "The plane can't go anywhere, and you can't go anywhere, until we get that megaphone back."

I sucked in my breath. It was time to stop staring in awe

at my Athletics and start shoving them. I stood up in the aisle
and faced the back of the bus.

"Okay, fellas, we got a megaphone missing," I said. "And
I'm standing here until we get it."

There was silence. Then a few snickers. A few giggles.
Some jostling from the back. I turned red.

"I don't know if you guys know this, but we aren't exactly
burning up the damn league," I announced. "I don't care
who took the megaphone, I just want it back so we can get
the hell out of here."

More silence. More snickers. I turned blue.

"I know some of you think you can be assholes . . . well,
I can be the biggest asshole of them all," I shouted. "And if
you've got a fucking problem with that, just call Charlie. I've
got five or six phone numbers where you can reach him. From
what I understand about a lot of you gutless wonders, you've
got those fucking numbers already. Well, go ahead, call him.
But he ain't here now, I am, and you'd better learn to live
with—"

Plunk. My speech was interrupted by the sound of something tossed out a back window of the bus. I looked outside,
and there on the pavement was a megaphone. "All right,
bussie," I told the driver as I climbed inside. "Let's get the
hell out of here."

As you may have guessed, it was Catfish who stole the
megaphone. I knew and the team knew, but I never did anything about it. As it turned out, I should have given him a
bonus for feeding me the slow curve that enabled this team
to see and feel my swing.

And so ended the formal introduction of the Oakland A's
to Dick Williams. I was never told how they reacted to it, but
then, I didn't need to be told. I saw. We won 12 of our next
13 games. Six days after my meltdown we went into first place
and were never caught. That was the difference between the
A's and the other five teams I managed. When you screamed
at the A's, they were man enough to understand why. And

good enough to know how to fix it. And smart enough not to take it personally. After all, chances are that sometime in the 24 hours before my scoldings, my A's had been screaming at each other.

If only the rest of the first year had been as easy as that speech. If only it had been a matter of just giving the team a jolt and watching us win those 101 games. If only my career at Oakland had consisted entirely of managing baseball. But it involved far more than baseball.

First there was my apartment. It was the first time—and the last—that I rented something without Norma seeing it first. I thought it was a fine place, in a Hayward complex just south of Oakland; a few players and coaches lived there, and parking was free. In my excitement to move in, though, I failed to notice two things. One, our actual apartment was located approximately 10 feet from the railroad tracks. Two, it was approximately 10 yards from the apartment belonging to Catfish Hunter. In short, we spent that year screaming to be heard on the phone, sleeping in a bed that shook, and worrying about Catfish playing jokes on our son Rick, who was all of 15.

That fear was realized during one Saturday afternoon cookout, after Rick complained that some watermelon seeds he'd swallowed were stuck in his throat. "Here," Catfish said, handing Rick something that looked like fruit punch. "This will wash 'em right down." It wasn't fruit punch. And only about an hour later our little Ricky brought those seeds back up. Couldn't even make it to the toilet. Those seeds hitting the floor sounded like a machine gun.

Of course, no matter where I've lived in my career, I've always enjoyed the feeling of security that comes over me when I walk into a baseball park. And Oakland Coliseum was no different. Although gray and drab, it came alive with both our team and some of Charlie's procedures. On my first opening day there, an April 7 doubleheader against the Chicago White Sox, we drew only 23,823 fans. And with good reason—there were just two ticket sellers. Charlie opened the front gate only, put a couple of people behind the caged windows with a little bit of change, and that was it. No promotions, no hoopla, no nothing. About the only sideshow was this leather-lunged fan who sat behind the dugout. After we lost the first game of the doubleheader and I was walking to home plate to turn in the lineup card for the second game, he shouted, "You still here?"

This theory of Charlie's that we were supposed to be our own promoters damn near ruined the most fun any of us had that first season. His name was Vida Blue. He was a 22-year-old lefty from Mansfield, Louisiana, a rookie so smooth and yet so rough that he resembled a jewel. After joining the team for the final month of 1970, he threw a no-hitter against Minnesota, so everyone knew he could pitch. But I had no idea how hard, and how gracefully, and how consistently, until the following year. Let me put it this way. By the 1971 All-Star break on July 13 he was 17−3. By August 16, with a month and a half left in the season, he'd won 22 games. There was no way he wouldn't reach that magic 30-win mark.

But then there was Charlie. Our attendance was running something like 35,000 people on half-price nights for games in which Blue started, and 6,000 people the rest of the time. Because of this, Charlie called me in September and insisted that I juggle the rotation so Vida would start seven of his last games at home. This screwed up Blue, who went 1−2 in the final month and probably would have missed the 30-win mark anyway, because he wound up 24−8. But it also pissed off the rest of my rotation, particularly Catfish, who was constantly being pushed back a day. I repeated to Catfish the same two sentences I offered other players who were becoming increasingly impatient with Charlie's tactics: "Yes, it sucks. But Charlie's the boss."

Not that Charlie's promoting did any good that year. We'd pulled so far ahead of everyone in the standings that nobody came to watch us that last month, even when Blue was pitching. It made Charlie so mad he became perhaps the first owner in history to cancel Fan Appreciation Day. When he changed his mind and tried to squeeze it back in, the fans showed how much they appreciated his contempt by avoiding the ballpark. We drew 2,667 for our final two games. Combined.

But how Charlie tried. The thing I first learned about managing under him—the thing all his managers learned—is that he loved the phone. He'd call me once a day, often at home, just to chat about the team. Maybe he'd suggest a change in the batting order or in the pitching rotation. They were innocent calls from a guy who wanted to make things better. But the calls were always there, every day, and I thought I'd become used to them until a fateful July 1, a rare off-day before my A's took on the California Angels at Anaheim Stadium, when I drove the family from Oakland to Anaheim to visit Disneyland. Appropriately, this is where I first learned how Mickey Mouse Charlie's style could be. We arrived in Anaheim about 3 P.M., checked into a hotel, and went to Disneyland, staying there until after midnight and returning to the hotel around 1 A.M. When I stopped by the front desk, my heart dropped. The receptionist's face was as shiny pink as the stack of messages in his hand. The stack must have been six inches high. "Mr. Williams," he said, handing me the stack, "a Mr. Finley has been calling." Sorting the slips out, I learned that Charlie had begun calling the hotel just after I arrived at 3 P.M. and had called continuously until 12:30 A.M., upon which he left the message "I will call tomorrow at 6:30 A.M." And damned if he didn't. Damned if he didn't always call back. I might be safe in a place like Disneyland. For a while. But eventually some pink-faced man would arrive with a stack of pink slips, saying, "Mr. Finley called."

But aside from such things as Charlie's phone calls, Charlie's stadium, Charlie's advice, Charlie's treatment of fans and players, Charlie's style, Charlie's lack of style—aside from all this, playing with the A's was easy. In 1971 Blue went 24–8,

Catfish went 21–11, and Reggie led us at the plate by hitting .277 with 32 homers and 80 RBIs. And on the field the season was fun. Reggie would go into a slump and come to the coaches nearly in tears. We, particularly Irv Noren, would talk to him about believing in himself, telling him to say "Screw you" to the pitchers, and then he'd go on a rampage. I would yell at shortstop Campaneris to quit trying to hit home runs—the 155-pound guy had had 22 homers the season before—and tell him to work instead on his fielding. He wound up hitting just five dingers, but he became one of the league's top five guys in turning the double play, which helped us more. More important, he stopped embarrassing great-fielding second baseman Dick Green.

Everything I did was fun. On our first trip into Boston, my first time back since being fired, a messenger boy told me that Mr. Yawkey wanted to see me in his office. I told the boy, "Tough shit. If Yawkey wants me, he knows where to find me." When I walked onto the Fenway Park field, I got an ovation. My team split a two-game series with the Sox, winning the second game 12–8. Our second time in Boston, with the fans howling, I got so mad at a call that I threw my cap about 10 yards, retrieved it, and then kicked it into the stands. That four-game series we swept.

We finally clinched the division on September 15—I use the word "finally" because we'd had a double-digit lead since June. Ironically, we clinched in Charlie's home base of Chicago, and the next day was an off-day, so our owner couldn't resist—the morning after our celebration he asked everyone to board buses and take an hour-long trip to his farm in La Porte, Indiana, for a party. I'm sure that party was very nice, but there's only one thing I really remember about it. Telephones. There were phones all through his house, phones on his back porch, phones in his barn, and even phones hooked to the trees on his acreage. I knew Charlie called me a lot, but telephones on the trees?

I couldn't dwell on the strange sight, because I had my

first championship series to play. Whereas the Red Sox had gone straight to the World Series after finishing in first place in 1967, there was now an intraleague playoff series to contend with. As the West Division champions, we had to meet the East Division champion Baltimore Orioles in a best-of-five series to determine the American League pennant winner and World Series participant.

Even though it was going to be a short series, Charlie showed his baseball smarts by putting together a thick scouting report on the Orioles. He even paid for it to be bound in beautiful green-and-gold books. Excited, I set up my rotation starting with Vida, then Catfish, then, with an off-day, Vida again. So much preparation, such high hopes.

I soon learned that playoff ball, particularly with the A's, is never so neat. We arrived in Baltimore before Game One in the middle of a rainstorm, which meant the first game would be postponed. This meant in turn that we would play three games in a row. And without an off-day, I had to abandon my plans to pitch Vida twice. Because of injuries, the only other starter I had left was a part-timer, Diego Segui, who had gone 10−8 in just 21 starts for me. I didn't like him in big games, but he was a tough bastard who'd take the ball anytime, so I had hope. I also had hope that we would win one of the first two games so our season wouldn't be depending on him.

Then things really got difficult. In Game One, Blue was throwing great and took a 3−1 lead into the seventh inning. Then he walked a guy, gave up a single and, two outs later, another single, making it 3−2. Curt Motton's RBI double tied the game, bringing up Paul Blair. I had Fingers warm in the bullpen and the game on the line, and I stood along the dugout steps and started thinking. Take Blue out? Leave him in? Out? In? Out? In? That's the way managers think, and that's how I was thinking, faster, faster, the question rolling around in my head so much that it made me dizzy. Damn. I finally had to decide. I figured Blue had still allowed just six hits and three runs and was still the best damn pitcher in the universe at that point. I figured Fingers wasn't quite ready for the situation yet, being the clubhouse patsy and the guy always tricked into giving away his money or putting on the wrong uniform. So I ignored my head and followed my heart. I left Blue in. He promptly hung one to Blair, who doubled down the third-base line for two runs to give Baltimore a 5–3 win.

Go ahead, Charlie, second-guess me. I'm sure that somewhere you're still second-guessing me. But that's the way I played, and that's the way I had decided to manage. There was rarely a question between my head and my heart—the statistics in my head usually overpowered everything. But when there was a question, the heart was going to win every time. And even for you, Charlie, this heart ended up winning a few.

But as far as the 1971 playoffs were concerned, the heart was nothing but broken. The Orioles hit four home runs the following day to beat Catfish 5–1 in Game Two, and then Brooks Robinson hit a two-run single off an overmatched Segui in the fifth inning of Game Three in Oakland to give them a 5–3 win and the pennant.

Reggie hit two homers in that final game, which is perhaps why he cried afterward. I hadn't handled my first postseason under Finley very well, which is perhaps why I felt like crying. I also heard that Finley was preparing to fire me, which made me feel like screaming. But for whatever reason, he didn't. Maybe it was because, as he was preparing the announcement, I was named Manager of the Year, beating out and pissing off Baltimore's Earl Weaver. Shortly afterward Blue was awarded Cy Young and Most Valuable Player, only the second player to win both in the same year. I think then Finley knew this team was no fluke.

I could tell because after the season, when I said we needed one more pitcher to put us over the top, he immediately acquired Chicago's Ken Holtzman, a great left-hander who impressed me not just on the field but in the clubhouse, where he became Fingers's guardian and helped him grow up. Or at least taught him to avoid being cheated in cards. Finley was so excited about my request for pitching that he took it a step too far, acquiring Denny McLain, the former 31-game winner for the Detroit Tigers who was 28 but overweight and out of shape. Before the season started, I had to send him to the minor leagues with a shoulder injury, just to get him out of the clubhouse so that his lack of discipline, which included gambling and such, wouldn't bring the team down. Looking at McLain pack up his gear, I remembered how far and how fast we can fall. I remembered Boston. That's why I could only look at him for a second.

Finley also impressed me that spring by not letting Vida Blue miss the season in a contract dispute. After his great year, Blue had decided to hold out for $115,000, while Charlie was offering just $45,000. I handled this like I handle all contract matters: I told the player I didn't give a damn who was right, I only wanted him to be ready for the season. So I secretly supplied Vida with balls and other equipment—we may even have found somebody to catch him—and I hoped. And sure enough, on May 1, after Vida had missed just 15 days of a season delayed by a strike, Charlie made him happy with a contract worth $63,000. And I was happy too. Suddenly a team that I believed could win a world title was together, and I continued thinking, Life with the dedicated Charlie Finley isn't so bad.

But the following season, things with Charlie became a little more tense. He had built the club, and now he'd settle for nothing less than the ultimate payback of seeing it become a world champion.

With great pitching from Hunter, Holtzman, and Blue Moon Odom, and great hitting from Reggie and Joe Rudie and Mike Epstein, a first baseman Charlie had picked up the previous season, we won 21 of our first 32 games and moved into first place virtually for good on May 27. It was the best thing that could have happened to the team—and the worst thing that could have happened to me. The winning, the excitement, the real possibility that we would make the World Series this time . . . it sent Charlie to the moon. Or, at least, to a place none of us had seen before.

Charlie's daily phoning became even worse. He began using phones like they grew on trees, calling me more than twice a day. He began calling me so much that when we went on the road, I was forced to share an adjoining room with another club employee so that we could make arrangements for one of us to be in the room to answer the phone. Not that Charlie couldn't find me even if I'd disappeared. One off-day I was playing golf, about to putt on the eighth green, when a pro shop worker brought out a phone message. Guess who? I told the kid I'd call Charlie when I made the turn at the ninth hole. The kid said Charlie wouldn't wait, and gently begged me to get in his cart and drive with him to the phone.

"Hey, Dick," Charlie belched when I picked up the phone, "how's the club?"

"Which club do you mean?" I asked Charlie. "I'm standing here holding a bag full of them."

Charlie also turned my clubhouse into a hotel lobby. One day I arrived at the park and spotted this tall skinny black guy sitting in the back. I figured he was just another new batboy until he knocked on my office door.

"Dick, I'm Allan Lewis, your new player," he said, sticking out his hand. "Allan," I exclaimed, "nice to meet you."

I stood up, smiled, asked him to wait outside the office a second, closed the door behind him, and then picked up the phone. "Charlie!" I nearly shouted when the old man got on the phone. "Who in the hell is Allan Lewis?"

Turns out he was our new pinch runner, a sprinter from Panama whose lack of baseball knowledge Charlie considered incidental. "Just call him 'The Panamanian Express,'" Charlie kept saying. I protested: "Charlie, we have no uniform for The Panamanian Express. No equipment. No locker."

Charlie just laughed. "Dick, wait until you see this guy run," he said. And so we saw. A few days after he arrived, The Panamanian Express took off from first base on a long fly ball, head down, arms and legs pumping, great form. And if only the ball had fallen in for a base hit. But the ball was caught, as Lewis learned upon arriving at third base. What's a Panamanian Express to do? He shrugged and ran across the diamond, across the pitcher's mound, back to first. Playing in parts of six seasons, all for Charlie, Lewis appeared in just 156 games and batted exactly 29 times. But hey, the guy could run.

And I shouldn't complain about just him. Charlie made 62 transactions that year, which has to be close to a record. All told, we put uniforms on 42 players. The worst part was that 12 of them played second base. Yes, Charlie didn't just try to influence my roster, he began trying to jimmy with my lineup, asking me to get a pinch hitter every time our second baseman batted. He figured that none of our second basemen could hit anyway, while all of them could field for a couple of innings. This was his rotating second baseman maneuver, Charlie's only in-game order that I felt compelled to carry out. After it cost us several wins by having the great-fielding Dick Green on the bench after three innings, and ultimately made a mockery of a playoff game, I finally ignored the order and prayed for my job. By then Charlie didn't notice, but only because he was too busy counting wins.

Charlie's eccentricities were visible everywhere. In the spring of 1972 he decided to schedule us in an exhibition game against a Japanese team in which a batter would strike out on two strikes and walk on three balls. So what if baseball had used different rules for 75 years? Charlie really thought this one would catch on, until our pitchers walked about 20 Japanese hitters and they beat the hell out of us. Call it an invention defeated by defeat.

That spring he also decided to start fooling around with an orange baseball, which we actually used in an exhibition

game in 1973. I'll never forget how former A's outfielder
George Hendrick, who we'd just traded to Cleveland, hit three
homers for the Indians with the orange ball but afterward
almost single-handedly killed the idea by telling then-Com-
missioner Bowie Kuhn that he couldn't pick up the spin on
the ball. I think he just did that to get back at Charlie. Call it
an invention killed by a grudge.

Charlie also acquired a fetish for mules. Don't ask me why.
Ask the mule. I'm referring to Charlie's trademark, appropriately named Charlie O. In 1972, after letting him clomp
around in the background of the organization for years,
Charlie decided the fucking mule should join the team. He
let him graze in the hospitality suites underneath the Coliseum during playoff games and even allowed him to lick the
ice sculptures. He let him graze on the field throughout the
left field foul territory. One problem. Before every game the
mule had this habit, probably nerves, of taking a big crap
down the left field line. It got so bad that I'd have to explain
things to the opposing manager during our pregame meeting at home plate. "The mule shits out there, and we can't
always be cleaning it," I'd tell him. "So if a ball rolls in the
shit, it's still in play." Right about then the opposing manager
would shit.

Charlie also suddenly had a thing for nicknames. He was
the one who first referred to Jim Hunter as "Catfish" and
who threw the "Blue Moon" in John Odom's name. But now
he began begging Vida to call himself "True" Blue. Vida
wouldn't do it.

Then there was Charlie's most noticeable promotion, a
gimmick so unusual that some of us have been reminded of
it every morning in the mirror for nearly 20 years. Late in
July 1972 we were on a charter flight from Boston, and the
team, as usual, was pissed off about something. This time it
was Charlie's rule about no facial hair. It wasn't that they
disagreed with it but that one highly visible member of the
team was ignoring it. Reggie had started growing a beard
and mustache and refused to shave it, and the guys were

mad that he seemed to be having so much fun. Catfish finally decided to address the issue in proper Oakland A's fashion. He decided to rat on him.

Catfish walked to the front of the plane where Charlie was sitting. "Charlie," he announced, "Reggie Jackson has facial hair. Lots of facial hair. And we don't think it's fair." Finley looked at Catfish and then gazed into space. "Oh, really?" he said.

By the time we landed in Chicago to drop Finley at his home, he'd concocted his solution. If facial hair had caused such a stir among the team, think what it would do for the fans. Not only didn't Finley reprimand Reggie, he offered $300 to anyone who would grow a mustache in the ensuing month and show it off at a promotion ingeniously called "Mustache Day."

And so the Mustache Gang was born—a baseball team that came to look like a protest march. The players were so confused by Charlie's edict that most of them also decided to grow their hair long. We became one messy group of players, which only helped to cultivate our image as a free-wheeling team. But we weren't that free-wheeling. A month later, as soon as he gave us our checks for $300 following the successful Mustache Day, about half the team ran into the clubhouse to shave. The other half—well, some of us kept our mustaches for the rest of the season. And for the next season. And the next.

To this day, as far as I know, several of those A's have never permanently shaved their mustaches. I'm one of them. You may have noticed another—a guy named Rollie Fingers. No, he didn't always own the most conspicuous mustache in sports. Like a lot of things with our team, his style started with Charlie.

• • •

Say this much for Charlie: we did have style, even if it bordered on the grotesque. This style, formed by Charlie's creative tensions and nurtured by winning, finally bloomed late in the 1972 season. We were good, we were constantly on edge, and we were unafraid to let that deadly combination explode where it may. For a period of about 15 months, from August 1972 to October 1973, the Swinging A's would be just that, swinging our way through baseball's history books and sensibilities, swinging at each other and at opponents, swinging for home runs and lawsuits, swinging so fiercely that when I look back on it, I sometimes have to catch my breath.

First, there were the fights. Sure, we had several basic brawls, your usual things with players doing more hugging than punching. But we also had coaches who brawled, like the time in late 1972 when my third-base coach Irv Noren, then 48, had his eyebrow cut open when he was blindsided by Detroit pitcher Tom Timmerman, then 32. Or the time that season when my bullpen coach Vern Hoscheit, age 50, injured his arm trying to climb an outfield fence in Milwaukee in order to land a few punches before a fight had ended.

Then there were the real fights. The ones among ourselves. Call it a result of Charlie's creative tensions mixed with incredible talent and egos. In one case, though, you could almost call it deadly. We were in Texas, and Reggie Jackson, as an assistant player representative, passed along the Rangers' request that only family members could receive family complimentary tickets, the ones in the good seats; friends could only receive the designated friends' tickets, which were in less desirable seats. But right in the middle of Reggie's little clubhouse speech, Mike Epstein, our big first baseman, walked past him and said to hell with that rule, he'd give family tickets to anyone he wanted.

And then he shoved Reggie. Out of nowhere, the son of a bitch just pushed him. And Reggie pushed back. By the time I could get through a group of players to them, they were rolling around the floor in the dirty socks and cleats, making a complete mess of the clubhouse. We broke them up and I brought them into my office. Now, these were two pretty big guys, and the Arlington Stadium visitors' clubhouse had a pretty small manager's office. We crowded to-gether and I started yelling at them about teamwork and they started yelling at each other again. And bumping each other. I backed up and prepared to jump on the desk to avoid being crushed, when they finally admitted they were faced with one of life's biggest reasons not to engage in a fight: no room. They stopped yelling, they agreed that they could hate each other without killing each other until after the postseason, and that was that.

And we played on. We clinched the division in 1972 with one week left in the season and finished the year at 93–62. Our playoff opponent was to be the East Division champion Detroit Tigers, who finished 86–70, that final number approximating their average age. It was a playoff I knew we should win, considering that only three members of their starting lineup were under 30, and that most of their fire came from a guy who would be spending the series on the sidelines—their manager, Billy Martin. But as we soon learned, never underestimate Billy Martin.

For that matter, never underestimate a postseason with Finley, who started things off by having the actor George C. Scott throw out the ceremonial first pitch in Oakland. A fine man, Scott, and one of Charlie's tough guy idols. Too bad that Scott announced, shortly before throwing the pitch, that he was a Detroit Tigers fan.

I actually have to thank Charlie for Game One, because when we found ourselves trailing 2–1 in the bottom of the 11th, I called on this guy Charlie had found in Venezuela to win it for us. His name was Gonzalo Marquez, he'd been with the team about a month and a half, and we were stuck with him when a minor injury to Reggie in August required a replacement. We put two runners on base against the Tigers in the bottom of the 11th, and to be honest, I had no choice. My batter was Dal Maxvill, not much of a hitter. I figured I'd give Gonzalo, who had batted just 21 times for us and gotten eight hits, a chance. Sure enough, he did just enough, grounding a ball to right field that scored two runs when right fielder Al Kaline threw the ball off the back of a sliding Gene Tenace at third base. Tenace jumped up, ran home, crossed the plate in a dance, and we were up one game to nothing. People were saying, "Oh, that Williams, what a genius." But it was simple. I needed a guy to put a bat on the ball, and if nothing else, Gonzalo could do that. For once that ball found a hole.

The second game was not as close as Game One—we won 5−0 behind Blue Moon's three-hitter—but don't forget this basic fact about the Oakland A's: a game doesn't have to be close to be full of all kinds of shit. Hell broke loose in the seventh inning, when Bert Campaneris stepped to the plate to face the Tigers' Lerrin LaGrow, a rookie with the shakes. Campy had already driven the Tigers crazy, singling and scoring after two stolen bases in the first inning, and singling and scoring on a wild pitch caused by his fake steal of home in the fifth inning. All this time Tigers manager Billy Martin was visibly cursing. Like all good managers, he loved to win in that fashion but absolutely hated to lose like that.

Up stepped Campaneris in the seventh, here came LaGrow's first pitch, and—thwack—it smacked Campaneris in the left ankle. You could hear the ball bouncing off the bone. The next thing you heard was the bat. A stunned Campaneris regained his balance and began swinging his bat like a lasso. Somebody on the bench screamed, "No!" But yes. He threw the thing. In one of the more chilling events in playoff history, he flung the bat directly at LaGrow's head. Just in time the kid ducked, and the bat bounced behind him.

And now hell really broke loose, with both benches clearing and the Tigers trying to climb over each other to reach Campaneris, who made one of the smartest moves of his illustrious career: he ran like hell. Afterward I sensed this incident was just getting started. "Dirtiest thing I ever saw in the game of baseball," Billy Martin smartly proclaimed. "He has to be suspended for the rest of the playoffs." Outwardly

First row, fourth from the right, that's me, the Pasadena high school baseball hotshot.
At the far left in the front row is another future major league manager, Bob Lillis.

This is the Larry's Ice Cream Store baseball team, which I played on while living in
Pasadena. I'm second from the right in the front row.

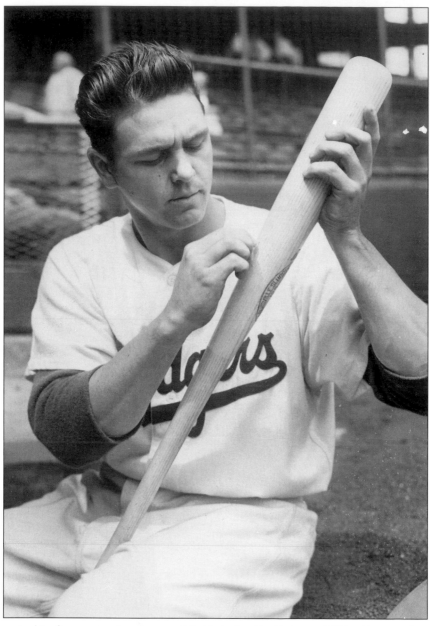

Looking for any edge, here I am as a kid with the Brooklyn Dodgers in 1951, rubbing a nail across the grain of my bat to dig out the bad wood. This practice is prohibited today—come to think of it, lots of things that used to give you an edge are prohibited today. *(Photo by Barney Stein)*

Here I am in Vero Beach in 1952 receiving a few hitting pointers from Brooklyn instructors John Corriden *(left)* and Andy High *(center)*.
(UPI/Bettmann Newsphotos)

In Brooklyn's Monarch Winery, 1952, I'm reciting one of my off-color limericks while Dodgers teammates Pee Wee Reese *(on my immediate left)* and Ralph Branca *(next to Pee Wee)* laugh.

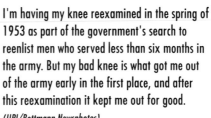

I'm having my knee reexamined in the spring of 1953 as part of the government's search to reenlist men who served less than six months in the army. But my bad knee is what got me out of the army early in the first place, and after this reexamination it kept me out for good.
(UPI/Bettmann Newsphotos)

A good throw would have gotten Al Kaline at third, but as you can see, I was lucky just to make the catch in this 1958 game. Can you believe the Orioles replaced me with Brooks Robinson?
(AP/Wide World Photos)

Believe it or not, I actually got stuck behind this roll of tarp, which I tumbled over while chasing a foul ball for Baltimore against Cleveland.
(UPI/Bettmann Newsphotos)

I'm glad somebody took this photo, if only because it proves that Mickey Mantle and I played in the same league. I've just tagged Mick out at third base during a game between my Kansas City team and the Yankees in 1959.
(UPI/Bettmann Newsphotos)

Take a good look at this, because it didn't happen often for me: I've just hit a three-run homer and am crossing the plate in front of catcher Yogi Berra at Yankee Stadium.
(New York Mirror photo)

That's my rear end showing in Yankee Stadium. While playing for Kansas City, I dove for this Marv Throneberry ball, which passed just out of my reach for a home run. *(New York Mirror photo)*

See how skinny I was in 1966 after my triple-A Toronto team won the Governor's Cup? That's the summer I lived on ballpark snacks. *(Toronto Star photo)*

This was one of the first times, and maybe the last, that Ted Williams and I talked during spring training in 1967.

Even though I paid my first major league fine, as cited here, out of my own pocket, the club reimbursed me, as clubs often do.

THE AMERICAN LEAGUE OF PROFESSIONAL BASEBALL CLUBS

520 BOYLSTON STREET   BOSTON, MASSACHUSETTS   02116

May 1, 1967

Mr. Dick Williams
Manager, Boston Red Sox
c/o Leamington Hotel
Minneapolis, Minnesota

Dear Dick:

This is to acknowledge receipt of your check for $50.00 payable to the American League.

Kindest regards.

Sincerely,

Joseph E. Cronin
President

JEC:ga

Me and one of my heroes—my mother, Kathryn.

My wife, Norma, cuddles our young son Marc in Fenway Park in 1968.

While in Boston I must have appeared in as many cartoons as Dagwood.

I'm trying to make a point with an umpire while Red Sox ace Jim Lonborg—who had seen this many times before—patiently waits for me to get the hell off the field. *(Photo by Richard Raphael)*

Boston catcher Mike Ryan and I argue with umpire Marty Springstead, insisting that Ryan had successfully made a tag in this 1967 game. As usual, I lost the argument.

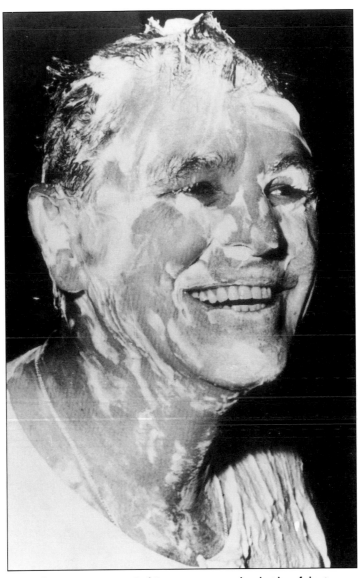

Back in 1967 my Boston Red Sox were so young that the idea of shaving still excited them. Here they've covered me with shaving cream right after we clinched the American League pennant on the last day of the season.

(AP/WIde World Photos)

The 1967 Red Sox, the Impossible Dream team. *(Photo courtesy Boston Red Sox)*

Norma and I are being honored here by the people of Peabody, Massachusetts, in a wonderful parade during the 1967 World Series.

With Dick O'Connell standing behind me, I show the press how happy I am to be signing a three-year contract with Boston after our great 1967 season. On my left is Tom Yawkey, apparently smiling but really just gritting his teeth.

Ted Kennedy, a politician with more than just a casual interest in the Boston Red Sox, presents me with a proclamation after the 1967 season. Seated at Kennedy's right is Speaker of the House John McCormack; at my left is Commissioner of Baseball William Eckert.

Commissioner Eckert presents me with my 1967 Manager of the Year award on Opening Day in Fenway Park in 1968. *(Photo by Russ Adams)*

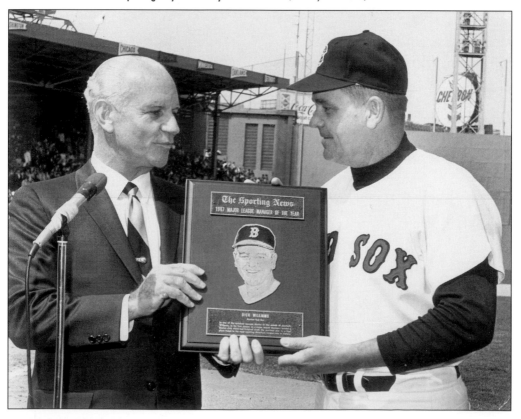

A happy moment with two of my Red Sox sluggers: Carl Yastrzemski *(center)* and Tony Conigliaro *(right)*. We weren't always so chipper together. *(AP/Wide World Photos)*

Hi . . .
I'm Dick Williams,
unemployed
baseball manager

... and when you find yourself
suddenly out of work, that's
when you really appreciate the
comfort of a savings account at
your local co-operative bank.

The Co-operative Banks
of Massachusetts

TWO BILLION DOLLARS AND GROWING STRONGER

If you think this 1969 post-firing ad is touching, you should have
seen the TV commercial.

I turned up my nose at Martin's actions. But inside I thought, Billy, you sly dog, you just wanted to slow him down. By getting him so mad that he might be completely stopped by suspension, you've accomplished more than your mission. As one hustler to another, I'm impressed.

Martin's words, combined with the umpires' report, made it back to American League president Joe Cronin. And I knew we were screwed. I knew we'd lose Campy.

For at least the length of his ensuing cross-country flight to Detroit, that didn't matter to Charlie. Following our Game Two victory, we packed up and flew out on what turned out to be probably the happiest flight of his life—and the worst flight of mine. It wasn't so much that Charlie brought his damn Dixieland band with us, ordering them to roam the aisles of our World Airways charter before takeoff and play this horrible version of jazz. Our takeoff was delayed about an hour by a bomb threat, and Charlie had that band playing during the entire delay. The tuba guy, the trombone guy, all those guys, squeezing and cramming and pushing their way up and down the plane. Great music, great guys. But it got a little old. The morning after landing in Detroit I went to the ballpark and realized the worst was just beginning. Campy was gone, suspended indefinitely. I figured, at the least, I wouldn't see him until after this series.

And we played on. My overanxious offense, looking for a sweep, struck out a then—playoff record 14 times to Detroit's Joe Coleman in Game Three, and we fell 3–0. Then came Game Four, when my developing image of the A's as a mature and wise team for the ages was shattered. I saw the truth: I was managing in a damn loony bin. After fighting the Tigers to a 1-all tie for nine innings, we scraped together two runs in the top of the 10th and were just three outs from a pennant. But entering the bottom of the 10th, the lineup card in my hand began shaking. Because of Charlie's rotating second baseman maneuver, I had flat run out of second basemen. I looked around the dugout and realized that the only guy available to play second was a catcher and first baseman who couldn't even play first that well, Gene Tenace. To the astonished look of teammates, I ordered him to second base. And then I slipped my hand under my cap, grabbed my hair, and pulled.

It's an old baseball axiom that if you play a guy in a position where he doesn't belong, when the game is on the line, the ball will find him. Always has, always will. And sure enough, after the Tigers loaded the bases with none out, Sal Bando was given a double play grounder at third. He turned and threw the ball on the outfield side to Tenace, who was actually trying to turn a double play. "Oh my God!" I screamed, like someone about to witness an inevitable accident.

As Tenace ran across the base, he tried to catch the ball and pivot at the same time. He did neither. Just as the ball was arriving at Tenace's glove, the runner, Gates Brown, slid into him, causing the ball to bounce off the glove and roll harmlessly toward the outfield while one run scored. A walk scored another run, and a fly ball by Jim Northrup gave the Tigers the win, tying the five-game series at two wins apiece.

I walked into the clubhouse with my eyes down and my ears burning. The second baseman maneuver really sucked. Lost in thought as I sat in my office on that October afternoon, I barely heard the ruckus in the clubhouse. I stuck my head out the door, and—oh, shit—there were Vida Blue and Rollie Fingers screaming at each other. I'd put Vida in the bullpen this series due to an injury to Darold Knowles. Maybe Rollie was mad because Vida had actually relieved him in this game. Just before the punches began to fly, they were separated by teammates, at which point I thought, How bad can one supposedly wonderful playoff day get?

When I returned to the hotel that night, I learned. Norma had just flown in from Oakland to join me, smuggling Campaneris with her. Charlie wanted the guy around—what could I say? At about 2 A.M., with Norma in her leopardskin robe covering a leopardskin nightgown and me in my boxer shorts, we climbed into bed . . . and heard a knock at the door. It can't be, I thought, grabbing my robe and going to the door.

It was. Standing in the hallway was Charlie. Looking over my shoulder into the bedroom, first thing he said was "Tell Norma to get rid of those pajamas."

"Right here?" I asked, too confused even to think about belting him.

"Don't be silly," he said. "I just don't want her wearing anything that looks like a Tiger. Bad luck, you know, and . . . "

"What the hell do you want?" I interrupted him.

"Time for press conference," he said.

And so it happened that Charlie became one of the first owners ever to throw a public, late night fit in the hotel suite of a manager whose team is facing the final game of the playoffs. Once the media had arrived, some of whom had been coaxed from the bars, Charlie summoned Campaneris. When I saw Campy walk in, I thought, Damn, only one game left and Charlie's still trying to make him eligible! While my shortstop sat in the back looking perfectly remorseful, Charlie ranted about how sorry Campaneris felt and how the league president, Joe Cronin, should allow him back in the playoffs. He was getting so worked up that I was secretly wishing that Cronin would hear this.

Wish granted. At the close of his speech a red-faced Charlie announced that we should make one last appeal to Cronin. I threw on some clothes, and Charlie marched me with my smirk and Campy with his sad face two and a half blocks over to Cronin's suite at a nearby hotel. Charlie began banging on the guy's door. By now it was nearly 3 A.M., and mad as I was at Charlie, all I could do was pray that the league's highest ranking officer wouldn't answer. But then the knob turned and my heart leaped and Cronin's wife appeared. Believe it or not, she invited us in. And then from the back of the suite appeared a man in an old-fashioned nightgown, which, come to think of it, I'd never seen on a man. I started to laugh, but thank goodness, Charlie's rantings immediately drowned me out. After listening to Finley for a few minutes, this poor harrassed Cronin wished us goodnight and closed his door. I went back to my suite and, like most nights as manager of baseball's last dynasty, I slept like a baby. That is, I woke up every two hours crying.

The next afternoon, in the deciding game, the Tigers, perhaps more rested, came out and scored a quick run in the first inning off Blue Moon. What happened next wonderfully illustrated a truism that will live with these A's through history: when it came time to play, they knew how to cut through the bullshit.

Second inning. Reggie Jackson walked. He stole second. He went to third on a fly ball. Mike Epstein reached first, and I thought, What the hell. Even though there were two out, I called for a delayed double steal. Tigers starter Woodie Fryman delivered the pitch. Epstein took off. Catcher Bill Freehan jumped up and threw to second. And Jackson dashed toward the plate. He arrived just before the return throw from second, sliding so hard that something popped. It wasn't the ball into Freehan's glove, it was Reggie's hamstring. He was safe. Tie game. But by the way he staggered back to the dugout, I knew he was going to be out. Oh, shit.

Two innings later a duly inspired Gene Tenace had his first hit of the series, an RBI single, which gave us the lead. With my starter Blue Moon Odom looking good, I figured we were all looking good. But of course that couldn't have been further from the truth. After the fifth inning Blue Moon ran into the dugout runway and doubled over at the end of the bench and began throwing up. Well, it sounded like throwing up. But nothing was coming out. "Skip," he said, "I can't go anymore. I'm sick." And with that he staggered back to the clubhouse.

No sooner did I order Vida Blue to get up in the bullpen than I heard it. The laughter. The jokes. Here it was, the final game of the playoffs, our entire season on the line, and these idiots were still making fun of each other. "I bet Blue Moon shit his pants!" yelled one player. Another added, "Those weren't the dry heaves, they were the dry chokes!"

As it turned out, it was no big deal. Vida Blue came in and threw his usual heat, and about an hour later he'd combined with Blue Moon on a five-hitter as we eventually won 2 – 1 to take the pennant and advance for the World Series to meet the Cincinnati Reds. The celebration actually began minutes before the final out, when a fan threw a beer can down at center fielder George Hendrick from the outfield bleachers—and Hendrick caught it. Then he caught the final out, upon which so many beer cans were thrown that all he could do was run like hell.

But man, we celebrated like hell. Who says the A's can only screw around? Who says we're all image and no inspiration? Those thoughts were running through my head as we danced for a few minutes on the Tiger Stadium field and then ran through that barrage of beer can missiles to the safety of our clubhouse. But once again I had celebrated too soon. As I walked through the clubhouse door behind Vida, my eyes shot to a corner where Blue Moon was sitting and congratulating everybody. Vida looked at him, smiled . . . and stuck his hand around his throat.

"Gaaaaaag, gaaaaaag," Vida began yelling at Blue, as if choking himself.

"Fuck you!" Blue Moon shouted back, and then put his head down and charged.

And then, before my unbelieving eyes, we had what was surely the first championship clubhouse fight in history. The two players tangled for a few seconds before being pulled apart, but the message was clear: we had to get to the World Series before we killed ourselves.

While flying to Cincinnati from Detroit for the World Series, I wasn't sure whether to be elated or worried. Yes, I was happy about making it to my second Series in five years as a manager. But no, I didn't want to go through another 1967 Series, where I'd suffered not only the pain of losing but the far worse pain of wondering whether I'd done enough. In 1967 I was as awed as the players, and perhaps sometimes I managed like it.

I would make certain that didn't happen again. So as we landed in the Cincinnati area, I decided that no matter what happened, the world would know that I was here, that I was not afraid of any silly World Series. More important, my team would know. Perhaps this attitude is why, eight days later, I had set unofficial Series managerial records for visits to the mound, pinch hitters, pinch runners, trick plays that embarrassed national heroes, near fistfights with my own players, and sundry other goodies. Sure as hell, they eventually knew the Oakland A's and I were there.

We were facing the Reds, but not the legendary Big Red Machine, and there was a difference. These guys were younger—Johnny Bench was just 24, for pete's sake—and lacked the veteran pitching. But they were favored by the experts, and I guess I can't blame the experts. Last time I looked, Pete Rose and Tony Perez weren't trying to choke each other. And not once during the postseason had manager Sparky Anderson felt like he wanted to explode.

I was immediately faced with a Series full of decisions. Who replaced Reggie? Easy. George Hendrick. He was just a kid but had shown great ability to chase down the ball. Who could be my catcher? A harder decision. I'd gone with Dave Duncan during the season because he was the better defensive catcher and had responded with 19 homers. But on a club where four other guys hit double figures homers, that number isn't so important in the postseason. And so during the playoffs I went to backup Gene Tenace because he'd hit a tad more consistently than Duncan (.225 to .218) and hadn't struck out as much. Tenace had responded with just one hit in 17 playoff at-bats, but that hit had come in that final game and had given us the win, and . . . Hmmmm, I wondered. Judging by his momentum and my heart, I went with Tenace.

Why did I just spend most of an entire paragraph explaining that? Because about 20 minutes into Game One, Tenace, who'd had five homers all season, hit a two-run homer off Gary Nolan, a 24-year-old pitcher who should have known better than to give him that high fastball. Then, about an hour later, in the fifth inning, Tenace homered again, giving us a 3–2 victory. How about that. Two home runs in his first two Series at-bats for the balding reserve who would rarely be heard from after these eight days. It was a Series record, not to mention a great story. I felt like a genius.

A day later, in Game Two, once again I got lucky and my players were good. We took a 2–0 lead after three innings on starter Catfish Hunter's RBI single and Joe Rudi's homer. With the score unchanged in the sixth, I made what many thought was a weird move by replacing first baseman Mike Epstein and his 26 regular season homers for my defensive expert, Mike Hegan. The move was a no-brainer. Hegan is only the best defensive first baseman I've ever managed, and that includes San Diego's Steve Garvey, who broke Hegan's 178-game errorless record through a fluke, which I'll explain later in the book. By bringing him in, I was showing Catfish my confidence that we wouldn't need any more runs to win this game, just a guy who could catch a grounder. However, Epstein didn't think I was showing *him* much. He cursed his way into the dugout, after which I didn't look at him the rest of the game. Selfishness in a World Series is the essence of scum and isn't worth a look.

Three innings later everyone had forgotten all about Epstein, considering we had just watched two of the greatest fielding plays in postseason history—one of them by Hegan. But first came the play that more people remember. With a runner on first base and none out in the ninth, we were still holding the 2–0 lead. Up stepped Denis Menke, in came a fat Catfish pitch, and away flew the ball to deep left field. We jumped to our feet, and amid shouts of "No! No!" we twisted and contorted our bodies in hopes of somehow willing the ball back to our side of the fence. Then, while in a crouched position, I saw it. Joe Rudi's body, his glove, his arm, an arm that seemed at least eight feet long, springing above his body like a burst of water from a fountain as he leaped against the green left field fence, the ball falling out of nowhere into the glove at the height of his jump, the white part shining against the brown leather, a catch, an out, a 350-foot unbelievable out.

Our cries became "Yes! Yes!" as we realized that Rudi had saved us at least one run, maybe two. Then only I was crying, "No! No!" again when I saw Rudi showing off the ball while giving the runner, Tony Perez, a chance to successfully retreat to first. Believe it or not, I still think about how his showing off the ball eventually cost us a run that inning as Perez later scored on a Hal McRae single. Like I've said, when you get this close, you can't let the little things kill you.

I didn't even have time to calm my nerves, as the next batter, Cesar Geronimo, hit a low line drive toward right field, a ball that sounded like a double. Before I could even say, "Oh, shit," there was Mike Hegan, blocking everyone's view of the pretty hit with a prettier dive that stopped it. He knocked the ball down and crawled through the cloud of dust to first base to make the second out. For my money, a more impressive play than the Rudi play, only you don't still see that play on highlight films, while Rudi will remain a part of baseball lore forever. Oh, well, I thought, as we eventually won 2 – 1, at least Hegan's catch will get Epstein off my back.

Wrong again. On the plane ride home, while everyone was either drinking or getting hit in the butt by one of Finley's trombone players, I turned in my seat to see a lurching Mike Epstein. "I feel you don't appreciate me," he said, slurring only every other word. "I've been busting my ass all season and you take me out of a fucking World Series game and I don't appreciate it. And I don't want this to happen again."

I could take everything but that last line. He doesn't want it to happen again, does he? And just who in the hell does he think he is? I stood up and—much to the surprise of everyone, who thought they were in the middle of a party—began screaming back. "You get your ass to the ballpark tomorrow and be ready to play! I'm the manager and I'll do whatever I want!" I wanted to slug the ass, and he wanted to slug me, and we nearly went fist city until we both realized we were leading this World Series two games to nothing! Here we are, two wins from a world title and the manager wants to kick the shit out of his first baseman and vice versa? We didn't fight, because even this team was not that crazy.

In hindsight, we should have fought. Maybe the sight of it would have better prepared our team, which sat restlessly through an off-day and a rainout before finally sleepwalking through Game Three on a Wednesday, October 18. Against Jack Billingham and Clay Carroll in a game that started in the twilight because Charlie insisted on playing a World Series game at night. We only saw the ball good enough for three hits and lost 1–0. So add this to the other times I wanted to kill Charlie. Night World Series games are fine . . . as long as they *are* at night. Charlie must have forgotten that when it's night in the big media areas of the East Coast—which is when the games must start because of television—the sun is still shining low on the West Coast. Low enough to cast long shadows and screw up hitters. Thanks to Charlie, his team was one of the first to get screwed by that rule.

Oh, well, there's one reason I'm glad that the game drew a lot of television viewers. On this one October night, in front of millions of viewers, I grabbed my 15 minutes of fame by fooling the shit out of Johnny Bench.

Perhaps you remember it. Eighth inning, runners on first and third, one out, Rollie Fingers pitching, Bench at the plate. On a two-and-one pitch, the ball was low and Bobby Tolan stole second, leaving runners on second and third. With the crowd getting restless and tension getting thick on the bench, suddenly I remembered something Billy Southworth had done when he was managing. I turned to my pitching coach Bill Posedel and told him, "If this next pitch is a strike, I'm going out there to the mound and act like I'm giving Fingers hell because he shouldn't be giving Bench anything to hit with first base open. I'm going to wave my arms and act like I'm calling for an intentional ball four. But instead I'm going to tell them to throw the damn ball right down the middle of the plate for strike three. Bench will never know what hit him."

Posedel responded like any faithful coach. "What the hell are you talking about?" he asked. The next pitch was a strike, and I didn't have time to explain. I ran to the mound to meet with Fingers and catcher Tenace, waving my arms and shaking my head. Then I explained my plan. I told Fingers, "Be sure you throw a breaking ball, because if it's a fastball and somebody figures out what we're doing, Bench can hit the shit out of it." And I told Tenace, "After you jump outside the plate for the intentional walk signal, don't jump back behind the plate so quick."

Fingers understood. Tenace, to this day, still may not understand. He just stared at me. And on the mound, with millions waiting impatiently, I explained myself again before returning to the dugout.

As Tenace stuck out his hand for an intentional walk and jumped out from behind the plate to make the catch, I still wasn't confident that they'd pull this off. Then I saw the pitch and I knew. Fingers threw a nasty slider headed for the outside of the plate. Tenace jumped back behind the plate. And Bench was ours. When Joe Morgan figured it out and yelled at Bench from third base, it was too late. Bench, thinking he was going to be walked, froze as the ball went across the outside black for strike three. The crowd roared, and as I learned later, fans in front of televisions everywhere were cheering in disbelief. Tenace ran off the field, also cheering, also in disbelief. Later Fingers told the media that he used to pull this play in Little League. Maybe he didn't know what the hell we were doing after all.

It's a shame that move couldn't have gotten us an immediate win. But the following night, in Game Four, four moves damn near like it worked perfectly to put us within one victory of a world championship. And although my applause grew with these Game Four hijinks, once again I plead luck.

It was the ninth inning, we trailed 2 – 1 with one out and nobody on base, the Series was two outs from being evened up at two games apiece. Clutching at straws, I sent up Gonzalo Marquez to pinch-hit for George Hendrick, simply because Marquez had a better chance to make contact. Sure enough, Marquez singled. Immediately I inserted The Panamanian Express, Allan Lewis, as a pinch runner. Gene Tenace then singled Lewis to second to eat up my next move. Looking for a base hit, I batted Don Mincher for Dick Green. Worked again. Mincher smoked a ball to right center for a single that scored the speedy Lewis to make it 2 – 2. With Tenace on third and Mincher on first, I then sent Blue Moon Odom out to run for Mincher, thinking that with his superior speed he could break up a possible double play. As it turned out, because of another move that worked, it didn't matter.

In place of Fingers, I send up one final pinch hitter. It was — be still, my heart — a guy named Angel Mangual. This is the outfielder who'd played in only 91 games for me that season because every fly ball hit to him was an adventure. Once he told me that I made him nervous. I told him, "Wrong, Angel. You make *me* nervous." I was serious then. And when I sent him up to pinch-hit, I was just as serious. We needed somebody just to make contact, and he could certainly do it better than Fingers. And sure enough, he did, making just enough contact to bounce the ball through the right side of the infield and into the outfield, where it died of malnutrition while Tenace danced across home plate with the run to give us the 3 – 2 win. How about that. Three pinch hitters and two pinch runners in the course of about 10 minutes and we pull one out of our butt. I was so happy afterward that I barely noticed Mangual in the corner, still brooding because he made me nervous. I guess I should have been thankful he wasn't slugging somebody.

If I'd known what would happen the next two games, I'd have celebrated that win more. The theory that managers who are heroes one day are inevitably goats the next day is even more applicable in a World Series. Because in Game Five, while trying to win the title in front of the home fans, trying to steal a ninth-inning victory like we'd stolen them all year, I got booed. The Reds led 5 – 4 in the bottom of the ninth when Gene Tenace walked. After Ted Kubiak couldn't bunt him to second, I inserted Odom again as a pinch runner, then brought up Dave Duncan as a pinch hitter for my pitcher Dave Hamilton. Duncan singled down the left field line, and Odom raced to third with still just one out. It was the previous night all over again. My charmed lineup card was working again. We were going to win the title without needing to return to Cincinnati.

And then Bert Campaneris hit a soft pop foul behind the first-base line. The minute I saw second baseman Joe Morgan going for it, I knew this was it. Our scouting reports said that Morgan couldn't throw well while running to his left. My third-base coach Irv Noren had studied the reports. He would be sending Odom home as soon as the ball was caught. And it was caught. And Odom ran. And . . . son of a bitch if Morgan didn't make a perfect throw to Bench to tag Odom out for a double play to end the game. No question, Blue Moon was out, although I was happy to see us end this game on a fighting note as Blue Moon disagreed with the call and jumped up and bumped home plate umpire Bob Engel. Afterward I defended our decision to send him home, all the while worrying that my luck had run out.

We left for Cincinnati immediately after the game. Typically, there was no jazz band on the plane, no mules, nothing. Suddenly this Series was all business, as was confirmed the next day when the Reds pounded Vida and three other pitchers 8 – 1, bringing the Series down to Game Seven. For most of the sports world, Game Seven of a World Series is the ultimate contest, the stuff of dreams, the meeting of two champions in a nine-inning showdown to decide, after six months of fighting, who will be the greatest. But that's just most of the sports world. As I walked to the stadium on that October 22 day, all I could think about was that Game Seven would be a time to work my butt off. A time to pay attention to detail like never before, every tiny detail, leaving nothing unturned in those nine innings, allowing for no excuses that could haunt a man for the rest of his career.

Perhaps this is why, after going to the mound 26 times in the previous six games, I went to the mound 16 times in this final game. I wanted a face-to-face with my pitchers before every tough pitch, every tricky situation. I must have lost 10 pounds from all the walking. The current World Series rule that a manager must take out his pitcher on his second visit to him in one inning—the same as in the regular season—should be called the Dick Williams Rule, because it was enacted after league officials got sick of seeing me stroll. But what the hell. I also visited Charlie in his Riverfront Stadium box seats next to the dugout. No, I wasn't asking advice—no way was I using more than one second baseman. I was just making sure I wasn't missing anything that he saw. Indeed, I was leaving no stones, or rockheads, unturned.

One more tiny, A's-type detail needed to be ironed out before the game. We were told that a fan standing in a ticket line vowed to shoot Gene Tenace if he played. The guy was arrested and searched, and sure enough, he was packing a pistol. We didn't tell Tenace, but we told his father, who said he didn't want Gene to know. And we played on.

We scored a run in the first inning on another Tenace RBI single, and then two more in the sixth on Tenace's and Bando's back-to-back doubles. Tenace got mad at me when I yanked him for a pinch runner after his double, but you didn't think we'd get through this game without at least one fight, did you? He screamed at me, but I screamed back, finally telling him that there had been a serious threat on his life. I asked him how much fun would it be to celebrate a world championship from the inside of a pine box? "Oh," he said.

We were still up 3–1 in the eighth inning, when I made my first of two controversial moves. With runners on second and third and one out, with the cold Johnny Bench batting and the incredibly hot Tony Perez on deck, we walked Bench to pitch to Perez. You could almost hear the groan from Oakland fans behind our dugout combined with the cheers of Reds fans. I had just put the go-ahead run on base, breaking all unwritten Series rules. But nobody understood. We had decided before the Series that no matter what happened, the future Hall of Famer Bench wasn't going to beat us. I couldn't live with myself if he did. Even if it did mean going against percentages. Like most moves of the heart, it paid off. Perez could only manage a fly ball that scored one run, which took us into the ninth with a 3–2 lead.

With two outs in the bottom of the ninth, and the same score, there was more controversy. Fingers hit Darrel Chaney with a fastball, for pete's sake, and we were in trouble again. One out from a title, Pete Rose coming to the plate, and I'm about to soil my pants. I wondered if Mickey Sinks was watching. I went out to talk to Fingers, with no intention of taking him out, even though Odom was up the bullpen. Fingers had pitched well, and he deserved this last hitter. Not knowing I felt this way, Fingers pleaded with me. "Dick," he said, "I can get him." His words were like fine music. I'd gone to calm him down, and instead he'd calmed me down. Despite more groans from behind our dugout, I left him in. And damned if he didn't do the job.

I can still see Rose's ball. Floating out toward Joe Rudi in left center field, floating, floating—boom. Rudi easily made the catch. We were the world champions. I had reached it. My mountain. My every-night-of-my-life dream. I could describe to you the pile on the pitching mound, the hugs and tears and screams. I could tell you how I ran from there to the box seats next to the dugout to the roof of the dugout, where I hugged Norma while Charlie hugged his wife, Shirley, and together the four of us danced in a light rain. I could tell you how I cried. Unashamedly cried out of exhaustion for the 43 years I had poured into reaching this one moment.

I could tell you all that, but it wouldn't begin to describe the feeling. That's what I remember most about that day, the feeling. After working every day for the last damn-near eight months, suddenly I felt like the best. The best of everyone, everything, in baseball. The best for the entire next damn year. The ultimate authority. The winners. That's the word I used most often in the ensuing several hours of wild celebration. Winners. I was finally, truly, no questions asked, a winner.

I was also sober, as most celebrating baseball players barely drink a cupful of the champagne you see them pouring on their heads. Not enough time, not enough room, not enough champagne. However, this was not the case with my son Rick, age 16 at the time. He stole one of two bottles of champagne off my desk and shortly thereafter got sick. If the people of Oakland wondered why our plane arrived later than scheduled that evening, it's because we had to hold the team bus while my son threw up on the wheels and then in the back commode. We also had to delay the takeoff of our flight so he could get his head out of the plane's toilet.

Charlie understood all of this. I knew he would. But soon after we arrived in Oakland, he began not understanding some things. Like how come several players didn't show up for the Oakland victory parade in front of 150,000 people. The no-shows included Vida, who hadn't forgotten about his spring holdout. Then Charlie got mad because, on our team's mandatory championship visit to the White House, President Nixon wanted to pose for photos with me, not Charlie. He put Charlie in the corner of the Oval Office and then turned his back on him and talked to me, even commenting that he couldn't believe Boston had fired me. "Very insightful, Mr. President," I said.

Charlie wanted us to pay him a little reverence at this

point, and I can understand. After all, not only had he built the team, but after the win he gave us each a full-size World Series trophy and a wonderful diamond ring and a film of the World Series, and even gave each wife a World Series charm with a diamond in it. By the way, the rings carried the unique motto S + S = S. Charlie told us that meant "Sweat plus Sacrifice equals Success." Several players said they thought it meant "Shit plus Shit equals more Shit."

• • •

It was a quick off-season and spring training, interrupted only by Charlie's controversial trading of George Hendrick because he didn't like his personal habits, and by his acquisition of a 24-year-old kid name Bill North from Chicago, the only player I've ever seen literally strut on to a world championship team. I saw North and thought, This will be fun.

The 1973 season began with another bad start. We lost our first three games, getting swept at home by Minnesota. Then we flew to Chicago, and on the bus ride from the airport to the hotel I heard North and Blue Moon Odom sniping at each other, and then sniping louder, and I thought, We're going to have our first fight before our first victory, and I'm just not ready for that. I turned around and shouted, "Keep your fucking mouths shut and your minds on the season. You don't start taking this thing seriously, I'll give you something to fight about." It wasn't quite the megaphone speech, and it didn't have quite the same results, as we went 3−4 on the trip and struggled throughout the season's first month and a half.

We finally climbed above .500 in mid-May and were actually playing well when the Kansas City Royals came to town May 18. But once again we couldn't let a good thing alone. It was time for new guy North, who fit in well here, to cause another scene. In the sixth inning against the Royals he singled to score the tying run, he stole second, and then he scored on a single to give us the lead. Everything was fine until North came to the plate in the eighth inning. The Royals' pitcher was Doug Bird, just another reliever. Or so we thought.

On Bird's first pitch North swung and missed and released the bat, lofting it next to the pitcher's mound. Losing the bat is a common, natural occurrence when a batter is fooled by an off-speed pitch. What happened next is not so common. Walking to the mound, just before he reached his bat, North stopped, turned, and nailed Bird with a right to the jaw. Bird dropped, but North didn't stop—he jumped on him and pounded him. I was watching this like it wasn't really happening, like it was some scene staged as a joke. What in the hell is Bill North doing pounding a guy after the guy throws him a strike?!

North was thrown out of the game, which only made me spend the final couple of innings wondering. Did I have an insane man on my hands? I mean, more insane than the guys I already had? First thing I did when I got into the clubhouse afterward was call North to my office. Before I could even ask him what the hell had happened, he told me. Three years earlier Bird had plunked North in the head with a fastball in a minor league game. It was no ordinary plunk, it cracked his skull. North, needless to say, hadn't forgotten. He apologized to me but claimed this was the first time he'd seen Bird since and he had no choice.

Now it was my turn to go crazy. "Since this was such a personal grudge, why didn't you just go to his hotel room, open the door, and pop him one?" I asked. "Or why didn't you at least tell us, and we would have gotten back at him some other way! Why the hell did you have to fight him by yourself, on your own, without any of us knowing? Billy, damn it, this is a team that doesn't just play together, it fights together!" Yes, I can't believe I made that last statement. That showed just what kind of team I believed I was managing.

With North threatening to steal the show, soon it was Reggie's turn to get into the act. On July 4 in Oakland against California, he went three for four with one RBI, but his bad outfield defense—something he later became famous for in New York—allowed three runs, and we lost 3–1. While standing at the postgame buffet, Reggie was mouthing off about his offense like always, when Irv Noren said, "Reggie, if you played defense like you play offense, we would have won this game." Reggie blew up. "How can you say that about me!" he shouted. "A man can't play around here and be happy! Why can't you just let us alone—quit acting like all of us have to be Babe Ruth or something."

Right away the media rushed to me for comments on the explosion, which I could hear even in my office. After talking with Noren, I announced that I agreed with my coach. As if you thought I'd say anything else. Just as I hope my coaches will back me, I back them. I told the media, "Reggie doesn't need to be so sensitive. And furthermore, Noren was right. If Reggie did play defense like he swings the bat, we'd all be better off."

The next day Reggie saw my quotes, and suddenly he's madder than hell, not at Noren but me. That morning, as we were boarding our flight to Baltimore, Reggie stopped as he passed me on the plane and said, "Don't even talk to me again. Put my name in the lineup card and leave me alone." Before I had a chance to tell him that I wasn't even obligated to put his name in the lineup card, he was gone down the aisle. We blew across the country that night on a ride turbulent with tension. Reggie wanted to kick my ass, and increasingly I wanted to kick his. And—oh, yes—we were in first place.

Finley loved this stuff. He loved people to be uneasy, uncertain, worried enough about their jobs and their egos to play their butts off. I preferred to treat them like men and hope they'd play their butts off because they wanted to win. But he loved it the other way, and proved this after our tension-filled flight arrived in Baltimore late that July night. After we reached our hotel, Charlie called me like always, only this time the news was different: all of my coaches were having their contracts renewed for the following year. I was glad, considering my contract ran through the following season, which meant we'd all be together at least one more year. I called the coaches to my suite and happily made the announcement. Twenty minutes later he called again—not unusual for Charlie, except this time he told me that I too would have another year added to my contract, carrying me through the 1975 season. I thanked him and hung up the phone and thought, We should get into shouting matches with Reggie more often. The next day I called Reggie into my Memorial Stadium visitors' clubhouse office, and we talked it out. He told me he was sorry, that things had just gotten hot. I told him I was sorry but that I'd always defend my coaches. And that was that. The Oakland A's fought hard but made up quick and then played even harder.

How did I survive this mental and physical minefield? The best answer I can give you is that, beginning in the middle of 1973, I didn't. Although it's difficult to relate this to anything specific on the field, my body began to collapse just before the All-Star break. On Thursday, July 19, I felt a pain in my gut. It was my appendix. Before I knew it, Norma was rushing me to an Oakland hospital to have it removed. It wasn't until I awoke after surgery that I realized I might have to forgo my managerial duties in the following Tuesday's All-Star game in Kansas City (I'd been invited to participate because my team had won the league title the previous year). I immediately decided that, having never made the game as a player, no way in hell was I going to miss it as a manager, even though I'd already managed the game once in 1968. You can never be in enough All-Star games.

And thus I wobbled onto the Kansas City field just five days after surgery, dressed in my finest Oakland white, hurting like hell but needing like hell to stand in that line along the first-base line for the introductions of the American League team. Of course, in planning this grand entrance, I completely forgot that the A's had once played in Kansas City before Charlie fled town. So here I was, in one of the more heroic moments of my life, getting booed off the field.

Things returned to smooth following the All-Star break,

and even were headed toward normal after Charlie picked up three players for my stretch drive—pinch hitters Jesus Alou and Vic Davalillo and second baseman Mike Andrews, my old player from Boston, now a free agent after being released by the White Sox.

By August every morning we were either in first place or no more than a couple of games behind, and it was actually seeming like a real baseball season . . . when all of a sudden, instead of being mildly irritated by Charlie, we felt sorry for him. On August 7 he suffered a mild heart attack. The way I found out was typical of Charlie: he called. He said he'd sneaked out into the hospital hall and used a pay phone because the nurses had unplugged the phone in his room. To nobody's surprise, he was out of the hospital in a week. From then until after the end of the postseason, he traveled everywhere by wheelchair. But since winning was his ultimate medicine, his pulse only quickened. And as I became the object of Charlie's ever-stronger devotion, my blood began to boil.

First, there was the phone call that almost cost me my job. Once while we were sitting down to dinner with a houseguest, Charlie called and demanded that we talk. Considering this happened virtually every night, I guess it shouldn't have been either a surprise or a big deal. But this time we had a guest. And dinner was ready. So I told Charlie, "The food is on the table, we have a guest here, let me call you back." It was an unusual request to make of Charlie, who gave me an unusual answer. "What's more important, baseball or the houseguest?" he asked, building to a scream. "If you can't answer that, if that food is more important than this job, I can always make a change." With my wife and our guest sitting there horrified, I screamed back, "Is that a threat or a promise? Go ahead, make your change!" And then I hung up. That night, when I didn't lose any sleep, I came to the conclusion that maybe I did want to leave Charlie. The next day he called me again like nothing had happened. But we both knew something had.

I also nearly lost my job in a fight over playing Reggie
Jackson as a designated hitter despite a hamstring pull because he wanted to catch Pittsburgh's Willie Stargell as the
major league's RBI leader, and I was happy to help him. But
he wound up falling two RBIs short, 119–117, and both of
us caught hell from Charlie for risking Jackson's health.
Charlie had no idea that swinging a bat wasn't hurting Jackson's hamstring. And I was getting the idea that I couldn't
take this much longer.

Because of what he called the pursuit of winning, Charlie
was doing even more weird things now, and these disturbed
me more than ever. After the September 1 trading deadline,
he traded Jose Morales anyway, ensuring that we would be
one player short during the playoffs. I became madder at
Charlie on this issue after Bill North tore his ankle ligaments
on September 20 and missed the rest of the season—he and
his .285 average and league-leading 53 stolen bases. Even
though we were allowed to replace him, we were running out
of capable players. Considering you couldn't count The Panamanian Express as a player, we were down from 25 to 23.

Keep the players insecure and keep them hungry—that
was Charlie's theme. We were united in our hate for Charlie
because of this, and probably played better as a result. But
we were getting damn tired of the man. We clinched our
division on September 23, and before the end of the regular
season we were forced to endure one last embarrassment. On
the last day of the season, in a home game against Chicago,
Charlie faked the Coliseum attendance figures so they read
7,422, which put him above the coveted 1,000,000 mark for
the season, at 1,000,761. How do we know he faked the
numbers? Because there couldn't have been more than a
couple of thousand people there at most. Players in the
dugout were wondering if the fans had bought the tickets
and then left. When the typical THANKS A MILLION announcement flashed on the scoreboard, the dugout erupted
in laughter.

Following that game we vowed among ourselves that these

playoffs and the possible World Series would not go the full 12 games as in 1972. Not because we wanted to show our awesome superiority but because we had to get Charlie off our ass as soon as possible. I added a silent prayer that this postseason would go more smoothly than the last. Yes, I wanted to win another world championship. But no, I didn't want to spend the rest of my life on a funny farm because of it.

Of course, who was I kidding? This time the bull started flying before the playoffs, which would be against the aging Baltimore Orioles. My first chore was to find a center fielder to replace North. When I announced that it would be my buddy Angel Mangual, who had played in only 74 games that year because he still gave me the shakes, Mangual decided to get even. He asked to be traded. Right in the middle of the damn week before the playoffs. Not only did he not want to play center field for me in the playoffs, he didn't want to play for the A's, period. At this point I could neither worry nor do anything about it. There was too much else on my mind. Like losing the first game 6–0, when Baltimore pitcher Jim Palmer stuck it up our butts with a five-hitter, all singles. The next day Catfish Hunter and Rollie Fingers paid the Orioles back by combining to hold them to eight hits while we won 6–3. Good thing we won, too, because in that game my buddy Mangual, who had decided he wouldn't quit yet, nearly gave me a heart attack by running into Bert Campaneris in shallow center field and knocking a sure popout out of Campy's glove, costing us a run. But we won, so I didn't kill him, and we headed back to Oakland feeling good about a one-game-apiece split.

Less than 24 hours in Oakland and we were feeling bad again, this time because Charlie went nuts over a rainstorm. Our field was so wet that Game Three was canceled, shortly after which Charlie ripped into American League president Joe Cronin for not waiting all night to play it. The rainout had cost him a rare full house, and he told Cronin just that, cussing and railing against him outside the dugout while I stood next to him, staring at the ground. I couldn't walk away, because that would be insubordination, but while I was being completely embarrassed by this outraged old man, I started thinking that maybe life wouldn't be so bad if I did just that. Walk away. At least I'd be able to keep my self-respect.

The rain kept coming down, and Charlie finally shut up. The next day, under decent skies, Campaneris gave us a two-games-to-one lead with an 11th-inning homer in a 2 – 1 victory. And so we were one game from winning a second straight pennant and going to a second straight World Series. As this team's history has proven, it was the worst possible place for us to be. Never able to do anything easily because we were uncomfortable being comfortable, we took a 4 – 0 lead in Game Four in Oakland and then blew it by allowing the Orioles to score four runs in the seventh and one in the eighth. Vida Blue gave up four of the runs in the seventh on Brooks Robinson's RBI single and Andy Etchebarren's three-run homer. Rollie Fingers finished us in the eighth by allowing a homer to Bobby Grich, giving Baltimore a 5 – 4 win and sending the five-game series to the fifth and deciding game. When we lose, we do it grandly.

And when we mourn a loss, boy, do we mourn. I walked into our clubhouse, past the unopened cartons of champagne, and it was like walking into a boxing ring. Fingers was cussing in the direction of Vida as if blaming him for Grich's game-winning homer. Vida was too shook up to yell, so Blue Moon Odom was yelling for him, cursing back in the direction of Fingers. Finally, they began slowly approaching each other. I was watching this and thinking, Heaven help us, we're going to have a clubhouse fight on the eve of the biggest game of our season. I considered jumping between them, but then I thought about my safety and decided to make a more forceful statement. I wanted Reggie to jump between them. He caught my glances and stepped between the two huge men and talked them off their ledge. I turned, walked into my office, sat in my chair, and put my head in my hands. This is what I'd worked all my life for? Who was going to talk me off my ledge?

Less than 24 hours later I was screaming and shouting, "I've worked all my life for this!" Because, true to our heritage, we'd won the big game with big game pitcher Catfish Hunter and big luck strategy. That last part refers to our final two runs being scored by reserves Vic Davalillo and Jesus Alou, both of whom I was using on the whim that veteran players are big game players. Our three-run total was more than enough for Catfish, who threw a five-hitter and survived a ninth-inning jam with some more old-fashioned wisdom. With two out, he allowed Brooks Robinson to crack a double and then fell behind Bobby Grich two balls and no strikes.

With all hell breaking loose in Oakland Coliseum—fans on our dugout, fans throwing things at their own players—I walked to the pitching mound, feeling like I was walking through a war zone. I gave Catfish baseball's version of survivalist training: "Let this idiot hit it. Don't walk him. Don't try to strike him out. Just let him hit it." Why would a manager give this seemingly backward advice to his pitcher during a close game? Because when the pressure is on, it's damn near impossible for a guy to strike anybody out and easier than hell to walk him. Your mind is working so fast that your arm forgets where it's going. Thus, fewer bad things can happen if the opponent is just allowed to hit the ball. "If you have to," I told Catfish, "lob the ball up there."

So he did. Grich grounded the ball to Campaneris, and we won the game 3–0 and took the pennant series three games to two. We rushed to the field, then realized that all the fans were rushing with us, so we turned and ran for our lives to the clubhouse. It's a wonderful feeling, a pennant, but this time I was so exhausted that I could barely lift the bottle of champagne over my head. All I could think about was that I wanted to win a second World Series title but without all the accompanying circus.

Our opponents, those "Amazin' Mets," were no longer the miracle kids of 1969, although they did have three good pitchers in Tom Seaver, Jerry Koosman, and Jon Matlack, and some fairly good hitters in young John Milner, Rusty Staub, and Cleon Jones. They also had some strong emotion—although no longer ability—from a 42-year-old Willie Mays. Their biggest advantage, though, was that we had Charlie.

Finally realizing that we were outnumbered because of his late season roster botching, Finley tried to add another infielder, Manny Trillo, for the World Series to make things a little more even. Commissioner Bowie Kuhn, of course, told him no. Charlie, who fought with Kuhn throughout both of their tenures, was, of course, very upset. So before Game One of the Series in Oakland, Charlie got on the loudspeaker and announced that he wanted Trillo but Kuhn wouldn't allow it. Embarrassing as hell, this announcement triggered a sequence of Charlie maneuvers that would land him in hot water with the Commissioner and, at the same time, get his team humiliated in front of a national audience.

Thus upset, we won Game One 2–1, getting both runs in typical A's fashion. In the third inning, with my pitcher Ken Holtzman on second base with a double, Campaneris scored him on a ground ball that Mets second baseman Felix Millan, freaked out by Campaneris's speed, threw wildly to first. Then Mets pitcher Matlack, freaked out by Campy's dancing off first base, put an attempted pickoff throw into right field, moving Campy to second. From there Campy scored on a simple Joe Rudi single. It was perfect A's baseball and, I like to think, perfect Dick Williams baseball. Bug you until you let us win, because you just can't take it anymore.

We were still on a high because of this sort of play as we entered Game Two. Little did I know that after this day I'd never be high about the Oakland A's again. It was just your basic World Series game: six errors, 28 hits, lasted four hours and 13 minutes over 12 innings of some of the worst play you have ever seen.

Cut to the 12th. With the score tied 6-all, as it had been at the end of nine innings, the Mets put two runners on base with two out. Up stepped Mays, who had been stumbling all over himself throughout the game (which was nothing to be ashamed of; remember, the man was 42 years old). Somehow he managed to bounce a ball over Rollie Fingers's head and into the outfield to score a run. Next up, John Milner, who hit a grounder to Mike Andrews at second. Yes, I know, Andrews had played in just 18 games for us since we signed him. But if every player on my team can't play his position in every situation, then I haven't done my job. With all my extra work sessions, even my substitutes should be sharp.

And Andrews was sharp. It's just that Milner's grounder hit something and skipped through his legs, and two runs scored. The next batter, Jerry Grote, also hit a grounder to Andrews. This time our first baseman, Gene Tenace, got his feet tangled up and pulled himself off the bag to make the catch, allowing the runner to be safe and a third run to be scored. The scorer gave Andrews an error, when it was clearly Tenace's fault, but I didn't call the press box and yell at the scorer, because I didn't give a damn. We'd given up four runs, and that was all that mattered. Or so I thought.

After our 10−7 loss—we scored a run in the bottom of the 12th—I walked past Andrews in the clubhouse and patted him on the back. He was sitting with his head down, staring at his still-laced shoes, mumbling, "My fault, my fault, my fault." I interrupted him. "Remember what I've said about physical mistakes," I told him. "They happen to everybody. It wasn't your fault. You're human." Then I entered my office and was sitting there quietly commiserating when in barged an angry Charlie.

"Dick," he fairly shouted as he slammed the door behind him. "We're putting Andrews on the disabled list and activating Manny Trillo."

"What happened?" I asked. "I didn't see Andrews get hurt."

"Oh, yes, he did, that son of a bitch," Charlie said. "He got hurt real bad."

Right then I understood what Charlie was doing. He was mad about Andrews's errors and was making up an injury so that he could replace him with his own second baseman, his beloved Trillo. That crap is pulled by almost every team during the regular season. But the World Series? This was sacred. And so was Andrews's right to make a physical mistake.

"Charlie," I shouted, "you can't do this!"

He pulled out a statement signed by one of our team physicians, Dr. Harry Walker. "It says here Andrews has a bad shoulder," Finley said. "So the hell I can't do it." He paused. "Let's call in Andrews and get this thing over with," he said. I nearly cried.

Before Andrews could get through the media mob to my door, I lost it. "Charlie, you are wrong, you are dead damn wrong!" I shouted. "You're getting rid of a man because of physical errors, which means you're getting rid of him because he's a human being."

About the time my face had lost all blood, Andrews walked through my door. His face was also white. "Mike," I said loudly, "I've got nothing to do with this."

Charlie explained to Andrews that he must sign this paper agreeing that he was hurt. "You had to be hurt tonight to make those plays," Charlie said. In one of the strongest moves of his career, Andrews fought the request. In that small office, with Charlie and the doctor breathing down his neck, Andrews refused to sign. He kept telling Charlie that he was fine, in no pain, that he knew he'd screwed up but that this wasn't fair. Andrews finally stomped out, still refusing to sign, with Charlie and the doctor stomping out behind him.

As I packed my bags for our immediate trip to New York, I thought the issue had been resolved. Charlie had tried to do one of the most heartless, gutless things I'd ever seen, but he'd failed. And maybe if I tried hard enough, I could forget about it. Then, about 45 minutes later, I walked outside to the bus, and there was Andrews, unloading his bags from the equipment truck and crying. It turned out he'd signed that form under further heavy influence from Charlie. And it had finished him. Both as a player—he retired following the season—and as a person who could remain strong without showing emotion. He had been torn from the inside out, and he was crying.

And that was it. I was in tears, and I was finished. At the moment I grabbed Mike's limp hand and wished him good luck, I decided that I'd need good luck too. Because I was getting the hell away from Charlie Finley. I was going to leave the Oakland A's whether they won or lost this Series.

Of course, I had somewhere to go. Much as I hated Charlie, I couldn't stand the thought of being out of baseball and wouldn't have made such a rash decision if that was going to be the case. So in the back of my mind as we climbed aboard our charter jet bound for LaGuardia Field, I thought, Yes, I will call back that guy and accept his job offer to manage the New York Yankees.

A couple of weeks earlier, through a middleman, I'd been contacted by the Yankees about replacing Ralph Houk, who was getting ready to be thrown out the door. Owner George Steinbrenner had nothing to do with it, he wouldn't involve himself with tampering, but I trusted that the job offer was real. And the thought appealed to me. Not the thought of the Yankees but the thought of going anywhere I could just manage baseball again without having to be everything from a telephone answering machine to a boxing referee. The Yankees weren't so crazy back then, you'll remember. Baseball's only zoo was in Oakland.

Yes, the Yankees idea was clearly illegal. I had one official year left on my contract and another year that Charlie had promised but not, thank goodness, put into writing. I was clearly wrong to answer their queries. But the minute I hung up after that call, I had a daydream about answering one of Charlie's phone calls with "This is Dick Williams, ex-manager of the A's" and then laughing like hell while I explained to him that I was history. Then I had another daydream where I was the one calling Charlie to tell him I was resigning, calling him five and six times a day with the news. And I thought, Whether this Yankees deal blows up or not, it's worth it to find out if there's really anything there.

Because we were in a pennant race, I initially put the thoughts out of my mind, telling the Yankees we would talk at the end of the season. Even then, I told them, I wasn't sure I could leave such a winning situation. But when the Mike Andrews incident occurred, I knew this would forever be a losing situation. World championship or not, much pride would always be lost under Charlie Finley, and it is pride, not victories, that helps us sleep at night. So as we flew east to New York for Game Three of the 1973 World Series, for the first time I felt like I was out of my body, watching somebody else in that first-class seat. Because for the first time I realized I would no longer be managing this team. By the way, Charlie canceled the movie *1776*, which he'd originally scheduled for the flight. Maybe, considering the furor over the Andrews incident, he thought it was too revolutionary.

He was right. The rest of the World Series was colored by his treatment of Andrews, beginning with the armbands I saw on many of my players' uniforms during the off-day workout in New York. The bands all bore Andrews's number, 17. Reggie Jackson looked at me and flexed his armband as I walked onto the field. I smiled and said nothing. He knew I approved.

But that was just the beginning. On Tuesday morning before that evening's Game Three, Commissioner Bowie Kuhn announced that Charlie could not activate Trillo, which we'd all expected, and that he had to reinstate Andrews, who would join the team Wednesday. Later, just before the game, Charlie called me and demanded that I tell the team his side of the Andrews story. So I did, and it was the hardest thing I've ever had to say. Even though I knew my players realized I didn't agree with Charlie and that the words weren't mine, they were still coming out of my mouth. To give even a quick and superficial account of Charlie's reasons made me feel cheap and dirty. By the end of my speech, once again feeling like I was watching someone else, I'd made sure everybody knew that what I was saying was bull. And then I decided, Hell, I can't last another minute like this, I've got to make sure these players know how to stand up for justice. I've got to make sure that if nothing else, they've learned how to kick some ass.

So I told them. I'd set a record by managing a Charlie team for three years without being fired, and that was enough. I was resigning after the Series. I told them, "This is the hardest thing I've ever done, but somebody has to stand up to this man, and it's going to be me." I added that if anyone leaked the story to the media, I would deny it.

And we played on. Because of Andrews's absence, we now had just 22 men, three fewer than the Mets. And we seemed awfully out of sorts. As a sign of things to come, Catfish Hunter allowed a homer to the first Met he faced in Game Three, Wayne Garrett, and then allowed another run after two singles and a wild pitch. It seemed the A's had finally met a distraction that was bigger than them, but we fought back to tie the game in the eighth inning. Then we actually won it in the 11th on Campy's RBI single after catcher Jerry Grote's passed ball nullified an apparent strikeout by Angel Mangual, thus keeping the inning alive. It was kind of a weird way to win, but I didn't care, because we weren't the same Oakland team that had begun this World Series, and I figured we might need this win later. Was I ever right.

My sense of impending chaos was heightened the next day when Andrews returned to the team, complete with press conferences and more tears. The Mets knocked us down in the first inning on Rusty Staub's three-run homer off Kenny Holtzman, and this time we never recovered, losing 6–1. To show how screwed up we were, the highlight of the game for us came in the eighth inning, when I pinch-hit Andrews for Horacio Pina to cause one of the most unusual scenes in World Series history—nearly 55,000 Mets fans standing and applauding an opponent. They gave Andrews a standing ovation before he saw his first pitch, and another one after he grounded out to third base. The most amazing thing wasn't that these tough New Yorkers were cheering for the enemy—it was that Charlie Finley was in the club box near the dugout cheering with them! People wondered if I had used Andrews just to spite Finley. If they could have heard me say, looking into the stands, "Take that, you son of a bitch," while Andrews walked to the plate, they'd have had their answer.

Our distracted play continued into Game Five, during which we could manage just three hits off Jerry Koosman and that hot dog Tug McGraw, who would irritatingly slap his glove against his thigh after big outs, causing our dugout to collectively want to slap a glove against his head. We lost 2–0 and now were one loss away from losing the Series, as we trailed three games to two.

Our flight back to Oakland for Game Six and (if necessary) Game Seven seemed to take all night. The players and press were wondering about me going to the Yankees. I was wondering if I hadn't won my last game as manager of the A's. The team's mind was on anything but baseball. At this point, down three games to two with so much shit flying, an average team wouldn't have a chance. A great team like us, though, maybe had a slim chance. But slim at best. Making things immeasurably worse was that the Mets, having put our backs to the railing, could afford to blow off Game Six. Yogi Berra could pitch a decent starter named George Stone—he was 12–3 that season—in Game Six. That would give their ace, Tom Seaver, an extra day of rest so that if there was a Game Seven, he'd probably be damn near unhittable, considering he'd allowed just two runs in eight innings in Game Three. And if Seaver faltered, number-two pitcher Jon Matlack would be rested and in the bullpen to back him up. Either way, we figured, the Mets had us whipped.

Imagine my surprise, and my team's surprise, to discover that we had figured wrong. Yogi decided to go with Seaver in Game Six, keeping Matlack on schedule for Game Seven. It was as if he'd decided to either win the Series right there, with a pitcher working on just three days' rest, or not win it at all. Yogi played right into our hands. And the Swinging A's were back.

In Game Six, Reggie Jackson lashed a double to left center to score a run in the first. Then he doubled to right center to score another run in the third. It was good to see him on the bases, because it was one of the few times in the past few weeks that we saw him alone. Claiming that his life was threatened, Jackson had been traveling everywhere with this bodyguard with big arms and tight shirts. I didn't complain. The way things were going for a while, I damn near put a uniform on the guy.

Finally given a lead thanks to Reggie, Catfish Hunter celebrated by allowing just one run on four hits in seven and a half innings. Then Darold Knowles and Rollie Fingers each got a big out with two men on base in the eighth inning to save it. We won 3 – 1, sending the Series to a full seven games again. And now that we've beaten Seaver, I thought, we've won it.

I also thought that for one game we could forget about Charlie. I thought that for one game, arrogant and swaggering as this team had been, we could think only of ourselves. And did we ever. In the third inning of Game Seven against an overmatched Matlack—I wondered what Yogi was thinking about right then—our pitcher, Holtzman, doubled down the left field line. Campy cracked a long home run over the right field fence. Rudi singled to center. Reggie hit the living crap out of the ball for a homer into the right center field stands. That was four runs, and that was enough.

Our only problem was that while we held a 5 – 2 lead with two out in the ninth, a fan jumped over the right field fence and stole Reggie's hat. Reggie threw down his glove and chased him, and just as he was about to catch him, another fan leaped down to steal his glove. After he recovered his equipment and took his position, I thought, How typical—just as everything seems to be falling apart, this crazy ball club puts it back together. Sure enough, a couple of Knowles pitches later, Wayne Garrett knocked a soft line drive to Campaneris at shortstop, and that was it. We were world champions again. The first team since the 1960–61 New York Yankees to win back-to-back world titles. One of the best clubs in baseball history. To hell with Cincinnati's Big Red Machine of the mid-seventies. To hell with the Brooklyn Dodgers, who everybody loved but who—everybody seems to forget—rarely won the big one. These long-haired, freaked-out, swinging, fighting, fantastic A's were better than anybody, maybe at any time. It was a dynasty. It was a miracle.

And I couldn't enjoy it. Just as the last out was made, it sunk in that no matter what I'd done, this wasn't my team, not really. The fact that I could leave them proved it. This was Charlie's team. And this World Series win, which we envisioned as showing Charlie up, only made him happier. I realized this as Campaneris made his catch, and so I did something that I sometimes regret. I didn't celebrate on the field. I clapped a couple of times, turned, and headed down the runway into the clubhouse. This was Charlie's team out there now. I was finished. And I wanted to get the hell out before I did something I'd really regret, like decide to stay.

I ended that notion in a postgame national television interview in the clubhouse. "This is a great day for me but also a sad day," I told the nation. "Because I am leaving the A's, for personal reasons, and not out of any dissatisfaction over my relations with Mr. Finley." Charlie then jumped in front of the camera, hugged me, and said, "You are a great manager, and I will not stand in your way." Remember those words. Not the part about the great manager, but the part about not standing in my way.

The time between my announcement and when I walked

out the door proved to be my most difficult time of the Series. Reggie hugged me, crying, and said, "I'm sorry, I'm sorry, I'm sorry." Other players pleaded with me to rethink my decision. I'd been so busy breaking up fights that I guess I'd never realized how much I was loved. And never realized, as I began crying myself, how much I'd loved in return.

The next morning, though, it took about five minutes for me to love being gone. That was the time I spent watching the television report about how Reggie and Blue Moon spent at least some of their postgame party engaging in a fistfight.

Within two days of the end of the Series, the word was out about my interest in the Yankees, although I had signed no contract. But Charlie's farm director, John Claiborne, knew enough to advise Charlie that if I was really going to leave, he ought to at least get some compensation for me. And so just before I flew home to Florida for the winter, Charlie delivered one last punch. The same man who had told me earlier in the week that he wouldn't stand in my way announced that I wouldn't get away without a fight. If the Yankees wanted me, he said, they'd have to compensate him heavily. I was so sick of things by now that I simply ignored Charlie, figuring something could be worked out or the man would be declared insane, one or the other.

But you don't forget about Charlie. No sooner was I laughing about the $7,000 Kuhn had fined him for his World Series antics than I was receiving a World Series paycheck with $1,700 deducted. Turns out Charlie had decided to charge me for every little expense during the season—not lodging and transportation and regular meals but things like lunches he'd asked me to buy for my coaches, and for *him,* and even long distance phone calls to Norma, which he'd never charged me for in the past. Just as I was getting over this financial hit, I discovered that our new World Series rings, which Charlie had claimed would dwarf our first rings, didn't even have a diamond in them! And instead of saying 1973 WORLD CHAMPIONS on them, they said 1972–73 WORLD

CHAMPIONS, which couldn't have meant a hell of a lot to guys who weren't on the 1972 team.

And baby, Charlie was just getting started. On December 13 my Yankee deal was finalized. It was a three-year contract promising control over much of the organization. I flew to New York, put on the shirt and cap, did the press conference, and then flew back to Florida, loaded down with Yankee souvenirs and scouting reports. I walked off the plane and nearly dropped everything when I heard Charlie was making a formal protest of my signing. I thought, That idiot! He's really going through with it!

All of a sudden I had to fly back north, this time to Boston, for a late December hearing in front of American League president Joe Cronin. This would be my first chance to actually meet George Steinbrenner, believe it or not. He had been too cautious to dirty his hands in something that was almost certainly against league rules. So he'd stayed out of sight, and only after I signed the contract did he talk to me. Even then, he told me to ignore and avoid everyone until the deal was done and approved.

So I flew to Boston for the hearing with my lawyer, John Remsen, and caught a cab to the hotel. Walking across the lobby, I heard this voice calling me: "Dick, Dick, over here, over here." Following Steinbrenner's advice, I completely ignored the man until suddenly he ran up and tapped me on the shoulder. It was Steinbrenner. Of course, we'd lost the hearing. Cronin made the announcement on December 20. But I knew we didn't stand a chance. I knew the Yankees would have to give Finley something. The question was, What would he ask for? "I still have all intentions of managing the Yankees," I told the media after the ruling, which stated that Charlie must give his permission for me to manage elsewhere.

But then Charlie made his announcement. Yes, he said, he'd give his permission for me to go to the Yankees—if they gave up top outfield prospect Otto Velez and pitching prospect Scott McGregor. When he said those names, I knew my world had been turned on its ear, because I knew the Yankees simply wouldn't agree to such a deal, nor should they. Like I've said, I don't swing a bat or pitch a ball, I don't actually win games for teams. I just get their players prepared so they can win. No way am I, or is any manager, worth two young prospects. And I knew then that no way would I be the Yankees' manager.

On January 3, 1974, the Yankees announced that their new manager would be Bill Virdon. And I was officially sunk. Now I either returned to Charlie for the last year of my written contract or managed only where Charlie agreed I could manage. The A's players wanted me to do the former. Reggie and Bando called me throughout the winter, trying to get me to suck it up for just one more year. "If it was a full year, I might do it," I said, realizing I had run out of options. "But you know that the minute I announced I was returning, Charlie would fire me."

It was about this time, in January, that an elderly man dressed in worker's clothes knocked on the door of our Singer Island home one morning. I thought it was the gardener. "Dick, I'm John D. MacArthur," the man said, giving the name of one of the richest men in the country. "I hear you are out of a job. How would you like to come work for me?" And that was how this phase of my life ended, with me taking on a job as an aide to a near-billionaire while waiting for another managerial offer that Charlie would approve.

My new job lasted only six months, and as you shall see, Charlie ended up having the last laugh by approving my move to the worst team I've ever seen, let alone managed. But hell, that's okay. No, really—I finally believe that Charlie deserves to laugh all he wants.

Time has a funny way of changing the way a man looks at things. So does the luster of two World Series rings. Looking back, while Charlie may have been a demon, he was a champion. Fine, say I'm getting soft in my declining years.

But hey, we won. For two years we may have been the best ever. Whatever hell he put us through, most of us have forgotten the bad things and only remember the good. Like the rings. Like our names in the record books. Like our imprint on a sporting nation's consciousness.

Would I manage those three years for Charlie again, knowing what would happen? After many years of thought I've come up with a two-word answer: hell, yes. Like I said at the beginning of this chapter, he may have been a maniac, but he cared about winning. Now that so few people feel like that anymore, Charlie, I appreciate how you felt. And to tell you the truth, Charlie, I sort of miss you. I hated you then, but my life is so quiet now that I sort of miss you and your winning madness.

Norma, who hates to hate anybody, sent Charlie a card on his birthday and on Christmas in 1975, then again on the same dates for the next three or four years. Last year, 14 years later, he finally sent a letter back. It contained some pictures of me, and on one of them he signed, "Thanks for Everything, Charlie." I never thought I'd say this, but—hey, Charlie, you old man, same here.

HELL'S ANGELS

After two consecutive world championships, what can a manager possibly do for an encore? How about agreeing to manage a team so bad that it could take batting practice in a hotel lobby without breaking a chandelier? That's what Boston pitcher Bill Lee said about my California Angels, whom I began managing June 26, 1974—the encore to my years with Oakland. The memory of victory parades and champagne still lingering in the back of my mind, thoughts of dreams fulfilled still deep in my heart, I came to the conclusion that I didn't have to take Bill Lee's shit. When I brought the Angels to Boston my second year on the job, I decided to prove him wrong.

In the afternoon before a night game I took my team down to the hotel lobby—after calling all the newspapers, of course. Then I broke out Wiffle Balls and plastic bats. And there, in front of people who began dropping suitcases on their toes, we took batting practice. I'm talking line drives off elevators. One-bouncers off the registration desk. After one particularly vicious grounder eluded a diving attempt by a bellman and rolled into the manager's office, out came the manager. Up went his blood pressure. "Out!" he ordered us.

"But why?" I said in a voice I hoped was loud enough for Bill Lee to hear. "We aren't breaking anything." The lesson of the story, and of my Angels career, is that a few hours later we were again unable to break anything, as Lee shut us out 6−0.

And so it went for my 341 games with the inappropriately named Angels, a group of players who were so bad that it took lobby workouts to make them funny. They only won 147 of the games I managed, losing the other 194 in such despicable fashion that this became my only job where I was left to wonder why in the hell I'd taken it in the first place.

Perhaps because I was offered the job while still in bed. I was in my Riviera Beach, Florida, home one summer morning at 6:30. The phone rang, and of course I thought somebody had died. I picked it up, and the man on the other end indeed sounded dead. It was Harry Dalton, the general manager of the Angels. He was calling from near their Anaheim, California, stadium—meaning the clock on his wall said 3:30 A.M. As I later learned, there were two reasons he was calling me that early: he had the kind of team that kept him up nights, and he was doing something against his will, something he was ordered to do by Angels owner Gene Autry. He was offering me his manager's job. If the lighted red numbers on my clock were correct, this occurred about 6:37 A.M.

Dalton was not a fan of mine, although I'm not sure why. Maybe it was something I'd said in the newspaper one time, maybe something I did on the field. In this game of constant tightrope walking, one action is all it might take to turn somebody against you forever. Possibly, Dalton didn't like me because I'd played with Baltimore back when he was first hired there—as an office boy, by answering a newspaper ad. In disbelief I had watched him rise meteorically to the top, seemingly through no fault of his own. In other words, Harry knew that I knew that he didn't know shit.

In the summer of 1974, when it came time to find some-

one to run his baseball team, I was the last person he wanted
to see. But Autry, an old cowboy who was attracted to an
outlaw like me, gave him no choice. By 1974 Autry had
watched his Angels compile a winning record just four times
in the 13 years since he had purchased them as an expansion
franchise. They lost simply because the players were like day-
old, marked-down doughnuts. They came cheap, and even
then they weren't worth the money. Autry was a singing star
who wanted to surround himself with baseball stars, but he
wanted them for a song. History will show that he later spent
gobs of money, even almost winning a pennant with his open
checkbook, and generally became one of baseball's true pa-
triarchs. But at the time I came on board he was a cheap-
skate.

Autry's tight spending habits weren't limited to baseball
players. The time his star horse, Champion, died, he called
Roy Rogers for some advice because he knew Rogers had
had his own horse, Trigger, stuffed. Autry asked how much
that procedure cost. "About $25,000, but that was 10 years
ago," said Rogers, probably touched that Autry would consider such an act. Rogers then asked, "So, Gene, what are
you planning with Champion?" Autry paused. "Bury the son
of a bitch."

That's just what his sealed wallet had done to the Angels.
He had buried the sons of bitches. That 1974 team was led
on offense by Frank Robinson, who was already 38. The top
pitchers were Nolan Ryan and nobody. All of this would have
been fine if the Angels had had a good scouting and farm
system, but they had neither. The only thing worse than a
wretched baseball team is one with no help in sight.

Naturally, I took the job without using my sight, even
though I had been enjoying my work with Mr. Mac, as we
called John D. MacArthur. The third-richest man in North
America at the time, he had a very complicated life, what
with 90-something businesses and damn near a billion dollars. Yet somehow he was able to do everything simply. He

would wake up each morning at 5 and meet me at 7 in his hotel restaurant, where, with a simple meal of coffee and a bagel in front of him, he would plan out strategies that would affect much of this country's economy, investing millions in some vast new project, buying one conglomerate and selling another, shifting huge amounts of capital around the country like a baseball manager shifting his outfielders. He would dress in old pants and shirts with lint balls, ready for any kind of work. Sometimes—don't laugh—he'd leave our meetings to straighten the nails on a new construction project. Once he left to find the guy who filled the local newspaper vending machine. It seems his newspaper was missing a section and he wanted his quarter back. Tight? Maybe. But then, how do you think he got to be so rich? Those quarters and straightened nails add up.

I enjoyed accompanying Mr. Mac to motivational meetings and seminars and observing his straightforward, no-bullshit attitudes. I did not enjoy flying to these conventions, because he would fly to them in an ancient plane with the back door open so he could smoke. But once we landed and moved through the mass of bodyguards and businessmen looking to kiss his ass, I saw his quiet but stern motivational style change many old money attitudes.

Only one problem with that kind of business world change: it takes too long. And after eight months of working with him, I realized that, much as I liked the man, I didn't like that scene. Unlike my world, there was no quick payoff. Not once did one of Mr. Mac's company presidents put on a last minute squeeze play and walk home that night with the profits. Not once did Mr. Mac make a position change and see results at the end of the week. If I was ever going to be a businessman, it would have happened between winter 1973 and spring 1974. But as I found my mind straying to the sports page and box scores during our morning meetings, I realized I would always be a baseball man.

So when Harry Dalton got me out of bed that June morning, in more than one way I jumped. I had already spoken to Calvin Griffith about managing his Minnesota Twins, but our conversation had lasted as long as it took me to say, "One hundred thousand dollars," and him to scream, "You're out of your mind!" That's how much money I wanted to return to managing, not so much because Norma and I needed new living room furniture as because I needed to puff out my chest again. I needed to make a statement again. At that point no manager in baseball history had made six figures. Simply, I wanted to be the first, and maybe somehow pave the way for managers after me. Besides, considering my record with Oakland, and considering the way I'd been forced into unemployment, I figured I damn well deserved it.

Harry Dalton's first response to my demand was something like "Aren't you still getting paid by Oakland?" "Well," I told him, "I am, and I'm not." Then I explained that I was so disgusted with Charlie Finley since the Yankees incident that I'd vowed not to accept one more penny from him. Not a one. So from the time I left the team following the 1973 World Series to the end of 1974 when my A's contract finally ran out, I didn't cash one of Finley's checks. I made photocopies and mailed the checks back to him.

Yes, I realize this might not have been a financially prudent thing to do. Taking that money, I could have played a lot of golf. Maybe even erased a lot of bad memories. But what if Finley phoned me at the golf course in April and ordered me to hurry on down to one of his minor league cities as a hitting instructor? I would have had to find the next flight. At that point I'd rather have found a high bridge.

So I made my $100,000 request to Dalton, which amounted to a $25,000 raise from the salary Mr. Mac was paying me, and a $35,000 raise from my final year at Oakland. I told them if they paid me what I wanted, I would come—"no questions asked." As I later learned, those are three deadly words. I wanted to show up the A's and the baseball world so bad that I didn't demand a look at the young Angels players. Or at their old players either. Hell, I didn't even fly out to California for an interview. My preparation for a definite job offer consisted of returning to the restaurant every morning with Mr. Mac and waiting for Harry Dalton to page me.

I later learned that it had taken Angels officials nearly six hours of wining and dining Finley before he gave them permission to talk to me. Dalton later phoned me and said fine, they would pay me $100,000 for each of three years to be their manager. Said it almost begrudgingly but said it anyway, which was the only thing that mattered. Or so I thought at the time.

And that is how I became the fifth, and dumbest, manager of the California Angels. I received an inkling of just how dumb as I was leaving my home for Anaheim. An old friend, former Detroit manager Mayo Smith, phoned me with a little hint. "Dick," he said, "I've scouted them and I know: they've got no talent in the major leagues and nothing in the minor leagues. Nothing." He paused. "But enough about me. Good luck."

If only I'd realized that history would still have considered me a good manager without a team or a big contract, now that I had already competed against, and defeated, the best in the business. But I desperately needed more competition, always more competition. For once in my life I should have been willing to sit peacefully on top of the mountain and enjoy the view without thinking, Okay, somewhere there has to be a bigger mountain. Instead, I found myself on an airplane bound for southern California in the middle of 1974 with the following new and fun facts at my fingertips: after eleven years of growth under the franchise's first two managers, Bill Rigney and Lefty Phillips, the Angels had risen from eighth place to as high as third—and then basically gone to hell, starting around the time Harry Dalton showed up as the boss.

Before the 1972 season, just after he took over, Dalton

hired Del Rice as his manager. Rice went 75–80 that year and was promptly fired, with his severance pay coming in the form of an ulcer. Dalton replaced Rice with someone who I thought was a pretty good selection, former Arizona State University manager Bobby Winkles. While at ASU, he'd produced a crop of great players—Reggie Jackson, Rick Monday, and Sal Bando, among others. He was a good fundamentals man and a good choice. And he was already on the Angels staff as a coach. He looked like he would easily make it as a big league boss.

But that winter Dalton acquired Frank Robinson in a trade with the Dodgers. Robinson was great in that ensuing 1973 season, with a team-leading 30 homers and 97 RBIs. But the future Hall of Famer, in an attempt to get a start on his next career, also tried to manage. Although he did later become a successful manager, that kind of thing never works when you're still a player. Soon the clubhouse became divided, which meant one guy was torn apart. You guessed it— Bobby Winkles. Even people not on the team were saying that the Angels were split into Robby's guys and Bobby's guys. Winkles wasn't helped by a basic dress and discipline code that even covered the way the players cut their hair. That stuff is fine as long as there's nobody like Robinson in the clubhouse telling the other players how bush league he thinks it is.

There was something bush league happening there, all right, but don't blame Winkles. The club went 79–83 in his first season. And then when he won just 30 of his first 73 games in 1974, they summoned me. "Can one manager turn around a bad team?" the media asked me. I answered, "An asshole manager can. And I'm one of those."

But upon arriving at Anaheim Stadium, realizing I would be working just a couple of giant steps from Disneyland, I decided to first get into the fantasy spirit of the place. I informed my players, "I guarantee you that as long as I'm here, we will not have a losing record." Not that they disagreed with me, but they promptly went out and lost our first 10 games together. The astute Autry summoned one of my coaches, Whitey Herzog, and confided in him with the most insightful words ever spoken during my tenure there. "Whitey," he drawled, "maybe I've hired the wrong man." Not being the kind of guy who likes to beat his head against walls, yes, perhaps I was the wrong man.

About our only early bright spot was that Frank Robinson apparently couldn't bitch, because I'd thrown him a major bone. In a move that I hoped would have Carl Yastrzemski—type ramifications, my first steps in the clubhouse were in the direction of Robby, whom I made the first official team captain in Angels history. If the younger players were going to follow him anyway, I figured, I might as well have him taking them in my direction.

Honestly, I thought it was a good idea. But like everything else I did there, it backfired. Soon after I arrived Robinson was shipped to Cleveland. Soon after that he was bitching at me, from Cleveland, for the $500 he said the Angels owed him as the traditional fee for being captain. He thought that if the Angels didn't pay, I should pay. The dispute moved me into a managerial class all by myself. Any boss can get in fights with his players, but now I was even taking shit long distance.

It got worse. Soon I was taking shit from players I'd never even met. Take the 1974 All-Star game, in which I was the American League manager. I had rejoined the league only a couple of weeks before the game, but I was still the defending World Series manager, so the All-Star team was mine. From my Angels I took Robinson and kid third baseman Dave Chalk, which seemed nice and safe. Little did I know that in Chicago, playing for the White Sox, resided a third baseman named Bill Melton, who, judging by snide little comments in the newspapers, thought he'd been snubbed. This was a feeling I wouldn't discover until two years later, just minutes before it stabbed me in the back.

I was also taking shit from old friends. My first trip back

to Oakland, in August 1974, should have been a triumphant return, right? I showed up with my lousy team and saw that Charlie Finley had ordered the following phrase emblazoned across the scoreboard, just for me: WELCOME TO OAKLAND, HOME OF THE 1973 WORLD CHAMPIONS. Just in case I forgot what I'd left. Then we got our butts kicked, and Finley ordered GOOD NIGHT, DICK onto the scoreboard. Afterward Reggie Jackson came over to our clubhouse and swore he would walk off the field if Finley tried that again. I said simply, "That's just Charlie. Typical bush league." But in my mind this was the last straw. Finally, for the first time since my Oakland disaster, I vowed to get him back.

That wouldn't be easy with my new club. We stumbled into the end of the season with a 36–48 record under me, which was just one game better than they'd done under Winkles. We were in sixth and last place, 26 games under .500 and 22 games out of first. What to do?

I thought about pushing Dalton to acquire an entirely new team, but that would have been a difficult sell even during those rare times he acted as if he liked me. I thought about appealing to Autry's sense of kindness— the same sense that had once brought Norma in out of the dark. Autry spotted her one night waiting for me in a lit phone booth in the darkened stadium concourse and insisted that she sit upstairs in his box until I finished getting dressed (i.e., finished fuming over another loss). He phoned her the next day from Palm Springs and gave her a gentle lecture on the dangers of lonely phone booths. This sense of kindness I could use, I thought. Maybe I could convince him that managing a team without any good players is as dangerous as a lonely phone booth.

I thought about doing a lot of things. I spent the winter wondering how in the hell I could get out of this contract. Of course, I couldn't. And deep down I knew I wouldn't. So I decided on the most logical solution: fight like hell until I wanted to stay. In other words, I decided to hire Grover Resinger.

If you're going to go through life with a first name like Grover, you had better be tough. And so it was with Resinger, an old-time baseball man who never made the big leagues but had enough minor league years to appreciate what it took to get there and how you had to fight to stay. Grover lived on a farm in Iola, Missouri, where he spent the winter with his pet wolf. He was 15 years older than me, although he looked twice that, and behaved as if he used to room with a guy named Doubleday.

You hate to lose? Not like Grover. Resinger hated to lose so much that he couldn't sleep nights. Several times during that 1975 season, after a late phone call with Norma, I'd step out of the hotel to buy the morning newspaper at 3 A.M. and see Resinger walking up and down the deserted city streets, his face shrouded in steam such as rises from manhole covers. I never knew the source of Resinger's steam, just as I never knew when he would erupt.

How about that day in Chicago during another half-assed batting practice when Resinger scared even me by jumping out from behind the batting cage, throwing his fungo bat into the air, and shouting, "Get the fuck off the field! You are embarrassing the game of baseball!"

Or that day in Anaheim when Dave Collins, just a rookie in 1975, was trying to hit home runs during batting practice. Resinger yelled at him so loud and so long that Collins began crying. If that was overdoing it, you couldn't tell from Collins's career. Last I looked, he was still playing, and still saying that Resinger's speech was the best thing that had ever happened to him.

Resinger was more me than me, which was a hell of an inspiration. Maybe this is why I walked into our Arizona clubhouse in the spring of 1975 and told my team, "You will never finish last again." This sounded so confident, so wildly optimistic, that people must have thought I'd been having some private soul sessions with Norman Vincent Peale. Sure, I'd eaten dinner with Peale once when I played with Brooklyn. He was all right, I guess. But he was no Grover Resinger, the source of my inspired confidence, the guy who kept a wolf for a pet.

Little did I know, however, that throughout the 161 games of the 1975 season the recipients of that pep talk would be intent on making a liar out of me. Not that they didn't try to win, but they had no opportunity. And don't ever believe that baseball bullshit that during the course of a long summer every team has a chance at the world championship. Believe me, sometimes you just don't have a chance.

These Angels were cursed with several things, beginning with what obviously bored reporters called an incubator infield. Indeed, we were young: first baseman Bruce Bochte was in his second season; second baseman Jerry Remy was a rookie; shortstop Orlando Ramirez was in his second season; third baseman Dave Chalk was in his second full season. It wouldn't have bothered me that their combined total of home runs was just seven, or that none of them batted better than .285 or knocked in more than 82 runs. I could have lived with that if I'd seen promise of improvement in the near future. The problem was, only one of them, Remy, really got much better. It was obvious that my Angels were the Peter Pans of baseball—nice, cute kids who would never grow up.

Our outfield was led by a guy named Lee Stanton, whom you may not have heard about, but who was a veritable Babe Ruth on this squad with a team-leading 82 RBIs and 14 homers—more than twice as many homers as anybody else on the team. We anchored the league in home runs that season with a big 55. Like other roadblocks in my career, though, this lack of power helped me discover a new path—in this case, a basepath. Because we couldn't hit, we ran. For the first of what would be many times with my teams, I decided to see what would happen if I ordered my runners to steal damn near every base they saw. Besides giving me something to watch every night other than bad swings, this strategy made a hero out of our other top outfielder, Mickey Rivers. Change that from "hero" to "star." Mickey will read this and think I'm calling him a sandwich.

He was so excited that spring when I informed the team of my running game that he burst out with "When it comes to stolen bases, this year I'm going to double my limit." But goodness, could Mickey run. He stole a league-leading 70 bases; our team stole an incredible 220, the most by any team since 1916. Problem was, stolen bases aren't the same as runs. Hell, in a stat that is unusual for one of my teams, we couldn't even steal home. We stole home five times in 1974 but not once in 1975.

And how we could have used a few guys crossing home plate. This poor hitting hurt not just me but, worse, the careers of one great pitcher and one future great, Nolan Ryan and Frank Tanana. My best memories of my short time in Anaheim surround those two guys: Ryan blowing away the league with the kinds of pitches and power I'd never seen before; Tanana doing just the opposite, screwing around and messing with the hitters' minds and my better judgment, and still getting people out.

First impression of Tanana: A week after I took over the team in 1974, he celebrated his 21st birthday. Normally I don't give a damn when my guys were born, but for this particular birthday his girlfriends arranged for a sign on the big screen in center field that read HAPPY 21ST FRANK TANANA. When the sign came on, the girls screamed. From the dugout I could hear their squeals and see Tanana's smug expression, and I nearly screamed myself.

Second impression of Tanana: His inconsistency got him taken out of the starting rotation when I arrived. He was so upset about being in the bullpen that when I brought him into a game, he'd just shit the ball up to the plate. Not knowing him, I asked if something was wrong with his arm. He smiled and said, "Nah. I just want to start." I stared at him. "Okay," I said, "you'll be starting in a couple of days . . . in Salt Lake City." Tanana, unsuited for that minor league town, just smiled back and never gave anything less than his best again. He was voted the league's best rookie pitcher in 1974 by going 14–19 with a 3.11 ERA and 180 strikeouts. In 1975 he was our team's best player, going 16–9 with a 2.63 ERA and a league-high 269 strikeouts. So what if he was single and ran the bars and broads hard and laughed at the manager? He gave me more than most of the team combined.

That is, with the exception of Ryan. Where Tanana would laugh, Ryan would glare. Where Tanana might dance around a hitter, Ryan would beat him with his legs. My most lasting impression of Ryan is just that: his legs. During the 1989 season many talked with wonder about the arm of this 42-year-old man, but they failed to see where the real magic was. Watch him wind up, see him release the ball, listen to him grunt—yes, he throws so hard he grunts like a tennis player—and watch him land. Then notice how his legs are stretched and bulging, every inch of them, and you will understand why nobody has done as well for as long. And after everyone else has gone home, sneak into the clubhouse and watch him work those legs with weights. Nobody has deserved that success more.

I wasn't with Anaheim more than three months when Ryan threw his third career no-hitter, a 4–0 win over Minnesota on September 28. I was impressed, obviously, but I was really blown away nine months later, when he threw his record-tying fourth no-hitter, on June 1, 1975, a 1–0 victory over Baltimore. What got me about Ryan's game wasn't his 100-miles-per-hour fastball or his grunting, so loud that it sounded like he was taking a shit right there on the mound. What impressed me was the way he ended it by freezing Baltimore second baseman Bobby Grich on a full count changeup. The biggest pitch of the game, and he had the balls to make it an off-speed pitch. Fooled Grich, his own teammates, the entire stadium. Not to mention that he fooled me, which happened so rarely with my pitchers that I remember his changeup like it was last week.

That incident contradicts another myth about Ryan, a myth almost as large as the one about the arm being his primary weapon. People think he wins all of his games with fastballs.

Wrong. With a fastball like that, you don't need to win your games with fastballs. He wins them with curves and change-ups and everything else the hitter can't hit when he's looking for a fastball. Whitey Herzog once proposed that Ryan come out and throw nothing but fastballs until somebody got a base hit. Ryan would never try it—his good baseball sense wouldn't let him—but I just wonder if he couldn't have gotten another no-hitter that way.

Oddly, in no way did Ryan fit into the vision I had for my pitchers. Not then, and not 15 years later, when I'm out of the game but he's still icing kids on changeups. Back then I ran a contest with my staff to encourage smart pitching. If a guy gave me 18 ground ball outs, or ground balls that should have been outs, and we won the game, I'd buy him a suit of clothes. Nolan heard about this contest and looked at me with a frown.

"Now, Dick," he said in that Texas drawl, "you know I don't throw ground balls."

"Okay," I said, thinking quick. "If you don't walk a man, I'll buy you a suit of clothes."

It never happened. Because batters were so afraid of Ryan, many times they wouldn't swing at close pitches. Those pitches would be called balls, and Nolan would always walk somebody. I always thought, Well, this is one prize Ryan will never win. But several years later, when he was pitching for Houston against my San Diego Padres, son of a bitch if he didn't throw a two-hitter without walking a single batter. I wondered why he was smiling at me so big when he walked off the field, and then it finally hit me. The next day when he arrived at the park, I arranged for a bottle of Dom Perignon champagne to be waiting for him. It could even be fun to lose to a guy like that.

Ryan also became one of my favorite people by sparing my life after one of my biggest managerial blunders. This should show you how much managing the Angels shook me up. We were in Chicago one day in 1976 and I was in my tiny office talking to the writers about how great Ryan had pitched the night before. At the same time, I was filling in my lineup card. I hope this explains how, an hour later at home plate, minutes before the start of the game, I turned in a card to the umpire that had Nolan Ryan listed as the starting pitcher. That's right— while talking about Ryan, I absentmindedly penciled him in, even though he had just pitched 24 hours earlier.

But no big deal, I can change the card, right? Wrong. Once you turn in a lineup card, the pitcher on that card has to face at least one batter. Making matters worse, the White Sox were being managed by my mentor Paul Richards, who resisted my embarrassed pleas to overlook the rule. "One batter, Dick," Richards said to me after I discovered my error. "There's nothing I can do. He's got to face one batter."

The game was beginning, so I ran back to the bench, and luckily for me, Nolan was sitting there. He was wearing tennis shoes and didn't have a protective cup inside his pants, but at least he was there. "Nolan," I told him, "I've got this problem . . ." Thank goodness he understood. He went out there and stiffly faced one hitter, who grounded out to shortstop, at which point I immediately yanked him from the game. After that, in a ritual that many baseball people found odd, I refused to let anybody in my office when I was filling out the lineup card. Now everybody understands why.

No telling how well Ryan would have done with somebody other than those prize Angels. The year I arrived he went 22–16 in 41 starts, but he could have gone at least 35–6, considering he had a 2.89 ERA. Then, in that horrible 1975 season, he went 14–12 in 28 starts, this time deserving to be at least 20–8 because of his 3.45 ERA.

And that was the story of my 1975 season—poor Ryan and Tanana were fighting with cannons, while their teammates were backing them up with popguns. Only once did I ever see any real thirst for blood, and that really didn't count. Because it was my thirst and the Oakland A's blood. Remember when I vowed to repay Charlie Finley for embarrassing me in Oakland in late 1974? By the end of the first month of the 1975 season with the Angels, I had that chance.

We were leading the A's 9–1 in the sixth inning of the second game of a doubleheader in Anaheim, and Mickey Rivers was on first base, and I decided, Up yours, Charlie. I sent Rivers to second base on a hit-and-run attempt. Our batter got a hit and scored all the way from first. And of course the A's were angry. When you're leading by a big margin, running like that is considered crass. Not just because you're openly challenging the other team or making a comment on their ability to throw you out. Mostly, it's because you don't *need* to run. You're winning by eight runs, you just need to keep your mouth shut and finish the game. You don't need to run, and the losing team doesn't appreciate it. Few realize that more baseball fights start because of a needless steal than because of a stupid beanball.

I should mention here that it's also considered crass for a team leading 9–1 to shout obscenities about the opposing team's owner from the dugout. Particularly when the owner's real name is being used, as in "Take that, Charlie, you son of a bitch!" Or perhaps even "Fuck you, Charlie!" I must admit, that night I let a few such things slip. Was I looking for a fight? You decide. Oakland reliever Jim Todd thought so. He was already mad because, after not allowing an earned run all season, we'd touched him up for five. Immediately after Rivers's steal, Todd's next pitch was directed at, and collided with, the top of Bruce Bochte's head.

First thing I did was run to home plate to check on Bochte. Every manager does that. I leaned down and saw that he still had both eyes. My job was done. Now I did something that most managers would not do. I charged the mound of a team I'd spent three wonderful years managing, I charged the mound and lunged at their 6-foot-2 pitcher, who was about 20 years younger than me but obviously without a gut in his body. He tried to run. I grabbed him by his belt and dragged him to the ground and started pounding on him. That's right, I took on Jim Todd, and—you guessed it—soon I was rolling around with what seemed like 50 of my former players.

Anybody who knows Dick Williams and saw this scene would think, He's a dead man. Like a cop locked in a jail cell with guys he's arrested. He's lying on a pitching mound and fair game for former players who surely are looking for his nuts with their cleats. But I guess the A's liked me as much as I liked them—or at least some of them did. My world darkened underneath a green-and-gold uniform, but the voice was friendly. "It's Reggie," the voice whispered. "I'm just going to lie here on you until this thing ends." I laughed and he laughed, and we just lay there like two kids playing king-of-the-mountain while all hell was breaking loose on top of us.

Then I felt it. Right in the back. I was being kicked. Ooof. Ooof. My worst fears were coming true. Somebody was finally trying to kill me. I turned to grab the cleat, but then the foot was being dragged away by Reggie. I looked up and couldn't see the face, but I later learned it was the A's center fielder, my buddy Angel Mangual. Oh, well. You really didn't think I'd get away without at least one bruise, did you? I guess I'm lucky Charlie didn't sic the mule on me.

I honestly thought this fight would both spark the team and, at the very least, get the A's off my ass. Silly me. The team continued to suck and ended the 1975 season on the wrong side of a four-man A's no-hitter. As if they wanted to share in giving me pain, on September 28 we were held hitless by the combined talents of Vida Blue, Glenn Abbott, Paul Lindblad, and Rollie Fingers.

Does that date look familiar? It was exactly one year after Nolan Ryan's third no-hitter. What all that meant to my future with the Angels can be summed up in two words: big deal. This was a team that was even too bad for omens.

But that winter a strange thing happened. We got better. This was because Harry Dalton did something I hadn't seen him do since I accepted that offer with "no questions asked"—

he actually tried to improve the team. Knowing how badly we needed experience and power hitting, he decided to stop watching and shrugging and finally picked up the phone. The date was December 11, 1975. When he finally hung up for good, we had acquired Bobby Bonds from the New York Yankees and Bill Melton from the Chicago White Sox. And I was ecstatic. The previous season, these two players had combined for 47 home runs, nearly the home run total for my entire team. So what if part of our cost was Mickey Rivers, who went to the Yankees? We had other guys who could run. We had no one else who could hit.

I went into spring training in a state of euphoria. No, managers don't always go into spring training feeling that way, no matter what baseball's poets may tell you. Sometimes you're so worried about the upcoming six months that just the smell of the Arizona sagebrush or the Florida rain makes you sick. But not me in 1976. We had a pitching staff led by Ryan and Tanana, we had an infield that was a year older, and we finally had power.

"This may be the best team I've ever managed," I told everyone that spring. Part of me truly believed it, and the rest of me figured that if I could get the players to believe it, it didn't matter what I thought. And the players would believe, wouldn't they? Wrong. This was my first and last major mistake as an Angels manager. This was not 1967. Baseball's era of heart was quickly becoming the era of the handout. Players, I learned for the first time in 1976, had begun believing only in themselves and their inalienable right to make as much money as possible for as little work as possible. As the wise Autry summed it up that year when he confided to friends, "You can't make chicken salad out of chicken shit."

In fairness, the first thing that happened to the Angels that season wasn't their fault. A couple of days before our opener, at an exhibition game with the Los Angeles Dodgers, Bonds's hand was stepped on at home plate. Broke the hand, broke my heart. Put him out for what could have been several weeks, but Bonds insisted on playing almost immediately. It was an incredible show of guts, not to mention a neat display of one-handed hitting. Too bad the rest of the team didn't react to the injury that well. They saw he was hurt, realized we wouldn't be winning many games at first, and right away they quit. And not just the kids, who were suddenly scared again. Except for Ryan, most of the veteran leaders quit too. Damn Bill Melton quit. Damn Tommy Davis, the former two-time batting champion in the early sixties, quit.

At the time I could have guessed Melton was carrying some sort of grudge against me. Why else would he have screwed around the entire spring and failed to get into shape and winded up claiming his poor fat hamstrings were sore? Surely not because he was trying to steal the Angels' money? "Stealing" is not too harsh a word. What do you call a .208 batting average with six homers and 42 RBIs during the year? He started the season fat and lazy and slowly progressed to fatter and lazier.

Now, as for Tommy Davis, I know his problem wasn't with me, because I don't think he realized that I was the manager—or, come to think of it, that this team even had a manager. I got my first hint when I caught the veteran outfielder in the clubhouse bathroom between innings, shaving. Another time I found him using the telephone in my office between innings. That was bad enough, but did he also have to give the operator my credit card number? Around the time I shoved Davis's cleats off my desk I realized that this was a team I could no longer control. They were a lethal combination of bad and uncaring, something I'd never encountered before or since. Right then, faced with the very real possibility that I might not last the year, I decided I'd better go down fighting. I had no idea how close I would come to doing just that.

Writing off the older players as lost causes, Resinger and I began driving the younger guys harder and harder. We yelled at them in the dugout, on the pitching mound, when their faces were stuck in their lockers, when they didn't think we could yell anymore. We yelled so much that when we shipped out veteran Joe Lahoud, he complained, "Those two guys ought to be wearing swastikas." I didn't take offense at that grossly insensitive comment, because I figured that Lahoud probably didn't even know what the swastika represented. It must have been something he'd seen in a comic book.

The harder we pushed, the more the players became withdrawn and unemotional. They let us walk all over them because they figured, rightfully, that soon enough our steps would carry us out the door. This hurt. Before when I cared, I won. Now, apparently, to care was to be uncool. To care was a waste of energy. Most of these players didn't want caring, as long as there were steady paychecks. Baseball's true modern era had arrived. And I was being crushed under its wheels.

By midseason the toll on me became evident. One afternoon we were coming out of Baltimore after losing on a stupid little play. Sitting in the car waiting for me was our announcer, Dave Niehaus, with his wife, Marilyn, whom I had never met. (By the way, Niehaus, whom I later rejoined in Seattle, is the best announcer in the business, as anybody who has heard his smoky voice and the wonderful stories he weaves between pitches will agree. Problem is, in Seattle nobody's listening.) Anyway, I was coming out of the stadium, so pissed that I was repeating, "Fuckit, fuckit, fuckit, fuckit, fuckit, fuckit." I climbed in the front seat, rolled up my window, and was now screaming it: "Fuckit, fuckit, fuckit, fuckit!" Yes, I'd lost my mind, I realized that. About this time Niechaus saw I had no idea that his wife was sitting in the backseat. "Dick," he said, "I'd like you to meet my wife, Marilyn . . ." Without missing a beat, I turned and said, "Nice to meet you," then faced the front again and screamed, "Fuckit anyway!" Just another day with hell's Angels.

After one such trip I was finally delivered from my misery. The ending wasn't pretty, but it makes me proud. I don't

know if I made any of my players wet their pants or anything, but by the time I finally got fired, they knew Dick Williams had been there.

It was the early hours of July 23, 1976. We had flown
into Los Angeles from a long trip, and we still had to take
this stinking 36-mile bus ride from the airport to our cars at
Anaheim Stadium. Grover and I were sitting in the front,
cursing under our breath while staring at our feet. Then I
heard this singing and laughing coming from the back, and
all I could think was, Do they have to rub it in?

"Quiet back there, all you winners!" I shouted.

The momentary silence was broken by a thwack! thwack!
I looked back and saw one of the bus seats busted and lying
in the aisle. Then I heard a voice.

"Fuck you," said the voice, loud enough to be directed at
the stressed-out manager in the front.

"Who said that?" I shouted.

"I did, you cocksucker!" shouted the voice, which became
a challenging body standing in the aisle, a body belonging to
Bill Melton. Oh, I thought, so he really does hate me, this
same Bill Melton I'd left off the All-Star team a couple of
years earlier. Before, I had just guessed it from his published
quotations during the previous year's All-Star game, and from
the undeniable fact that he had come here and screwed both
me and his teammates by not giving a damn. But now I was
certain he hated me. I may have been whatever he meant to
call me, but the instant he said it I realized that Bill Melton
was a gutless quitter who put his personal feelings ahead of
the team's.

"You're suspended!" I shouted back at him.

"This is the happiest day of my life," he answered.

The sarcasm and insubordination were like a punch to
my midsection. When people say they're blind with rage, now
I know what they mean.

"You got a problem with me," I screamed, "I'll meet you
outside this bus!"

There. I'd said it. I'd actually challenged a major league player to a fight. From that moment on, I knew my career as a California Angels manager was over.

No, we didn't fight. I met him in the parking lot of Anaheim Stadium, and we just screamed some more before each of us went home to a sleepless night.

I got up the next morning at 9, visited Harry Dalton at the stadium, explained the incident, and then went home. At 4 P.M. he called me as if there were something he'd forgotten to tell me in the office. There was. I was fired. Thanks, Harry, for saying it to my face. Thanks for letting me spend the entire morning with you not knowing.

That night Dalton told the media, and I quote directly here, that Dick Williams "wasn't ready to come to grips with the needs of a young club. He reached a point where he felt he was above the losses, that they tainted him personally."

He got that backward. I wasn't "above the losses," I was forced to sit right in the middle of them. It was the worst three seasons of my life, and I was actually relieved to be relieved. Grover Resinger also quit, retiring on the spot. Even when I called him to join me in my next managerial job, he said he was staying retired. Said he couldn't stand to even be around today's players, much less coach them. I guess he preferred spending time with his wolf.

The next morning, with no players around, I cleaned out my office and quickly left. I'd learned when to walk away from a bad accident. There were no goodbyes with the Angels, no drunken wakes, no final speeches. I hauled the last box of personal belongings out to the truck and turned to a lineup of stadium maintenance people who had stopped sweeping because they figured, wrongly, that they were watching some kind of history. It appeared they wanted a discourse on my career, so I obliged, however briefly, with a yell that straightened the hair on their mops: "Fuckit anyway!"

FOREIGNER

The beer was cold around my fingers. The top of the seat embraced my head. I closed my eyes on the airline magazine article about an obscure businessman, shut my ears against the drone of the engine, and for a minute I was back on a dugout, laughing and crying in the rain. For a minute I was in the World Series again.

Smooth sailing. I opened my eyes and smiled as if at a private joke. Another World Series? Why not? I had the world below me, Montreal in front of me, and, most important, Reggie Jackson alongside me.

It was the winter of 1976. A couple of months after leaving hell's Angels, I'd become the manager of the Montreal Expos, a typical job for me. In other words, they were an eight-year-old stinker that had never had a winning season. Soon after joining up, I'd led them to Reggie, then a free agent who could sign with any team. He was 30 years old, a prime player in his prime, coming off a 27-homer, 91-RBI season for Baltimore, even though he hated it there. Think how he'd do in a place he loved. He didn't love Montreal yet, but he loved me, and that was a start.

En route to visiting another potential team, the New York Yankees, Reggie agreed to visit my new employer and discuss becoming an Expo. Since he lived in Phoenix and I lived nearby in southern California, I agreed to fly to Montreal in late November with him. His agent, Bob Walker, was afraid to fly, so a few days earlier he had left Phoenix to drive in a mobile home all the way to Montreal with some of Reggie's friends. Also on the airplane with us, just in case Reggie got lost going through customs, were Walker's wife and Walker's assistant, his personal secretary.

This frazzled entourage somehow managed to meet in Montreal at the same time—Reggie in his fur coat and Walker in his Winnebago. Unfortunately, the most important part of this junket didn't make it on time. In fact, it didn't make it, period.

I'm speaking of Reggie's suitcase. Ordinarily, a single bag would seem to be of little significance, but by the time it was diverted in Toronto and ended up in an Ottawa airport more than 100 miles away from Reggie, it became something of huge importance. So huge that the Ottawa officials demanded that the bag be searched before it was turned over. It was locked, so Kevin McHale, the son of Expos president John McHale, left our weekend with Reggie and traveled to Ottawa with a key that our star prospect thought might work.

Unfortunately for the Montreal Expos, the key did work. It fit perfectly, allowing the bag to be popped open beneath the customs inspectors' beady eyes. Outside of Reggie's presence they were able to examine part of his personal life, to paw through *his*—Reggie Jackson's very own—fine sweaters and expensive shoes. God knows they could have touched his underwear. When Reggie found out about this, he was righteously outraged. Welcome to Canada, eh.

In the end, this little incident cost him no more than a bad mood. It was me and the Montreal Expos who paid the real price. Reggie quickly ended his weekend of parties thrown by the Expos with this pleasant statement: "This is a very nice place. We'll see what happens." Translated, that meant: "No fucking way am I playing in a city where people get to stick their fingers in your suitcase." He and his buddies finished their tour by making a few tacky jokes about French phrases and then left town, never to return.

After realizing what a loss this would be for the city's fur industry—it could have been supported on Reggie's shoulders alone—it quickly sank in what a loss this might be for the franchise and my career. Suddenly, I saw no more World Series, no more dancing. I saw only that popped-open suitcase, and then I wondered if a man could ever ease the heartbreak of one of life's great missed opportunities. It would take some mighty powerful drugs.

Did I say "drugs"? Ah yes, that word readily comes to mind whenever I think about my time in Montreal. It marked the beginning of my drug phase, so to speak. No, I've never gotten high on anything stronger than Chivas on the rocks. But sometime in the seventies drugs swept through baseball like a December tide, tainting everyone in the game—users and nonusers alike. It was in Montreal where I first realized that, try as I might, I just could not get out of the way.

Simply put, I had to relearn this game I loved. Greenies became something other than rookies, hangovers became something players could get before a night game. Before penciling a player into the lineup, I could no longer just ask how he felt. For the first time in my 10-year managing career, I had to look and listen. If a player's eyes were red and swollen, he was benched. If his hands were shaking, he was benched. If he mumbled incoherently to me, he was benched. If I yelled at any reporters afterward for asking why . . . well, I hope now they understand.

I was yelling because I *didn't* understand. Not in Montreal, nor later in San Diego, where the problem was just as bad. I didn't know how the drugs worked, or why they worked, or why a guy would want to compete against somebody else when he couldn't see straight. If these guys wanted to do drugs, that was their own personal business. But why did they have to keep coming into my clubhouse and putting on a uniform after they did it? Why couldn't they have just quit and done their drugs somewhere else, leaving me alone with players who cared? I know this attitude may sound unusual, but you try going from locker to locker checking pupils for dilation and then let me know how you feel about it. You watch a guy blowing a game because of a missed fly ball and then spending 30 minutes blowing his nose. You try it, then tell me how how I'm supposed to feel. A good word for that feeling is "betrayed."

My experience with the drugs was doubly bad because the rest of my four and a half years in Montreal was so pleasant. I loved the city. I loved turning baseball's worst team into one that won 95 games three years later, and 90 games the year after that, finishing in second place both times, only losing both the 1979 and 1980 pennants on the last few days of the season. Most of all I loved washing the aftertaste of the California Angels—similar to that caused by a hand-tossed garlic pizza—out of my mouth forever.

It was because of the Angels that Montreal became the only place I've ever actually applied for the job. In September 1976, less than two months after getting booted past the Anaheim Stadium broom crew, I was on the phone to the Expos' front office people, who were then in the middle of yet another summer of turmoil. After seven years with Gene Mauch, who took over the club when it was an expansion team in 1969, management decided before the 1976 season that something else was needed. During those seven years they hadn't won more than 79 games nor finished higher than fourth place, although don't blame any of the third-base coaches, particularly the one in 1970, who you'll remember was me.

So after the 1975 season they dumped Mauch and brought in rookie manager Karl Kuehl, and what happened? In 1976 they won just 55 games, which is a whole lot less than 79.

They lost 107, which was the highest number I could ever remember seeing in a final standing, wins or losses. Karl was fired when the team was 43 – 85, so he was only partly responsible for their horrendous record. Charlie Fox finished the season but was brought in with the understanding that he would take over as general manager afterward.

With Fox being a good old-time baseball man, and the farm system stocked with good players thanks to recent top draft picks—this time I checked—Montreal seemed like a great place to call. So, funny as it felt, I did. I called John McHale and acting general manager Jim Fanning and told them that when they started looking for a new manager, put my name into the *chapeau*. It was the right thing to say. McHale flew me to meet him in Chicago during the last weekend of the season. We talked on a Friday morning in a restaurant at the Water Tower. He made me an offer on the spot, and I told him I'd have to talk to Norma. He said I could call him Monday. We shook hands, and I boarded a Friday afternoon flight for California. Little did I know I'd be talking to McHale again within hours, because no sooner did I walk into our home and pose the question when Norma interrupted with "We're outta here!"

Today she tells me her quick response was because of our great memories of the 1970 season. As a coach then, I had no pressure, few outside commitments, nothing but time to spend roaming the narrow streets of old Montreal or going on outings with Norma and the kids in the beautiful countryside. For a family needing to recover from the stress of Boston, the summer of 1970 was wonderful, and Norma said she was hoping to re-create that. I think her quick response involved something else, though. She knew how much I still hurt from the Angels and that I should get as far away from them as possible. An eastern Canadian city in a different league seemed pretty damn far.

I called McHale Friday night and told him I couldn't wait until Monday. I wanted the job immediately. He said fine, and flew me back to Montreal a couple of days later. On that Monday we made the announcements at a press conference: I was the manager, Charlie Fox was the general manager, and this team would not lose 107 games again. And, oh yes, I would start out in a good mood. And why not? With a team that couldn't get any worse, I knew I had a couple of years to play with. And what promising players I had as tools. Waiting for me to find a place for them in my lineup card, among others, was the kid outfield of Andre Dawson, Warren Cromartie, and Ellis Valentine . . . and a catcher named Gary Carter.

And during what would certainly be a tough couple of years, there could be no better place to work. One of baseball's trendy subjects these days is the Expos' problem attracting and keeping good players because the franchise is in a French-speaking city in a foreign country. Yes, the problem is real. But the players' reasoning is bull. To the people of Montreal, where I've spent, on and off, six years of my life, I would like to offer this reminder: modern-day baseball players don't like your city, not because of your city but because they are baseball players. They live in a small world in which they have accepted certain things as absolute truths. To the modern-day player, a foreign country is Cleveland. A foreign phrase is "My turn to buy." A fancy restaurant is someplace their agents take them, agents whose turn it is to buy. To the modern-day player, culture is a portable compact disc player. History is a box score. Literature is a thick book he leaves on his clubhouse chair for all to see, a book he may one day even read. And for the modern-day player, differences are not to be tolerated.

The modern-day player doesn't hate Montreal so much as he's afraid of it. He's afraid that people who have gotten along for hundreds of years without him will criticize him in a language he doesn't understand, then charge him high prices for a meal the size of an appetizer. He's afraid of having a good experience that doesn't have room for him at the absolute center. When you accuse players of this ignorance, they talk about not playing there because of Canada's higher tax rate. They talk about this because their agents tell them to. Then they move to California, where they're taxed almost as high as you are in Canada.

Despite what your heroes say, Montreal is a wonderful place to spend a summer. From 1977 through 1981 we lived everywhere from a mountain home to a cuter-than-hell little place on an island. We went to picnics and festivals where, even if everybody couldn't communicate so well, everybody did know how to offer up a toast. And another toast. We learned the basics of French from a Spanish priest—don't ask for a play-by-play—and the basics of Canadian partying from the Expos fans. They may not have known much about baseball back then, but they knew a hell of a lot about good cocktail parties, and so what if they mixed the two?

There's a beer garden in the main concourse of the Expos' Olympic Stadium home, and often Norma would find fans there who left their tables only when the Expos loaded the bases. Win or lose, after every game that beer garden became a singing, dancing mass of people who had certainly gotten their funny-colored dollar's worth. Norma would take the meticulously clean subway to the games, party with the people, and then drive home with me. Note: the words "Norma" and "subway" had never before appeared in the same sentence.

To let you know a little better how I feel about the area, not once during my first two years did I think of fleeing back to the United States, even though we won just 75 games in 1977 and 76 games in 1978. This was because, as we entered that 1979 season, Charlie Fox and I had helped put together a team that would make people actually come to the park to watch baseball. A few innings of it, anyway.

Our resurgence started, believe it or not, with a guy named Barry Foote. He was the catcher when I arrived—a fact I learned not from looking at highlight films but from talking to the Expos pitchers. Despite batting just .234 with seven homers and 27 RBIs—do you know how hard it is to be a regular and have just 27 RBIs?—the pitching staff loved Foote. He called a good game, they told me. He was good for morale, they said. None of them could have known that I used to play this game, because apparently none of them guessed I saw right through their sugar and spice and realized that they wanted Foote because he was their friend. Foote wouldn't push them, wouldn't challenge them to be better. He'd buy them beers. That's why they wanted Foote and not the other competitor for the job, a kid so enthusiastic he was actually nicknamed The Kid.

Right away I was leaning toward this other guy. Who better than I to know that you can be a winner and not be liked? Then Foote came to spring training in Daytona Beach overweight and without a contract. He refused to wear a uniform until he signed. I said fine, burn that uniform. He was traded to Philadelphia and never heard from north of the border again. Despite howls you could hear to Miami, I named the other guy my catcher. And last I looked, 13 years later, Gary Carter was still somebody's catcher.

To those who give me credit for giving a probable Hall of Famer his first chance, I say I couldn't help myself. Carter reminded me of a young Dick Williams, only nicer. He spent his time in the dugout cheering like hell and his time on field cocky as hell, living by the verbal challenge and the pumped fist. The pitchers hated him. But then, maybe it was good they hated somebody. The last time they were happy, they lost 107 games.

Moving around the horn, the next important piece in our contending years' team was second baseman Rodney Scott, one of my all-time favorites, whom we acquired from the Chicago Cubs mostly because he could do things like steal third base nine times in one season with the pitcher holding the ball. At shortstop—well, first let me tell you who we didn't have. In a transaction as important as that involving Foote, one of the first things I did upon arriving was bench short-stop and chronic complainer Tim Foli. Somewhere in base-ball history he became known for hard play, but let me ask you this: How hard does a guy play when he refuses to play on the final day of the season because the local writers didn't vote him the team's Most Valuable Player? Foli pulled this on Charlie Fox at the end of 1976, even though he didn't lead the team in batting average, homers, or RBIs, or anything else worth mentioning. I take that last statement back. After his little stunt he led the team in gutlessness, and I wanted nothing to do with him.

Enter Chris Speier. He was the shortstop who'd played for San Francisco when Fox managed them in the early sev-enties. The minute Charlie realized I was going to back him up by canning Foli, he began working on acquiring Speier, which he finally did in the spring before the 1977 season. Although Speier was a nondescript blond kid who got lost in the glitter associated with other great players on those late-seventies teams, he gave our club much of its fight, as you will see later.

Speier was flanked at third base by another underpubli-cized player who did nothing but hit the shit out of the ball, Larry Parrish. He had such great years during that time—with at least 15 homers and 70 RBIs for three of my sea-sons—that some said Parrish could hit with his eyes closed. I've got proof that he did. One day our opponents, I forget who, brought in a relief pitcher who telegraphed his pitches from a stretch position. Soon all of our batters knew exactly what he was going to throw just seconds before he threw it, and we were hammering him. We loaded the bases for Par-rish, which worried me, because now this guy would go from a stretch position into a regular windup and wouldn't give himself away so easily. Parrish stepped to the plate, and lo and behold, the guy stayed in his stretch position. We sat back waiting for Parrish to crush one, and—boom—he hit a liner to center field, and the ball was caught just before the wall. He came back to the dugout muttering, but not about the catch. "That damn guy," he said about the pitcher. "I'd have figured him out a lot better if he hadn't gone into his windup." To this day I don't know what pitcher he was watching. I'm sure he had his eyes closed.

With all the hot lights that surrounded the next three guys, it's little wonder few people lauded Parrish or Speier or Scott or even me. I'm talking, of course, about the envy of the league, kid outfielders Dawson, Cromartie, and Valentine. I mention Dawson first—I'll always mention Dawson first, because he was everyone else's third choice. Of the three, he was always the slow learner, the one who'd need the most work and wouldn't go nearly as far. Our scouts would sit around and collect foam at the corners of their mouths while talking about Valentine's natural all-around ability and Cromartie's incredible bat. "And," they would always say, about 20 minutes later, "we've always got Dawson." As if Dawson didn't even belong in the same speech.

You know what happened. You could have never left that beer garden and still know what would happen. Dawson, working every day with coach Ozzie Virgil on his fielding, working endlessly with coach Pat Mullin on his hitting, became a future Gold Glover and Most Valuable Player and one of baseball's leading citizens.

Then there was Cromartie, who talked so much about his future fame that I swear he chipped his teeth. He was a great player but could have been even greater if he'd managed to control both his mouth and his actions. One of his best plays under me was a good example of his misused aggressiveness. He sneaked into that big orange monstrosity of a Montreal mascot suit—the creature is called Youppie—and ran around the bases during a rain delay. The fans loved it, but the guy who was supposed to wear the suit got fired.

That's a mascot for you, always getting somebody in trouble. The Chicken and all those things are great for the game, as long as they stay in the stands. For a clearer definition of

my feelings about mascots, ask the Phillie Phanatic, the Philadelphia baseball team's mascot. Once when he began bug-
ging me on the mound as I was changing pitchers for San
Diego, I told him, "You don't leave this mound right now,
you little green shit, I'm going to kick your ass." While the
unknowing fans cheered, he ran like hell. But at least Youppie lasted longer than Cromartie, who had played his way
out of major league baseball by 1984 and chose to end his
career in Japan, where they couldn't understand what he was
yammering about.

Finally, there was Valentine. I mention him last because
that's where he finished. He was always the nonconformist,
but nobody dreamed where that way of life would take him
. . . or take part of this team, and much of our dream. Ellis
Valentine was an extraordinary baseball player who became
a thief. He stole from his own ability because of his lack of
motivation and his unreliability. And he stole from his heart.
Stole from his teammates' trust. Stole from everything important to him until he no longer had anything when he needed
it. Like that great arm, that splendid bat, that will to win.

I suspected him of using drugs, although I never saw him
do it and he denied it when the accusation surfaced in New
York. Apparently he finally conquered whatever demons
possessed him when he was in Montreal. He's had a fine
comeback, and I applaud him. But at the time I could have
killed him.

This brings me to the theme song of my years in Montreal—players on drugs. As this former bench-warming big
leaguer who would have given vital organs to have his right
shoulder back understands well, the biggest crime of baseball
players on drugs is the waste. The absolute waste of something so precious men have spent their lives despairing because they didn't have it. The waste of an athletic ability so
great you can be a winner just by being yourself.

Whatever the truth about Valentine's alleged drug use,
there were plenty of other Expos who did drugs. Because

their involvement was limited, they shall remain nameless. Who understands better than I how people can occasionally fuck up? But suffice it to say, by the end of my second year there I knew my biggest opponent wasn't the Philadelphia Phillies or the Pittsburgh Pirates but the drugs.

This problem became real one night when Ozzie Virgil decided to take a shortcut from our dugout to the bullpen. Instead of walking down the right field line, he ducked underneath the stands and back to the field through a side door. I didn't think anything of it, but after the game the coach grabbed me and said, "There's something you gotta see." I followed him back behind the dugout and underneath the stands and—phew!—I grabbed my nose and stared at a sight that would haunt me for as long as I worked there. In a secluded area underneath the box seats, in a space just big enough for a couple of guys to stand, there was a towel spread across the concrete floor. On that towel were numerous butts. And you could close your eyes and know they weren't from cigarets. They were from marijuana joints. And judging by the cleat marks around the towels, those joints weren't being smoked by the fans. "Oh, shit," I said, over and over, loud and then softer. "Oh, shit."

I could handle a player who couldn't bunt. I could handle a pitcher who was afraid to throw inside at hitters. I could handle just about any problem you could imagine when it came to running nine innings of a baseball game. But how in the hell did I handle players who were smoking dope in uniform? How in the living hell did I handle a relief pitcher who may have been getting high two innings before being called to get somebody out?

I saw the towel and smelled the smoke, and . . . No, I wasn't mad. I wasn't disappointed. I was plain scared. So I passed the buck. After a sleepless night deciding that my job was to manage baseball games, I visited John McHale and told him about our discovery. Basically dumped it all in his lap. Call me a wimp if you will, but he was the team's ultimate boss, the man with the most authority. Managers can't suspend players or call the cops without team presidents. Managers really don't have the authority to do anything but manage. So I gave the problem to McHale.

And he tried to fix the problem. At first. Sort of. McHale called several clubhouse meetings, saying we wouldn't tolerate substance abuse. He held private meetings with several players suspected of being ringleaders. He took it a giant step further by hiring detectives to tail some of those players.

But what happened? That area under the bleachers remained covered with a towel and fresh roaches. We later learned the players called it "the launching pad." Soon the drug use had grown so much that the launching pad wasn't big enough anymore. Most of the action took place in the massive parking lot next to Olympic Stadium, where our guys would buy and sell from the opposing players. All of this was in addition to an increasingly popular player ritual of getting a pep pill known as a "greenie" from some of our trainers before a game, and then another pill afterward to help them calm down. There were so many players filing in and out of our training room with their hands cupped that it got me wondering if maybe these pills weren't legal. Then I decided not to ask. In trying to win ballgames back then, there were plenty of things I didn't ask. Maybe it's because I just didn't know if the answers would help us win. That doesn't make it right. It just makes it me.

McHale tried, but he couldn't stop the wave of drug abuse. Soon the drugs began affecting not just the users but also the rest of us, in ways you'd never imagine. I never touched any of the stuff, but somehow the idea of my players being fucked up worked its way inside me and gnawed like an ulcer, turning me into the kind of paranoid who glances around dark corners before making the turn. This is when I started checking eyes and hands and voices.

And this is when Ellis Valentine knocked on our hotel door one morning in Chicago and asked to borrow Norma's hair dryer. Normally, this would be—well, normal. Maybe a player has a girl in his room and she wants to dry her hair and he needs some help. No big deal. Norma smiled and handed over her plastic gun. But while Valentine and whoever were down the hall doing whatever with the hair dryer, Norma and I began thinking it over. What if he was going to use that hair dryer for something other than drying hair? What if he was going to stash some dope in there and hope that we could successfully take it across the border on our way home, at which point he'd borrow the hair dryer again? What if we were being set up to be smugglers? Okay, so maybe we had been watching too much TV. But what if Ellis Valentine also watched a lot of TV? What if he had also seen how easily this hair dryer trick could be done? This is how *the players'* drugs had distorted *my* view of the world.

And so it happened that, once before an afternoon game against the Cubs, in the middle of a pennant race, the manager of the Expos locked himself in his hotel room and took apart his wife's hair dryer, piece by piece, searching for dope. Didn't find any. Valentine, poor bastard, had just wanted to dry some hair. I felt bad until I realized that the Montreal police had been finding stuff on many players. The club's response? McHale, having finally thrown up his hands at any possibility of stopping the plague, kept the arrests covered up or ensured that the charges were dropped. And that was Expos management's ultimate solution to this problem. They threw a blanket over it.

Nowadays, through increased education and awareness, baseball's drug problem has been minimized. Back then we just hid. McHale, the players, even I did. Do I feel bad that I didn't beat some of these drug users over the head with a 32-ouncer and then get the police and the press on a conference call? Sometimes. If it happened again, would I react differently? Probably not. It goes back to my curse, my job, my life: winning baseball games. I can see precious little else. The blindness hurts. The blindness costs. But in my 20 years

of managing I have learned, if nothing else, that this blindness is irreversible. When I look back, all I can do is pray for
the things I've missed, and be thankful for the things I haven't,
and not even try to wonder whether it was all worth it.

Besides—and this will irritate the hell out of everybody
who thinks they finally have an excuse for my Expos teams—
the drugs alone did not make the Expos just barely miss winning two straight division titles. They had a lot of help from
our rotten pitching. Sorry, but I have a hard time defending
the veterans of our 1979 and 1980 staffs, Bill Lee and Steve
Rogers. The best I can say is that while both were weird, at
least one was honest about it. That one was Lee, whom we
acquired from Boston after the 1978 season. When I managed him in his first big league season with the Red Sox in
1969, he seemed a little funny, but all rookies do. Ten years
later the borderline fool had crossed that border. There are
a million wacky stories about this guy dubbed "Spaceman,"
but just two concerned and affected me and the club.

Once when I needed Lee to pitch, he showed up at the
clubhouse with bruises and cuts, looking like he'd just left a
10-rounder. He told me he'd been hit by a taxicab while jogging. How had he gotten to the clubhouse? I asked. The guilty
cabbie had driven him. Lee said he'd even tipped him. I tried
not to faint before telling him to sit out the game. Later that
season, on a trip, I spotted him jogging along a marina and
shouted to him, "Be careful, you don't want any boats to jump
out and hit you!"

Another time Lee walked in with lacerated legs and groin,
claiming to have run into a fence while jogging at 3 A.M. A
little investigating revealed that the only thing accurate in his
statement was the 3 A.M. part. Early the previous morning,
while Lee was at a girlfriend's apartment, her husband un-
expectedly arrived and Lee was forced to eject from a sec-
ond-story balcony by climbing down a trellis, which broke and
dumped him on an iron fence. So I guess the fence part was
also right.

Lee went 16–10 with a 3.04 ERA for us in 1979, but think how much better he would have done if completely sane. In 1980, sidelined by those weird injuries, he went just 4–6 in 18 starts with a 4.96 ERA. He finally retired a couple of years later, and has since been haunting the real world with things like a joke presidential campaign, which is at least more harmless than a joke pitching campaign.

Our only consistent starter in those years, and in fact the most consistent starter in the history of Expos baseball, was Steve Rogers. He spent his entire 13-year career in Montreal and became a grand baseball hero—almost as popular in that town as a third-string hockey goalie—by establishing a phenomenally low career ERA of 3.17 yet seemingly always being in the big game. If only people realized that in 13 years of pitching his win-loss record was just three games over .500, at 158–152. If only they realized that his record didn't match his ERA not because we were a weak ball club but because he was a weak-kneed player. I'm here to say Montreal's pitching emperor had no clothes. Steve Rogers was a fraud.

As just two of many examples, remember how, in 1979, he started two games in the season's final five days and lost both, getting bombed by Pittsburgh 10–1 and losing an admittedly tough 2–0 decision to Philadelphia? We wound up in second place, two games out of first.

I wish some of those adoring fans could have accompanied me to the pitching mound while Rogers occupied it. He'd be standing there crossing his legs and breathing so fast and heavy, almost hyperventilating, that I figured he either had to use the bathroom or was getting ready to throw the batter a lump of coal. He didn't like the big situations, the pressure situations. That would have been fine, except that in those situations an entire team and city and even nation were counting on him.

Okay, so Rogers used to publicly rip me pretty good. And okay, so after I was fired in 1981, he called me "a worthless human being"—but didn't put his name to the quote, instead hiding behind that terrible phrase "a source." That's not why I'm ripping him. It's not even because he'd tell everyone I was arrogant, brash, and a pain in the ass (I will always defend the truth). No, I am ripping him because during his Montreal career he ripped off the fans. He took advantage of his position as a good player on a bad team by refusing to help that team get better. I call it the king-of-the-mountain syndrome. A player knows that if his team becomes good, he won't stand out so much, he will lose his revered status and, hey, he might even have to prove himself in a big game. Rogers spent his entire career there pitching as if he wanted to stay king of the mountain.

I can sum up my feelings about Steve Rogers with this: he made one of the dumbest, most selfish plays I've ever seen in a professional baseball game. Ever. We were playing Pittsburgh and had the bases loaded, trailing by one run with just one out. The opposing pitcher fell behind Rogers three balls and no strikes. Rogers, who finished as a .138 career hitter, was given the "take" sign, meaning he wasn't supposed to swing at the next pitch, no matter what. Hopefully, the pitcher would walk him and tie the game. At the very least, even if the ball was thrown right down the middle, Rogers would still be ahead three balls and one strike. And that's where the ball was thrown, right down the pipe. But Rogers didn't watch it. His ego didn't let him. He decided to try to bunt. And he succeeded. A bases-loaded, surprise, one-out bunt. I am not making this up. The ball went right back to the pitcher, who threw to the catcher for the second out, and the catcher threw to first base for the last out. The Pirates had escaped—with a lot of help from Steve Rogers.

This play, unique in my experience, was so dumb that I never even asked Rogers why he did it. It would be like asking a man why he's walking around with a turd on his head. What could he possibly tell me that would make sense? And players wonder why I stand at the end of the dugout and stew? Actually, I should be thankful Steve Rogers possessed this kind of reasoning. It may have been his idiot off-the-field move that started this team on its two-year push in 1978, my second year. The club still hadn't grown up, and I was trying to keep patience and refrain from kicking too much ass when Charlie Fox decided to kick it for me.

One day before a game, while I was outside watching batting practice, Fox wandered through the clubhouse until reaching his prize acquisition Chris Speier. The shortstop had been struggling, so Charlie decided to hit him with a little old-time motivation. He told him, "Swing that damn bat, would you? Get the damn bat off your shoulders."

They were old-time words that would have been no big deal to an old-time player. But Speier took offense. Charlie turned and walked away, seemingly toward the clubhouse door. But he took a detour into my office. There he heard Speier's voice saying, "Fuck you, Charlie." Speier, like most players who trash their boss, never realized that Fox was in the area. Or had such good ears. Or such a bad temper. Fox took off like a tiger. He wheeled out of the office and around the corner, stormed up to Speier, and grabbed him by his uniform shirt with some more old-time words: "What did you say, you little cocksucker?"

Speier realized the remark had been ill-timed and was quickly backing down when here came Steve Rogers, our player representative in baseball union matters. Rogers pushed Charlie and yelled, "Get your hands off him!" Knowing Rogers had finally gotten himself into a jam where I couldn't help him out, Fox actually sort of smiled. Then he reared back and, to everyone's astonishment, slugged Rogers. Landed a beautiful right hook to his jaw. The pitcher staggered backward, and the clubhouse lit up.

In all the commotion I couldn't tell whose side the players were on. But a couple of hours later they were all on the side of inspiration, as that night Speier became one of baseball's few players to hit for the cycle, going five for five in the game. "Hey, hey!" shouted Larry Parrish in the clubhouse afterward. "Every day we should pick somebody for Charlie to yell at! What a great hitting team we'll have then!" Parrish paused. "Nah," he said. "Rogers's jaw couldn't take it."

I hate to tell this story lightly, because the punch cost Fox his job. He was soon transferred to the scouting department, and McHale moved down to take over. But in a funny way, I feel the punch got this team going. Suddenly the players were thinking like, This is real controversy, somebody besides the manager can get pissed off around here . . . hey, maybe we really are a baseball team! Beginning the following year, they certainly played like it. The Expos' blood got boiling right from the start, when I stuck our new acquisition Rodney Scott at second base and benched team favorite Dave Cash. Oddly enough, Scott came into my office and told me I should move him to shortstop, let Cash play second, and bench shortstop Speier. I heard Cash was saying the same thing, and even making it out to be some kind of racial issue. Since when is benching one black guy for another black guy racist? I love the way some players think.

But then, I loved it that Cash's benching pissed everyone off. Finally, the team was getting united behind something, that same old something that has united all of my teams: their dislike for me. Off the bench that 1979 season, Cash hit a splendid .321, while Scott and Speier played great together in the field. With a great year by Larry Parrish (.307, 30 homers, 82 RBIs) and at least a .275 average from the three young outfielders, we had a good start, and on September 6 we peaked with a club record 10 straight wins. We spent the next couple of weeks playing well under pressure—my favorite thing to watch—until September 25, just six days before the end of the regular season. On that night we led the Pittsburgh Pirates by one-half game.

Then, thanks in part to Willie Stargell's two homers off a young 23-year-old Scott Sanderson, Pittsburgh beat us 10–4. And the next night, crowd favorite Rogers lost 10–1. The losses put us one and a half games out of first place. A couple of days later, entering the final Sunday of the season, we had pushed that margin back to one. Besides a Sunday game against Philadelphia, we had a rain-caused doubleheader to play in Atlanta, but only if we won the final day and Pittsburgh lost. But Rogers was beaten 2−0 by Philadelphia, the Pirates beat the Chicago Cubs, and the season ended. In Rogers's defense, Steve Carlton was great that day. And even if Rogers had shut them out, the score theoretically would only have been 0−0. Or would it? Trying to break a shutout when you're trailing 2−0 is a lot harder than when the score is 0−0. Just once I would have liked for Rogers to be the one throwing the shutout in that situation.

Even if the season had been ultimately painful for us, it was wonderful for the people of Montreal. The club's surge had suddenly made all those empty Olympic Stadium seats sell for up to $100 a pop on the streets. We ended up drawing more than 2,000,000 fans for the first time in franchise history. Our radio broadcasts were going all over the country, so people stopped worrying about having to listen to announcer Duke Snider—who was a bit dull at times—and cared only about listening to the team. And in the middle of it all there was that great letter I received. From a Canadian, of course. It read: "The Pirates have a city of supporters—you, sir, have an entire nation behind you." Now, I thought, if only I could get the team's general manager behind me.

McHale began to question me almost from the moment he shipped out Charlie Fox, and our fine 1979 season did nothing to stop it. Maybe it's because he was overworked trying to cover up for various players we suspected (or knew) were doing drugs. When we suspended them, McHale would have to go to the trouble of telling them to go home, telling everyone to lie about why, and then pleading with them to stay straight upon their return. Through it all we managed to win 95 games, which only made me wonder what we could have done if everyone had been straight.

McHale was testy about how I wouldn't kowtow to players

he admired, about how I wouldn't promote better communication. It never seemed to occur to him that the object of this game was winning, and that's what I was doing. No matter how I was doing it.

Maybe he was also mad about my performance during a particular baseball winter meetings session in Hawaii during those Montreal years. New York Yankees manager Billy Martin, Kansas City manager Whitey Herzog and his wife, and Norma and I were sitting at a hotel bar. Behind the bartender you could look through this huge plate glass window and see under the water of the hotel pool. What happened next I can only attribute to the fact that this bar must have made its mai-tais with scotch. I excused myself to go to the bathroom, then sneaked upstairs and jumped into the pool. To the surprise of my fellow managers, Dick Williams swam up to the glass behind the bartender, flapping his arms and holding his breath. And then Dick Williams was turning his back and pulling down his pants, showing the entire bar his bare bottom. (I refer to myself in the third person here because this is the way the story was told to me the following day when I awoke with a headache and a touch of amnesia.)

It should have stopped with the mooning, but the other managers were jealous. Next, Billy Martin jumped in the water and swam past the window with a just-purchased hot dog sticking out from his trunks. Then Herzog jumped in with two eggs in his trunks. As he swam into view, he dropped the trunks just as the eggs popped out. The people in the bar gave us a standing ovation, with cheers as fervent as any we'd heard on the field, which should tell you something.

My problems with McHale increased during the 1980 season, which was much like the 1979 season, except we finished just one game out of first place after leading the division for 81 of 179 days, longer than anyone else that season. We suffered the same problems as in 1979—poor pitching down the stretch, and just enough inexperience that we still didn't deserve to be champions. Once again we lost it in the final weekend of the season, this time falling to champion Phila-delphia and putting them two games ahead with one to play. Having a good team is one thing. Being able to win a big game is something entirely different. A lot of people will say we also lost because of injuries to the likes of Larry Parrish and Ellis Valentine and newcomer Ron LeFlore, but that's bull. Everyone in baseball has injuries. Injuries are lame, torn, broken, sprained, fractured excuses. My overall reasoning for 1980 was to say, Remember, this was a team that had lost 107 games just four years earlier.

Soon, though, McHale stopped listening to this theory, partially because of the way I treated a couple of his pets, pitcher Ross Grimsley and outfielder LeFlore. When looking for reasons why a manager gets fired, always consider the players he feuds with: if the general manager has either ac-quired those guys or nurtured them, then maybe they're part of the reason for the firing. I don't think Grimsley or Le-Flore alone caused me to get the ax, but a couple of incidents involving them certainly helped.

Grimsley became a local hero in 1978 by becoming the first Expo to win 20 games, going 20–11. Problem was, two years later, at age 30, he'd completely lost it. The man was throwing coal. After 11 appearances in 1980 he was 2–4 with a 6.37 ERA and no signs of improvement. This being a pen-nant race, we had to dump him. I didn't see a hero in him, not even a 10th pitcher. I saw a 6.37 ERA, and if anybody else saw different, I apologize. McHale and other officials agreed that he needed to be released, so I called Grimsley into my office to give him the news.

His reaction was typical of the modern-day player. "You bastard," he shouted, "I'll get even with you!" My reaction was typical of the old-time manager. "Why make promises you might not keep?" I shouted back. "Why not get even with me now?" I stood up, he backed away, and that was the end of it. For that minute. Later the incident lived on in sto-ries about how Dick Williams released a player and then challenged him to a fight. Stories that made me wish that, at the very least, I had taken a punch at him.

Seven years later Grimsley and I met again, after I started managing the Seattle Mariners, for whom he was a minor league pitching coach. He saw me in that first spring training and was as nice as he could be. After seven years they all are. The modern-day ballplayer, you see, also thinks he should never be held accountable for his actions. But sure, I'll forgive them, just as I hope they forgive me. When I say I try to win with no strings attached, I mean it. When a fight is over, it's over. I'll forgive. I just won't forget. You can bet your ass I won't forget.

Then there was Ron LeFlore. In 1980 McHale traded for him, I put him in my outfield, and six months later, at age 32, he had set a new Expos stolen base record with 97. He had batted a decent .257 and scored 95 runs. And oh, was I glad to see him leave through free agency at the end of the year. Expos management loved him, but they didn't see him like I did. They didn't hear his rabble-rousing in the clubhouse, his constant bitching about the food or the laundry or the managing, even though I played him in every game he was eligible for. They didn't see his late night forays into strange parts of town, which wouldn't have been so bad if he hadn't taken the team's younger players with him.

This was a man famous for being signed to a baseball contract out of prison—remember how Lavar Burton portrayed him in the movie about his remarkable life? Everybody loved LeFlore's character in the movie. But in reality he acted too much like a movie star to help our team unity. One day toward the end of the season I summoned him to pinch-run if a certain batter got on base. He said fine, but several minutes later, when it was time for him to take the field, he walked out from behind the opponent's dugout. What the hell was he doing over there? A little ninth-inning socializing?

In a magazine interview just before he left the team, LeFlore accused the Expos of practicing racism. At the time, five of my eight starting position players were black. Now, the modern-day player's trendy excuse for poor performance is often racism. Not only is that wrong, it's incredibly selfish in that it causes the real racism in our game—in the hiring of front office personnel—to get tossed aside. So LeFlore's comments were true in a larger sense.

All of this contributed to a rocky start in 1981. Having finished so close for two straight years, I wanted to make sure that we didn't go into another October kicking ourselves over one or two games. I placed more importance on individual games than ever, meaning my confrontations with players increased, meaning McHale's lack of support quietly became more noticeable, until finally he laid it out right under the players' noses by flying to Chicago on May 21 to hold a "summit meeting" with me. At the time we were 21–18 and too busy bitching to worry about playing.

The summit was actually positive, with McHale talking about understanding slumps (I should hope so) and understanding how my methods for winning had worked before and should work again (I should hope so). But the best part of the meeting came at the end, when we decided that if this team was looking sick, we'd get rid of the infection. And that is how, eight days later, we finally traded Ellis Valentine. We sent him to the New York Mets for relief pitcher Jeff Reardon.

I was thrilled with the deal (although I wondered if Valentine would get himself killed in Manhattan). I was thrilled with no longer having to answer questions about suspensions, excused absences, and generally different rules that applied to a guy who just didn't play by the rules. I was thrilled that I'd no longer have to watch unfulfilled potential. I was thrilled . . . until I met Reardon. He later became a feared reliever, but at the time he was just another complainer, and his complaints, ironically, helped start the tide that washed me out of Montreal forever.

Essentially, Reardon said I didn't pitch him enough. Maybe

it was because the minute he joined the team, his father had a heart attack and I excused him to fly home and tend to him for a few days. And then a couple of weeks later I excused him to go home again. And a couple of weeks later, again. How can I pitch a guy when he is, justifiably, going home all the time? For once in my life I'm actually being a nice guy, and what happens? Reardon complains, and McHale, of course, listens. Why would he trade for him if he wasn't going to listen to him? See my earlier observation about general managers and their pets.

My position was helped when the season was broken up by seven weeks of a strike . . . No, I'm not going to talk in detail about any damn strike, you get bored enough reading about the stuff in your local newspaper. All I will say is that the strike lasted seven weeks, which is a long time to be in third place, four games out of first. And it's a long time to be away from players who love only one thing more than hating you, and that's winning.

When we returned to work August 10, they'd forgotten about the winning part. All they did was hate me. Steve Rogers started constantly bitching about me. Maybe that's one reason he won just 12 of 22 starts that year—too busy bitching. Warren Cromartie bitched about me so much that management forgot he bitched about everybody. I heard them talk, and from McHale's occasional questioning comments I knew he was listening.

The bottom line was that my team was tired of me. I'd been in Montreal longer than any other stop in my managerial career, and the players, after being kicked along through two bad years and two good ones, just didn't think it was worth it anymore. The irony was that I'd helped them mature to a point where they could win without me. So that's what they wanted to do, and that's exactly what happened.

On the morning of September 8, at 9:30, McHale phoned me at our Philadelphia hotel and told me to come down to his suite. For what happened next I give him credit. I knocked on his door, and he opened it with "Good morning, Dick, we're making a change." Fired me right in the hallway. Fired me the way I would fire somebody. No superficial greetings, no coffee, no danish, no bull. Just the ax, quick and hard. He then invited me inside, at which point I realized I hadn't asked him a rather important question. "For the record, John," I finally said, "why are you firing me?" Little did I guess he would say, "Because we're sick and tired of hearing about how you're going to manage the New York Yankees."

I struggled to hold on to my chair. The New York Yankees? What was this, 1974? What the hell did he mean about the New York Yankees? I asked him, and he referred to some recent newspaper stories that said I'd be going to the Yankees after my contract expired this season. I hadn't paid attention to the stories, because—well, you know how much attention I even pay to my wife during the baseball season. I might have read them closer if I'd talked business even once to George Steinbrenner since I tried to join him from Oakland in 1974. If I'd taken just one phone call from him.

But I hadn't. And so McHale's reasoning stunned me. "C'mon, John," I asked, knowing I was asking too much. "Tell the truth." He paused. "Dick, that is the truth," he said, before excusing himself and telling the media something entirely different, and likely more accurate: that I was being fired for lack of communication and poor clubhouse skills and all that other stuff I'm always getting fired for.

At the time the team was 44–37, having finished in third place in the first half (so designated after they finally settled the strike) and currently one and a half games out of first place in the second half. Jim Fanning, our farm director, who hadn't worn a uniform as a manager since I wore a uniform as a player, was called out of the front office to make sure the team finished the season without fucking up too much. While he watched, they won the second-half championship, won the mini-playoff with Philadelphia, and then came within one game of the World Series, losing the real five-game National League Championship Series to Los Angeles on Rick Monday's legendary Game Five, ninth-inning, tie-breaking homer. Off, of course, Steve Rogers.

I watched that homer on television, and I mourned. Problems aside, this was still the team that I'd damn near raised from childhood. This was a team I'd taught everything I will ever know, so much that when it came time to win a big one and I was gone, they could do it with a manager they barely knew. They could do it virtually by themselves.

I mourned because, like I said, five years in one place is a long time. A man can't give so much of his life to something and then take his hands and heart away so quickly. Besides, the Expos had earlier voted me a one-half playoff share. I had big money riding on the son of a bitch.

McNightmare

The office was filled with leather and self-assurance. The man behind the wooden desk, with his gray hair and pale skin, was filled with authority. Outside were stately palm trees and royal sunshine and, several miles away, an ocean. All of which made me wonder, What's that empty french fries bag doing in the garbage can?

It was the winter of 1981, and I was preparing to make a decision that would eventually give me a new heart for this game. And then, four wonderful years later, break that heart. The man behind the desk was Ray Kroc, founder of McDonald's fast food chain and owner of the San Diego Padres. Standing around him were a couple of people as strange to me as Ronald McDonald: Kroc's son-in-law Ballard Smith, who also happened to be the club president, and Jack McKeon, the general manager, who smelled like a cigar. Come to think of it, he dressed like one too.

Spread out in front of me was the strangest thing of all. It was a contract to manage the Padres, the laughable, impossible-to-love Padres. In their previous 13 seasons they'd won more than 73 games just once, and that was only because at that time they had a pitcher, Gaylord Perry, who threw a Brylcreem ball. That was 1978, and in the three years since then the Padres had gone a combined 182−251, winning just 42 percent of their games.

In a strike-shortened 1981 they'd finished 26 games out of first place. I asked myself, How can you play just 110 games and still finish 26 games out of first place? The fans must have wondered this too. The Padres had averaged just 9,439 fans per game that season; in five of their last 12 seasons they had drawn under 1,000,000. This was a franchise that had behaved like they were managed by a television announcer. Oh, yeah—they were. Jerry Coleman bossed them in 1980. They say he was late for a spring workout that year because he was busy filming a car commercial. Since then the team had become an Alka-Seltzer commercial.

But what the hell, I thought, even with all these strange things around me, why not? The two career factors most important to me at this stage were in place: the money was good, and the team surely was willing to accept a little instruction. In other words, the players knew if they didn't listen, the world wouldn't blink when I engineered the firing of every one of their sorry asses.

And so I looked down at the three-year contract, I announced for a second and final time that I'd agree to sign it . . . and then I was interrupted by a voice from behind the desk.

"All right, let's celebrate!" shouted Ray Kroc, who then pointed to Ballard Smith. "Why don't you run over to the McDonald's and pick us all up some food. Dick, your order?" Run over to *where*? The club president getting sent out for Big Macs? Oh my God, what had I done?

A little history first. I wouldn't even have been in this position if George Steinbrenner had remembered his own phone number. A couple of weeks earlier, while I was sitting in my Tampa home unemployed and trying to forget my French, the Padres had called and invited me out for an interview. After a forever flight, I had a forever meeting with the boring Ballard Smith and the stinky Jack McKeon, so naturally I wasn't tremendously impressed. I flew back to Tampa, and the next day Steinbrenner called me, also about a job. I wasn't sure what job, because he already had a manager named Bob Lemon, but I joined Steinbrenner at a Tampa Bay Buccaneers football game. It was too crowded in his luxury box to talk, so I was told to meet him at a certain time the following night in a deserted bank parking lot.

I blindly followed instructions— hey, the guy pays well— and ended up standing alone in back of this southern Florida bank in pitch darkness. As I was wondering just how badly I could want to work for anybody, the soft hum of a luxury car sounded behind me. A set of lights blinked once. I turned and tried to peer through a front window, then realized I didn't need to see the driver's face to know who it was. The car's front license plate read ʏᴀɴᴋ 1. George Steinbrenner, inconspicuous as ever.

I climbed into the front passenger seat, and Steinbrenner began whispering about taking me to a little restaurant where nobody would know us, where we could get our business done. We pulled up in front of this dimly lit joint, walked inside— and the entire room erupted with cries of "George, George!" and "Good to see you, Mr. Steinbrenner." Hell, some of these people even knew me. George Steinbrenner, inconspicuous as ever.

When we finally talked business, it was big business: the Yankees' manager job. George said he was interested in me replacing Lemon. I started dreaming about how great it would be, and I was dreaming all the way through the cup of coffee when I realized he hadn't offered me the job. So I decided to play my hole card—Ballard Smith, which is like playing a joker. I told Steinbrenner that I'd like to talk to him seriously about the Yankees, but that it was only fair to say I was also considering the San Diego Padres. Steinbrenner perked up and invited me to his office the next day at Bal Harbor Inn in Tampa, presumably for another incognito encounter.

At his office we talked some more, and while I still got no

offer, I did get a promise. "We are very interested in you, so let us know before you do anything with the Padres," Stein-brenner said. He wrote down his phone number on a piece of paper, I stuck it in my wallet, and the next day I took it with me on a second interview to San Diego.

That second session with the Padres was the first time I'd seen two grown men choke on their clam chowder. We were at the La Jolla Beach and Tennis Club—myself and Ballard Smith and Jack McKeon and Joan Kroc, Ray's wife, who had just entered the negotiations picture. I wasn't sure what the hell she was doing there. The team still belonged to her hus-band, even if he was aging and apparently growing sick. After about five minutes of conversation she said something you might not expect from an owner's wife: she didn't know any-thing about baseball. "Not a darn thing," she said. "No kid-ding?" I said.

But sometime during the first course she proved she knew a lot about Dick Williams. Just as we were beginning to dis-cuss the contract, she waved her hands, silenced Ballard and Jack, and blurted out, "Let's not haggle. We'll offer you a three-year deal at $190,000 a year and extend it to five years with a raise if you do well your first year. Okay?"

Oh. So *that* was what she was doing there. McKeon had dropped his spoon in his soup, while Ballard had these little fish-shaped crackers coming out of his mouth. This disgust-ing little scene later proved to be an omen. But at the time I just thought, Hmm, as long as I don't sit too close to them, I could work for these people.

I told Joan that her offer sounded wonderful and I'd probably take it, but that I needed to do one tiny thing first. Which was, although I didn't tell her, to call Steinbrenner. Back at my hotel later that afternoon, I pulled out the tiny slip of paper from my wallet, picked up the receiver, and dialed—and the line was busy. One of those real quick busy signals you always seem to get when you're calling big shots. I waited a few minutes and dialed again. Now I got a recording: the number was no longer in service. I called again. Same recording. I called a friend of Steinbrenner's, Tampa *Tribune* sports editor Tom McEwen, and asked him what had happened to George's phone. He asked what number I'd dialed. I told him. He laughed. "That's not George's phone," he said.

I figured the wrong number had been given to me by accident, a possibility I later confirmed. But in my career I had endured too many accidents. A sure bet was waiting. I phoned Ballard and said, "Let's do it." That is, of course, after I asked, "Are you eating?"

The next day we drove to Ray's office, located behind a McDonald's near La Jolla. Ray demanded a celebration snack and Ballard ran to buy it. I ordered a quarter-pounder with cheese, fries, and a large Coke. Ray ordered a milkshake. Ballard ate whatever Ray and Joan told him to eat. As Ballard passed out the little ketchups, I thought, No sir, I'm not in Boston or Oakland anymore. I wasn't even sure I was in big league baseball.

And so began the McNightmare chapter of my life, the one that reads like a novel. The others, I suppose, read like industrial explosions. But in San Diego, more than any other city I've worked in, my stay had a definite beginning, a climax, and an ending. I spent 1982 and 1983 helping bring the franchise to respectability for the first time in its life. I peaked with a 1984 pennant. Norma and I were happy enough that we never wanted to leave. But then I went through a disastrous downfall in 1985 and finally was forced to quit on the first day of 1986 spring training. In the course of this most exciting and unnerving and ultimately shattering time in my life, I learned several things: Never trust guys whose first names are last names. Never trust guys who smoke cigars. And if you're feeling safe and secure like you finally have a home, never trust yourself.

In the beginning you never would have guessed it. It was all so simple. My lineup was awful, filled with players who had been going through the motions, thinking nobody would notice since they lived and worked in the big shadow of those guys 120 miles up the road, the Dodgers. The Padres were never criticized by the manager or the media. Like many other folks who had moved to San Diego, they'd come to retire.

So simple. McKeon, a former manager who made more moves as a general manager than he'd ever made on the field (possibly because as a general manager he was always awake), was more than willing to change all that for me. He helped me get rid of most of the malcontents, brought in some tough bastards who cared, and in general acted like he wanted the franchise to succeed. If only I'd known, there was just one thing he really wanted. My job. But I'm getting ahead of myself.

In 1981, the year before I arrived, the opening-day lineup featured Terry Kennedy at catcher, Randy Bass at first base, Juan Bonilla at second base, Ozzie Smith at shortstop, Luis Salazar at third, and an outfield of Ruppert Jones, Gene Richards, and Dave Edwards. Three years later the team that I took into the playoffs and the World Series had just one of those starters—Kennedy. Unfortunately, he gave me more gray hairs than any of the guys we sent away. Kennedy didn't have a mental or physical problem but an equipment problem. He needed a diaper. He would whine when he didn't feel he was getting enough attention and cry when he felt he got too much.

Take what happened in 1984, when the league concocted this home run contest, pitting one representative from each team against another in a pregame show. It sounded silly, but there was pretty good money involved. And by the time it got down to the final four players, there should have been some pride involved too. But not with Kennedy. Nobody on the Padres will ever forget how, just before a semifinal match with San Francisco's Jeff Leonard in front of the San Diego Jack Murphy Stadium fans, our man decided he didn't want to compete anymore. He said he was tired of it, it was stupid and beneath him. He even warned his teammates, who had started getting excited about this contest—hell, we were even coming out and watching from the bench. He told us he was going to try to hit homers only to left field, where, being a left-handed hitter, he couldn't hit homers. So what happened? When it was his turn in the semifinals, he promptly stepped to the plate and popped everything up, shaming himself and disgusting the entire team.

Amid a group that eventually developed more character than even I could have imagined, Kennedy always had to be different. When Steve Garvey became such a popular player for us, bringing fans and national media back to San Diego, Kennedy resented it. His locker was next to Garvey's until, at one large media session involving Garvey, he made a big scene of packing up and moving far across the room. Said he didn't like to be crowded. And the time we ran outside to slap hands with the several thousand cheering fans following our return home in the middle of the 1984 playoffs, guess who was the only player who didn't want to go? Our catcher-in-the-cry. That he pulled full-season career highs of .295 with 21 homers and 97 RBIs in my first year with the Padres is the only thing that kept him around for the pennant. He certainly did nothing else to deserve it.

Other than Kennedy, by the time we reached 1984 the rest of my starting position players were new. At all my other managerial stops I'd molded winners out of players who were already present. Doing it the San Diego way was perhaps a more difficult feat, considering there was a chance that guys wouldn't hate just me but also each other.

Our rise from baseball's rubble started at shortstop in the Topps Trading Card Hospitality Suite at the winter meetings in Hollywood, Florida, in 1981, shortly after I'd signed my contract and eaten my quarter-pounder. To be exact, it started at the bar, with me and old friend Whitey Herzog, now the Cardinals' manager, sipping a couple of scotch-and-waters.

"So how's the new job?" Herzog asked. Because I knew he and McKeon had already talked, I understood he was really asking, How's your shortstop who hates being a Padre? He was talking about Ozzie Smith, who wanted to make a million bucks but the Krocs wouldn't give it to him. Whitey knew all about how Ozzie had put an ad in the newspaper for a winter job to supplement his income, sort of as a joke. Then Joan Kroc called him and said he could be her gardener, which was really worth a few yuks. Whitey knew that was the last straw for Ozzie, who now really wanted out.

"Well," I told Whitey, "my job would be a lot better if I knew who our shortstop will be next year."

"Funny you should mention that," Herzog said. "We've got to get rid of our shortstop too."

That would be Garry Templeton. I knew all about him too, because I knew all about the city of St. Louis. Templeton was the kind of player who played hard without looking like it. Ran hard but looked like he was walking. Made great plays but made them look too easy. Only got his uniform dirty when he absolutely needed to. St. Louis was the opposite kind of town. The fans there don't understand clean uniforms, even when that fact represents great skill. I grew up there, so I know St. Louis. It's the kind of working class town where everybody sweats, so they want to see you sweat. The fans will fill Busch Stadium and adore you . . . as long as you do your best to be just like them. To be a working man.

Templeton also had another strike against him in St. Louis, a problem he's never publicly discussed, probably because he could never fix it. Templeton is black, and St. Louis is—well, let's just say it was the last city to accept Jackie Robinson. St. Louis would never, ever accept a black shortstop who looked like he wasn't hustling.

Whitey told me that the shortstop would have to listen to fans drop the n-word on both him and his wife. Templeton later confirmed how fans would sit above the Cardinals dugouts and spend the entire game insulting him into an anger he'd never known he possessed. His wife, Glenda, couldn't take it and finally moved back to his home in southern California in the middle of what turned out to be his final season in St. Louis. Garry couldn't take it either, but he had no choice. Until the one day in 1981 when he literally took matters into his own hands by giving the crowd the finger and then publicly grabbing his nuts. Herzog had to drag him from the field that day in what the nation thought was a show of anger with his shortstop. Wrong. Herzog was afraid Tempy would do the only fair thing and leap into the stands and attack some of those racist assholes. So for everyone's good, Templeton had to be traded.

After hearing how much abuse he'd taken, and how long he'd lasted until he snapped, I fell in love with Templeton. About four drinks after Jack McKeon joined us at the Topps bar on that winter day in 1981, the trade was made. It wouldn't be formally completed for another month, but it was Ozzie Smith for Templeton, plus some other guys thrown in. Controversy be damned, I had a shortstop who would take us to the World Series.

Sure, Templeton sometimes looked like he was dogging it, and some fans in San Diego later had the same reaction as fans in St. Louis. But I soon saw how he'd spend 30 minutes wrapping his sore knees before games, and how those knees would be swollen and red after games, and how he never asked out of the lineup. I saw a team leader. Sadly, most fans didn't see it my way until the 1984 postseason, when Templeton became a towel-waving cheerleader.

Also joining our team during my debut 1982 season was this little fat guy from a local college who Jack McKeon had insisted on drafting in the third round the previous year, even though most scouts thought his bat was slow and he'd never be able to field. Four batting titles and three Gold Gloves later, maybe you've heard of the guy. Name of Gwynn.

McKeon's promotion of Tony to the big leagues in my first year proved to be the nicest thing anybody has ever done for me. I don't think I've ever had a player who worked harder and cared more and was more deserving of his rewards. Par-

ticularly in the field, where Tony was originally a hack. He
knew he had to work on being even a decent fielder, so he
worked until he became a great one. And don't think his batting titles came naturally either. With that big butt and funny
walk, nothing for him was ever easy.

Take Gwynn's first season, on an August night in Pittsburgh. He wasn't playing, so he was down at the end of the
bench talking to pitcher Eric Show. With Show being a high
thinker (translated: strange agent), it was only natural that
instead of baseball, they were talking about politics. Show was
quizzing Gwynn on what he called Twenty Things Every
American Should Know—questions about Congress and stuff
like that. Poor Tony couldn't figure out any of the answers.
Most people couldn't, which was Show's point. But to make
things worse, when they reached the 20th question, I shouted
for Tony to enter the game as a defensive replacement. He
ran to left field with, as he later explained, his mind still
spinning. He dove for the first fly ball hit to him and broke
his wrist. So much for quiz shows that didn't involve the
manager.

Even the public acclaim that Tony rightly deserved didn't
come easy for him. This always bothered me because I was
so fond of him. His peers knew he just might be baseball's
best player, but the San Diego fans always seemed to cheer
louder for a guy like infielder Tim Flannery, who'd broken
in with the Padres three years before Gwynn. The reasons
for this inequity are as simple as they are stupid. Flannery is
the ideal southern Californian. He surfs. His hair is blond.
And, of course, he is white. The players used to call Flannery
and his wife, Donna, "Ken and Barbie." The way the San
Diego fans reacted to them, you'd have thought they were
Charles and Di. They gave Flannery standing ovations on
opening day, with every hit, with every dive at third base.
They'd cheer so much you wondered if you were watching
Babe Ruth with a tan.

You were not. This is not to say Flannery isn't a great

Charlie Finley tells me a little joke while preparing to give Vida Blue a personalized license plate on Vida Blue Day in 1971. Charlie's generosity attached a blue Cadillac to the license plate.
(Oakland Tribune photo)

In a sense, the manager always stands alone. Here I'm surveying my 1971 Oakland A's during batting practice.

I'm being thrown out of a game in Oakland by John Flaherty, the same umpire who'd handed me my first major league ejection a few years earlier in Boston. Mike Epstein, my first baseman, is so upset about it that he has to clean his fingernails to stay calm.

Like manager, like son. During the 1971 Oakland season my oldest, Rick, tries to teach me a little strategy. If he'd been more than a part-time batboy, I would have benched him for it. *(Oakland Tribune photo)*

This cynical manager gets a little lesson in faith from Billy Graham during the 1971 playoffs. *(Oakland Tribune phto)*

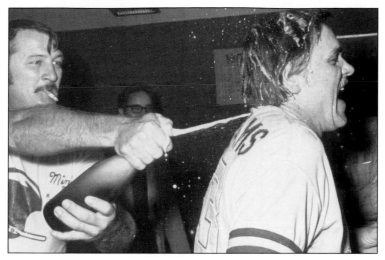

A Don Mincher sucker punch never felt so good as when he nailed me with champagne while we celebrated clinching the 1972 American League pennant.
(UPI/Bettmann Newsphotos)

Here are my Oakland A's and me being introduced at the opening of the 1972 World Series in Cincinnati. The injured Reggie Jackson—stylish even when not wearing a baseball uniform—is easy to spot. (AP/Wide World Photos)

Clowning with Cincinnati
Reds manager Sparky
Anderson before one
game of the World
Series.
(AP/WIde World Photos)

Tiny bubbles. During the
1972 Series I talked too
much to have time for
big ones.
(AP/Wide World Photos)

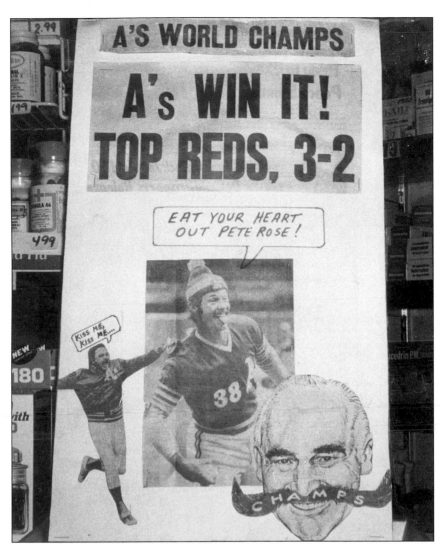

The spirit of Oakland, home of the 1972 world champions of baseball.

The above side depicts the hometown of the A's in raised sculptured letters, atop a baseball, with the A's logo in Kelly Green enamel beneath the American League Championship tally of playoff games! At the base, (where Mr. Finley's name appears), the recipient's name will appear in raised letters!

A crowning touch to the top is a beautiful, gleaming full one carat diamond of the finest quality and color to commemorate a great achievement set in a white mounting. The background is a beautiful playing field of shamrock in the form of an (emerald green) spinel. The 19 and 72 numerals serve as dividers for the words: World Champions.

Winning the best of seven in a dramatic finish sportsfans will long remember. The final tally is illustrated on the above side in raised and polished letters above an authentic reproduction of Mr. Finley's signature. And what better words to remember than his famous formula S + S = S,

"Sweat plus Sacrifice equals Success!"

Charlie Finley gave us these sparkling rings following the 1972 World Series win. But afterward things around the A's were never so bright again.

The fishing near my Singer Island, Florida, home was the best ever in the winter after the A's 1972 triumph.

(AP/Wide World Photos)

The 1973 All Star classic was almost like an Oakland home game. Here I am *(standing at right)* with six members of the American League team: Reggie Jackson and Catfish Hunter *(kneeling)*, Joe Rudi, Bert Campaneris, Sal Bando, and Ken Holtzman *(standing, left to right)*.

Here's the team that beat the New York Mets in the 1973 World Series being congratulated by President Richard Nixon. I'm standing next to Charlie Finley at the President's left.
(White House photo)

I like this sport because the trees I antagonize can't yell back. I've just finished a round with Sam Snead *(second from left)* and a couple of amateurs in Palm Beach, Florida.
(Photo by Bill Blakeney)

1974 Angels

Portrait of a disaster. I'm sitting in the middle of the front row, surrounded by the 1974 Angels, unable to escape.

Why is this man laughing? Life with the Angels wasn't particularly funny—or fun.

(Photo by Sheedy and Long, Sports Illustrated)

That's me in 1974 with . . . would you believe? . . . Whitey Herzog. So he really did have hair once.

(Photo by J. D. McCarthy)

MONTREAL EXPOS MANAGER DICK WILLIAMS 9-29-80

After a few years in Montreal I could almost pass for a native.

(Illustration by Taylor Jones for The Charleston Gazette)

A couple of fighters. Sugar Ray Leonard and I shake hands before his match in June 1980 in Montreal with Roberto Duran.

It might look like I'm hugging the Expos mascot, my good friend Youppi. Actually, though, I'm choking him. *(Journal de Montréal photo)*

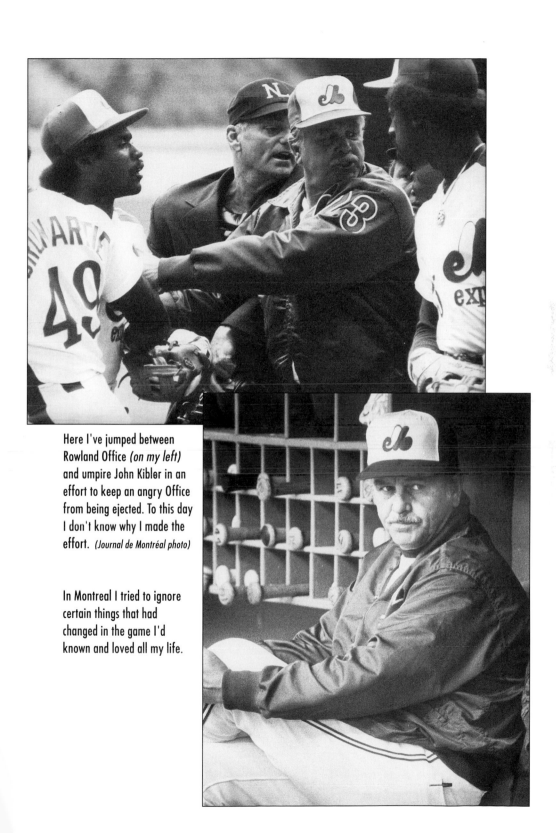

Here I've jumped between Rowland Office *(on my left)* and umpire John Kibler in an effort to keep an angry Office from being ejected. To this day I don't know why I made the effort. *(Journal de Montréal photo)*

In Montreal I tried to ignore certain things that had changed in the game I'd known and loved all my life.

I could have sworn—I *did* swear—that a ball hit by Steve Garvey in this 1984 Padres-Cubs playoff game went over the fence in fair territory. As you can tell, umpire Terry Tata disagreed. The instant replay, as I recall, showed that I was right and he was wrong—so it was a home run . . . but it wasn't. *(Photos by Martin Mann)*

After we won the 1984 National League pennant, Goose Gossage and I decided to dance. *(Photo by Martin Mann)*

Norma and me outside our home in the Coronado Cays near San Diego during happier times with the Padres.

I constantly tried to make things add up with the Seattle Mariners. Finally they just wouldn't. *(Seattle Mariners photo)*

The end in Seattle. Once again, shortly before getting fired from my last major league job, I was walking alone. *(Seattle Mariners photo)*

Earl Weaver and I exchange lineup cards before a Senior League game in 1989 between his Miami Sun Sox and my West Palm Beach Tropics. *(Photo by Denis Bancroft)*

Senior League star Toby Harrah slides into third base, and I show that I'm not too old to get down with him. *(Photo by Denis Bancroft)*

Whatever it is I'm saying to this Senior League umpire, the real message from me is this: No More Mr. Nice Guy.
(Photo by Denis Bancroft)

guy. He's the best. But he never was a great player, as he knows himself. And he's certainly not the kind of player around which a pennant winner is built. Above all, he's not even in the same category as Gwynn, who it seems got cheered only when he reached a batting milestone or threw a guy out at home plate from the right field corner. Flannery wouldn't recognize the sound of a boo; Gwynn couldn't forget it. In any controversy Gwynn was always the bad guy, the one taking abuse from the right field bleachers. My only gripe with the otherwise wonderful San Diego fans is that they will never let Tony Gwynn forget that he doesn't look like Tim Flannery.

Besides adding Templeton and Gwynn, my first year coincided with the first full year for another future 1984 hero: outfielder and second baseman Alan Wiggins. His recall from the minor leagues, which would later help us win our pennant, was also the start of some big league trouble that plagued my entire Padres stay. This trouble didn't affect our winning, but it did raise questions in my mind about the running of this baseball team.

Joan Kroc now speaks out against it, and all the Padres openly condemn it, but back then nobody in the organization was doing a damn thing about it. Drugs. Once again. For a moment I thought I was back in Montreal.

It had started before I arrived—ironically, with Wiggins's predecessor at second base, Juan Bonilla. It was Bonilla's broken wrist that gave Wiggins his first chance in 1982. Bonilla would be with us just one more season before being unceremoniously dumped, and with good reason. Not only had he been caught with an illegal substance, but he'd damn near been caught buying the stuff while in uniform. Often before home games in my first year I'd glance to the right of the dugout and into the pit where the groundskeepers sit. Every time I looked over, it seemed, there'd be one guy who wasn't a groundskeeper. I never thought to ask who it was—had enough problems without worrying who was holding the rakes. But after Bonilla was released, I heard people in the clubhouse talking about that guy. Finally, I asked somebody, "I know who you're talking about—what's the big deal?" "The big deal?" my source said with a smile. "That guy was the one who sold Bonilla the stuff." I asked if Ballard Smith knew about this. I didn't get an answer. After thinking about it, I decided I didn't want one.

I had brought former Montreal second baseman Rodney Scott into town at that time in hopes of having him replace the injured Bonilla, but Kroc wouldn't take him. Reason? He'd admitted to a newspaper that while he never did drugs, he'd once taken a puff off a joint. So Scott was out. Instead, the Padres management wanted Wiggins, a guy who'd been caught with drugs when he was in the Dodgers organization, then traded to us and caught with drugs again when he played for our triple-A Hawaii team. Why this guy was ever brought up to my Padres, I'll never know.

After a night game in 1983, my second year with Wiggins, one of the clubhouse guys came up to me with this bag of white powdery stuff. As I stood there speechless, he explained that when he was getting ready to throw Wiggins's baseball pants in the washing machine, the bag fell out. Unbelievable. The stuff was in the man's baseball pants! What was he going to do, snort a line while a guy was coming in from the bullpen? Later that night Wiggins came back to the clubhouse flustered, and asked to check his pants because he'd forgotten something. By then somebody had dumped the stuff, so the clubhouse guys told him they hadn't found anything. The front office was later informed, but guess what? They did nothing. Like they thought Wiggins's problem would just go away. I know, I should blame myself for not being more forceful about getting Wiggins out of there. Call it in-season tunnel vision. That curse.

Later that summer—big surprise here—Wiggins was caught throwing a marijuana joint out the window of his car. The front office was finally a little embarrassed, so they placed him in a rehabilitation center to give him one more chance. In 1985 he threw away that chance by failing to show up for three straight games in Los Angeles while we were still in first place. He tested positive for drugs and entered another rehabilitation center. The minute he was released, he got sent to the minor leagues and then dumped off on Baltimore. But by then he'd already sufficiently disrupted the team, and the Padres management had already started me wondering. How could it have gotten that bad? How could such a vehement anti-drug activist like Joan Kroc—who was gradually assuming control in place of her ailing husband—preside over a baseball team with a problem like this? Ultimately, my answer was that she didn't know. In matters of drugs, as in all other things involving this team, she was just plain naive. She'd never bought the team, never wanted it—she'd plain inherited it and had no choice but to run it. And she just didn't know.

Somebody, of course, should have kept her informed. But that somebody, Ballard Smith, kept her naive so he could keep himself powerful. As Joan later admitted, Ballard hurt her in plenty of ways, which we will discuss later. This chapter still has some fun.

Back to that 1982 team. With the additions of Templeton and Gwynn and Wiggins, who was great when straight, we got off to a pretty good start and played decently all summer. I was still feeling out the players' egos and attitudes, so I didn't crack a whip. But by then, with my reputation, I didn't have to. Most guys kicked ass simply out of fear that I'd do the same thing. The 1982 season was no Impossible Dream, but a young Eric Show won 10 games and a young Tim Lollar won 16. There was definitely promise here.

My biggest problem was that besides promise there was also Ruppert Jones. Despite being our best player for the first half of my first season, the seven-year veteran symbolized everything that was wrong with these Padres. They possessed no toughness under pressure, showing no belief in themselves, which showed a lack of work ethic needed to unearth that belief. For a couple of sorry days in July, this franchise malaise was exemplified by Ruppert.

It was just after the All-Star break. Jones had been our

team's representative and was flying high. But beginning with the first game of the second half, the fastballs were too fast. The curves were too quick. What he'd been seeing so clearly for three months suddenly got fuzzy. This game can do that to people. Shit happens. Now it was Ruppert's turn to eat it. In his first eight at-bats after the All-Star break, he struck out. Eight times? Yes, eight times. He went up, down, up, down. The day after number eight, he didn't show up at the park. We called his wife. She said he was on his way. Turned out to be the longest drive to the office in history. Three days later he showed up dirty and smelly and mumbling. My best buddy, coach Ozzie Virgil, intercepted him halfway to his locker, turned him around, and ordered him home to sleep it off.

The next day Ruppert arrived and explained to us that somebody had slipped him a knockout drug that kicked his ass for three days. The drug, I had heard about—just an old-fashioned Mickey. But three days? No way. In any case, it was apparently the only way he knew to escape his fall. But it was not Dick Williams's way. Jones found this out the following year. He didn't play well enough to compensate for the risk of losing him to whatever he was doing on the street, so we dumped him.

I had hoped the team would learn about self-discipline by watching me get nationally burned by cigarets. An explanation: Feeling the pressure of being a new manager again, on one 1982 Saturday afternoon during a game I lit up in the Dodger Stadium dugout runway. Damned if NBC wasn't putting the game on national television, and damned if their cameras didn't catch me puffing. Announcer Tony Kubek said, "That looks like a cigaret, doesn't it?" His partner, Joe Garagiola, tried to cover for me: "No, I think it's a pencil." Kubek shot back, "If it's a pencil, then it's on fire."

You can bet I heard from the league office the next day, with a telegram and a $250 fine for smoking on the field. I paid the fine and threw away my smokes and didn't take an-

other puff for six years. In other words, I took the opportunity to discipline myself. I'm sure the players noticed this,
because—not to destroy anybody's illusions—a lot of them
smoked, and many of them had taken puffs closer to the
field than me. Hell, after an inning has ended on a surprise
double play or other fluke, I've seen guys hustling to their
positions still holding a cigaret. When they realize it, they
flick it to the ground, where it will lie smoking for half an
inning. Many fans have noticed such tiny wisps of smoke.
Some blame it on something thrown from the stands. During
night games, romantics may think it's mist. Dream on. Chances
are, it's a Winston 100.

Despite my personal missions, after going 81–81 that first
season I worried that there still were Padres who didn't understand my way. I realized I would have to work harder.
The players of the early eighties didn't listen as well as those
of the late sixties. I would have to speak louder. First, though,
McKeon spoke for me. He went out in the winter following
the 1982 season and signed a guy who, while he didn't do
much for us on the field, certainly helped the guys believe in
themselves in the clubhouse. I'm talking about—hide the
women and women—Steve Garvey.

I'm not going to dwell on Garvey's recent birth control
problems. They're none of my business. Not once in our time
in San Diego together did I catch Mr. Clean with the Wrigley's Doublemint twins. Instead, I wish to use this space to
debunk an even greater Garvey myth: that the guy led us to
a championship. Garvey did a lot of things for this team, such
as give it leaguewide credibility and professionalism. But lead
he did not. And play consistently well he did not. He had left
his best days at Dodger Stadium, from where we'd taken him
as a free agent. The fact that nobody wanted to acknowledge
his flaws made it all the more irritating.

It irked me to watch the rest of the team busting their
humps while Garvey, who was so pretty-pretty with the media, received all the attention. Not that he wasn't a great guy.

Certainly, he's one of the nicest and most professional men I've ever met. But what he actually accomplished on the field as a Padre and what the public thinks he accomplished are two very different things. He couldn't drive the ball anymore. He couldn't move well in the field anymore.

While with the Padres, he bullshitted his way into, among other things, a major league record he didn't deserve. Remember his 193-game errorless streak, from the middle of 1983 to early 1985? For a first baseman, it's the longest in baseball history. But it's also the most crooked, because it was handed to him. I'm speaking of an incident early in the 1985 season. Man on first, sharp ground ball to Graig Nettles at third. The runner was fast, the throw was high and tipped off Garvey's glove, and the guy was safe on an infield single. No big deal. But because Garvey lollygagged behind first base and had trouble picking the ball up, the runner on second went to third. According to baseball's official scoring rules, a runner can never advance a base without a reason: either a hit, or a stolen base, or a wild pitch, or a balk . . . or an error. In this case, plainly, it was Garvey's error. Yet incredibly, the San Diego scorer made no call. He didn't give Garvey an error, didn't give the runner a stolen base, nothing. He offered no official explanation as to why the guy advanced.

No, giving the batter a single was not an official explanation, because the runner wasn't going on the pitch and therefore couldn't have gotten from first to third on a single. Because of the no-call, history will show that the runner went all the way from first to third on the infield single. Go figure. The scorer was simply afraid to call the error on Garvey. He was afraid to mess with a legend. So was the entire city.

This play particularly angered me because the record for consecutive errorless games that Garvey eventually broke belonged to Mike Hegan, my first baseman at Oakland, who may have been the best-fielding first baseman ever. Hegan would attempt to, and did, reach more ground balls in one month than Garvey could reach in a year. You don't make errors if you don't take chances, which makes Hegan's 178-

game streak from 1970 to 1973 even more amazing. And which makes Garvey's record a fraud.

A good test of the fielding ability of your first baseman is how many times he'll field a sacrifice bunt in front of home plate and attempt to throw to second or third to get the lead runner. Even if the first baseman doesn't get him, the effort shows confidence in his ability and a sense of daring that's needed in all good fielders. But Garvey never tried. Not only wouldn't he throw to second base, he'd never even look in that direction. He'd pick up the ball and automatically flip it to first, playing right into the hands of the opponents. Every opposing club bunted in his direction, and now you know why. We'd have a number of fancy plays called to stop the bunts, but he'd never follow orders and throw the ball to second or third.

Today the hot talk about Garvey is whether he's really the philanderer that those two women who claimed he impregnated them say he is. I never saw any of that. Despite his on-field flaws, off the field he seemed as clean as his image. I never saw him in bars, never saw him hanging around hotel lobbies, never saw him when he wasn't neat and polite to everyone. In fact, the only problems I had with him in regard to women didn't involve his girlfriends but his ex-wife. Cyndy Garvey would call me in my office, cursing Steve to high heaven and trying to force him to pay what she claimed was overdue child support. Hell, what did she expect me to do? I couldn't even force him to field a bunt. I would always listen—it's funny to hear pretty women curse—and then walk into the clubhouse and tell Steve that she'd called. By the sour look on his face, I was sure he knew why.

But Garvey did help us. After he joined the team in 1983, our attitude grew brighter. He worked hard, influenced the kids, and made it easier for us to get rid of more veterans who weren't producing and not caring as much. It was no coincidence that 1983 was the last year for such Padres as outfielders Ruppert Jones, Gene Richards, and Sixto Lezcano.

The 1983 season was also the final year for one of my all-time favorites, pitcher Chris Welsh. I say this not because I liked him but because I liked what his attitude did for my clubhouse influence. When I was through dealing with him, the Padres realized that we play only to win and only as a team. Or we get the hell out. We were in Pittsburgh. Welsh was on the mound with a man on first base. I thought the guy might steal, so I called a pitchout, meaning Welsh was supposed to throw the ball outside so the catcher could grab it and have a better chance at throwing out the runner. Welsh promptly threw the ball over to first base to hold the runner on. He obviously forgot that on a pitchout we don't want to hold the runner on first, we want him to attempt a steal. He forgot our first rule of a pitchout: never try a pickoff. It was a mental mistake. You know how I feel about mental mistakes.

Out to the mound ran my pitching coach Norm Sherry with a verbal reminder. From my seat in the dugout I could see Welsh talking back. That was fine, I'd never had any rule against on-mound discussions. When Sherry returned, I calmly asked him, "So what did you guys talk about?" Sherry got this funny look on his face. "You sure you want to know?" he asked. Now I had the funny look. "What did he say?" I demanded. "Well," Sherry explained, "he said if you didn't like the way he did it, you should get someone else." "Oh," I said. "Is that what he said?"

I told Sherry to get somebody loose in the bullpen. The minute Welsh reached the dugout at the end of the inning, I told him I was taking him out of the game. Afterward, in the clubhouse, I asked him if he really had said that. He said yes. I told him, "You've pitched your last game for me." And within a couple of days we'd dumped him.

The conflict between Welsh and me became the talk of the clubhouse. That was good. It united the slouchers in their hate for me, which meant they'd probably play harder, if only out of spite. You know how I love that attitude. And the reasonable folks became united with me in my love for winning. And after all, Chris Welsh wasn't Cy Young. As I've said, the people who have the most trouble with me usually aren't the most productive. Welsh was 0−1 for us in seven games that season before we shipped him to Montreal, where he went 0−1 in 16 games, with a combined season ERA of 4.42. His career ended two years and two teams later with a record of 22−31 with a 4.46 ERA. Case closed.

And so we ended the 1983 season with half of the guys hating me and half of them respecting me but all of them playing hard. We'd finished 81−81 again, but it was a good 81−81, and you had to be blind not to see that our team's future was bright. That year had marked the debut of out-fielder Kevin McReynolds, and it was Tony Gwynn's first season breaking .300. Our pennant-winning outfield was completed the following year when the trade with the Chicago Cubs brought in Carmelo Martinez, who had the confidence to hit any pitch that didn't hit him first and the power to hit it long. With veterans (Garvey and Templeton), hot kids (McReynolds and Martinez), and plain great players (Gwynn), our team's future was now.

As for my future—well, once again that was a different story. My problems with the Padres began at the very beginning of this rush to greatness. At the end of that 1983 season McKeon pulled two fast moves on me, which at the time I failed to realize could be so deadly. First thing, he added his buddy Harry Dunlop to our staff full-time as the bullpen coach. Dunlop had joined the team on a temporary basis late in the summer, so I didn't pay much attention to him until that winter, when McKeon suddenly told me Harry was going to be hanging around permanently.

I thought, Why is McKeon suddenly messing with a good thing? We have a chance to win a pennant, and he's bringing in new coaches? I wanted to tell McKeon no, and I should have. A manager should be able to surround himself with his own people, if for no other reason than to protect his back in the clubhouse. Why do you think Ozzie Virgil has been with me all these years? Besides being a great third-base coach, he's a great friend who fights most of my criticism and calms most of my angry players.

A guy selected by the general manager might not be so willing to protect you. After all, he is your boss's buddy. And soon he could influence players the wrong way. If this coach is telling the players that his buddy the general manager doesn't agree with the manager, why should the players agree with the manager? Ultimately, it's the general manager who hires and fires them anyway. An outsider coach, in other words, can turn a manager into an outsider. Maybe the outsider coach will be a good guy, but if he's not your pick, you never know. In this regard, Dunlop proved to be a walking worst case scenario. Because Dunlop, I learned a couple of years later, was McKeon's spy.

In that same winter of 1983 my discomfort with Dunlop was compounded when I learned what had just happened to one of my most trustworthy coaches, Bobby Tolan. McKeon called and told me that Tolan had requested a minor league managing job and was being reassigned to a double-A team in Beaumont, Texas. I thought this odd, because Bobby had always worked well as my hitting instructor and seemed perfectly happy. But hey, if a guy wants to be a manager, I won't stand in his way. Turned out he didn't want to be a manager. When I saw Tolan that spring, he asked me why I'd requested that he get managing experience. I told him that was bullshit, I'd never requested that. Then I asked him, "Why didn't you tell me that you wanted to be a manager so bad?" Tolan told me *that* was bullshit, he'd never said that. I think McKeon had wanted Tolan gone, and he evidently lied to both of us to grease the skids.

This stunned me. Again, why fix something that wasn't broken? I was getting comfortable and happy and ready to charge to the pennant. We all were. Why would McKeon mess with it? But it was too late to do anything, or even worry much about it. The 1984 season was upon us, and suddenly we were contenders. And after all, in that winter of 1983

McKeon had granted my most important request as a Padres manager. I'd wanted him to acquire the one piece I felt could strengthen us in the clubhouse and make us damn tough on the field and put us over the top. All of my championship teams have had that one piece, and it hasn't been coincidental.

I like to call it a PWCP—a Prick Who Can Play. I'm talking about a guy who may not lead chapel services, who may not hold daily press conferences and call the media by their first names, who may not shed tears when young guys get cut and old guys are forced into retirement. These PWCPs may not be the nicest guys in baseball. But often they're the toughest, the ones who care the most about winning, because that's all they care about. While the public may not understand them, teammates respect them and managers love them. The PWCPs, who may break bats after strikeouts and furniture after losses, are a constant clubhouse reminder of why we play. And how bad it is to play badly.

Before the 1984 season I asked McKeon for just one PWCP, but he got me two: Goose Gossage and Graig Nettles. Gossage was signed as a free agent over the winter to be our right-handed bullpen ace, but he became much more. He became our conscience. Nettles was acquired in a trade at the end of spring to be a veteran influence at third base, but with his sarcastic wit and his red neck, he became another me. The way I figured it, if McKeon had gotten those guys, he couldn't be all bad. And thus our glory season began.

I knew our everyday lineup would be good enough to win. You're around long enough, you know. We had Kennedy catching, Garvey at first base, Wiggins at second base, Templeton at shortstop, Nettles at third base, and McReynolds, Martinez, and Gwynn in the outfield. I knew our bullpen would be fine thanks to Gossage.

The only thing that worried me was our starting pitchers. Not that they were bad, just bizarre. Take three of our starters: Eric Show, Dave Dravecky, and Mark Thurmond. They picked the middle of that season to be seen at a local fair passing out information on the conservative John Birch Society. It took about five seconds for the word to spread that they were, in fact, John Birchers.

Their political affiliation didn't bother me, or apparently anybody else on the team. But it created a public relations ruckus that distracted us. I had to spend half of my time talking about how I didn't give a damn about their conservative beliefs and the other half sending questioners to Templeton, who told me that the blacks on the team didn't give a shit about it either. In fact, Templeton told me, those three were some of the least bigoted guys he'd ever played with.

I finally put the talk to rest late in the season, after we returned from an eight-game trip in which we went 6−2, with Show, Dravecky, and Thurmond combining for the six wins. Somebody asked me if I was happy with the trip. "I'd have been a lot happier if we had another Bircher pitching for us," I said. "That way, maybe we'd have won the other two games." I don't care what a guy believes in, as long as it includes himself.

And really, of those three guys, only Show was truly weird. I'll never forget how, on September 11, 1985, he sat down on the mound in Cincinnati after giving up Pete Rose's record-breaking 4,192nd hit. Just plopped his ass down on the dirt while baseball's new all-time hit leader was celebrating on first base. How embarrassing. If he was tired, he could have come into the dugout. There was no reason to belittle our team and himself and detract from Rose's glory. Not that the record could ever be diminished. Hell, I was so excited when it happened that I wanted to run out of the dugout and jump on Rose myself. Of course, I didn't. I settled for an autographed picture instead.

Show, you know, was the one who recruited the other two guys as Birchers. And he was definitely the most militant, often leaving his controversial books and pamphlets on his locker-room chair in hopes that nosy teammates would pick them up and be influenced. He was outspoken on the pitching mound too. Once when I went out to remove him from a game, he threw the ball to me before I reached the mound. It was the act of a quitter. So I tossed the ball back to him, saying, "I don't want this son of a bitch." And, of course, I left the struggling Show in the game to get absolutely hammered.

My favorite on-mound conversation with my weird staff that season occurred with starter Tim Lollar. He was pitching a hell of a game in Philadelphia, leading 3–0 in the eighth inning, when he allowed two monster homers on two consecutive pitches, the second homer longer than the first. With Gossage in my bullpen, I jumped off the bench and ran to get Lollar out. Upon reaching the mound, I congratulated him on a good performance, told him that he'd had enough, and then waited for him to hand me the ball. And waited. About 10 seconds later I said, "Okay now, give me the ball." He looked at me apologetically. "Uh, Skip, I can't," he said. "It's rolling around the upper deck somewhere." Turns out the umpire hadn't thrown him a new ball yet. We laughed like hell and hoped that the local television cameras had gone to a commercial. As it was, the Phillies thought we were showing them up.

That crazy 1984 staff, like all modern-day staffs, wouldn't have been complete without a whiner, somebody who could form the perfect Little Leaguers battery with catcher Kennedy. Remember Andy Hawkins? This was the first full season for the Waco, Texas, native, who looked big (6-foot-4) and talked tough (in that Texas twang) but wouldn't fight the hitters if his snakeskin boots depended on it. He was afraid to throw the ball inside and afraid to challenge a guy by throwing it past him. "The Timid Texan," I called him. Even when he was good, he was timid. Take 1985, when fans might remember him opening the season with 11 straight wins. It was the most consecutive wins by a major leaguer at the start of a season in 26 years. But they were what I call protected wins, because we got him out of there in the sixth and seventh innings, before he could lose the games. Before the going got tough and the not-so-tough would spit the bit.

One day in 1984 Hawkins came into my office and asked, "Please stop calling me 'The Timid Texan.' " I stared at him. "Fine," I said. "Then please stop pitching like one." I lived up to my part of the bargain and never called him that again. He stewed awhile and then lived up to his part in October by allowing just one run in 15⅔ postseason innings. But my methods never work, do they? And Hawkins was probably still mad at me for pushing him when, a couple of years later, as a free agent, he became the highest paid Yankee pitcher in history.

With my talented but unusual team intact, our 1984 year began on a down note when owner Ray Kroc died on January 14. He had been sick, and his death was not unexpected, but it still shook those who knew him as a man who both loved and respected the game and its importance in society. He had bought the team in 1974 when it was moments away from being sold and moved to Washington, D.C. He put his ass on the line then, and he kept it on the line every day by promising the fans that his players would try—or else. As complacency swept through the game, he became angry. Like me. Ray Kroc and I thought alike and cared alike.

One particular consequence of Kroc's death must have depressed many of the San Diego fans: the club would now be run by his widow, Joan. A wonderful lady, like I said. But she didn't know, or care, about baseball. So things were in Ballard Smith's hands. That kept the entire city awake nights.

We started that regular season slow, even by the Padres' wretched early season standards. Perhaps because their spring training facility in Yuma, Arizona, is too relaxed and too close to San Diego (just three hours by car), this organization traditionally has the slowest starts in baseball. Our start wasn't the worst in club history, but it was one of the most disappointing, as we lost seven games in a row from May 11 to May 16 and fell to 18 – 18, in fourth place.

Ah, a Dick Williams team playing less than 100 percent. There's nothing like it. By the seventh straight loss, I'd been kicking enough ass that the clubhouse was in an uproar. I'd been confronting players on the field and in the dugout and in front of their lockers. And they were finally reacting. In one corner Kennedy was sucking his thumb, in another corner Gossage was howling at the writers, in another corner Wiggins was getting the shakes, and in the middle of it all Eric Show was trying to quiet everybody down so he could preach. Just the way I liked it: a team that was being pulled apart under my tension and would soon be pulling together with the common goal of revenge. A team on the verge of coming together just to show me up.

And beginning May 17 it finally happened. Wiggins set a club record with five stolen bases, we finally won a game, and we never really faltered under pressure again. On June 10 we defeated Cincinnati 12−2 and went into first place for good. Two months later, on the morning of August 12, we were 69−47, with a 10½-game lead on Atlanta and the pennant sewed up. Remember that date, August 12.

Until that time, it had been a darn near perfect season except for one thing—this imperfect manager. True to my history, the more we won, the more I expected us to win. The safer we were in first place, the more I demanded and the tougher I grew. In other pennant races it was the love of winning that made me surly. In this one it was the understanding of what winning was all about that drove me. The years had taught me how difficult it is to be a contender, let alone a champion. I wanted my players to realize that playing so well didn't just happen. Why else hadn't I been in a World Series in the last 11 years? Having been in the big games, I knew that the more you win, the more work it takes to win. And I was going to get that message through to my players if it killed me. Which it nearly did.

The first thing to return was my temper. Not that it had ever left, but true to my pennant race personality, I exchanged "mad" for "fighting mad." Nothing illustrates that better than what happened that August 12, a Sunday afternoon in Atlanta. The record books will remember it only as a Braves 5 – 3 victory. Sickos, however, will remember it as the day when baseball became a war game, when pitchers became gladiators, batters became targets, and one manager was tagged as evil. In no baseball game in history have so many heads nearly rolled. Literally.

We had just beaten the Braves three out of four games to knock them 10½ games out of first place and, essentially, eliminate them from West Division contention. In our Saturday night win Alan Wiggins had bunted twice for base hits, which the Braves thought was rubbing it in, but which was really just Dick Williams baseball.

Wiggins came to the plate to start the Sunday game. On the mound was Pascual Perez, who had hit only two batters in his previous 135⅔ innings. He was a wild man, but he was not a wild pitcher. Until then. His first pitch hit Wiggins in the back. And that reminded me of two unspoken rules of this game.

Rule Number One: if a pitcher is trying to hit you, he throws it directly behind your back, because the natural tendency on an inside pitch is to back away from the plate. Knowing that Wiggins may have inadvertently embarrassed the Braves in the previous game, I felt this rule was in effect.

Rule Number Two: when Rule Number One is in effect, get the bastard. In this case, Perez.

And so before my team even took the field for the bottom of the inning, I said loudly, "We know what we've got to do." My starting pitcher, Ed Whitson, one of the toughest guys in baseball, was already mad enough. I didn't have to say anything to him.

Whitson waited a couple of innings until Perez came to the plate, and then—boom!—he threw it right at Perez's back. Except Perez knew it was coming, and he was backing away even during Whitson's windup. So Whitson missed. Then

suddenly, strangely, the sky was eclipsed by . . . John Mc-
Sherry, the home plate umpire who is the most grotesquely
overweight man in the world of sports. This includes sumo
wrestlers, who compared to McSherry are veritable reeds. (I
developed a permanent mental impression of McSherry once
while he was running to first base from home plate and three-
fourths of his ass became visible above his belt. It was enough
to get him arrested for possession of 20 pounds of crack.
Ugh, what a sight. I called him "The Santee Silo" because he
lives in a place called Santee. For reasons I'll soon get to, I
could call him something a lot worse.)

After moving out from behind home plate—took him no
more than 20 minutes—McSherry warned both Braves manager Joe Torre and me that with the next close pitch we'd be
thrown out of the game. If you know Whitson, you know
how long I remained in the game. About 10 seconds. He
threw at Perez again and missed him again, so Whitson and
I got tossed out of the game. But before I walked back to the
clubhouse, one more time I said it: "We know what we've got
to do." And then I disappeared. What happened next I had
nothing to do with. I made no more announcements, issued
no more orders. I did nothing but watch the game on the
clubhouse television set. Yet because of what happened next,
I was given one of the largest fines—$10,000—and suspen-
sions—10 days—of any manager in baseball history. You see,
all hell broke loose.

In the sixth inning we still hadn't hit Perez, so our relief
pitcher, Greg Booker, gave it his best shot. Perez took off
running again, and Booker missed, but Booker and acting
manager Ozzie Virgil were tossed from the game. I was
watching it all on TV and thinking, About the only thing the
afternoon lacks is a good brawl. Two innings later our reliever Craig Lefferts took care of that.

With one pitch Lefferts became our season's Most Valuable Pitcher. Because he finally hit Perez. Plunked him square
on the back with one of the best pitches I've ever seen. It was

a curveball that actually followed a fleeing Perez out of the batter's box. Son of a bitch just couldn't get away from it. And then a hockey game really broke loose. The benches cleared, the players threw real punches, there was real anger. At least, that's what I saw on the clubhouse television set. I really did stay in the clubhouse the entire time. I knew that if I went outside, I'd be in for a big suspension, and I knew that a pennant-contending team couldn't afford a benched manager. I yelled to my players in the clubhouse, which was getting crowded because of all the ejections, that they shouldn't go on the field either. Not because they shouldn't kick the shit out of the Braves, but because they were also facing suspension.

After Perez had been hit, and a fight started and stopped, I figured it was over. The Braves, and hopefully all of baseball, had finally gotten the message. The Padres would no longer be intimidated. Not by other teams, not by umpires, not by fate, not by anybody.

Then a not-so-funny thing happened. In the top of the ninth inning, Torre ordered his pitcher, Donnie Moore, to hit my batter, Graig Nettles. And so Moore hit him, on his second pitch. I saw this on TV, and I couldn't believe it. The incident was over, but Torre started it again. Did he ever. My warning couldn't stop my players from running past me down to the field to kick Torre's or anybody's ass, some guys wearing nothing but baseball pants, undershirts, and scowls.

The brawl that ensued was horrific. Amid the usual rolling around by players on the field, Atlanta fans started throwing things, so Ed Whitson and Kurt Bevacqua scrambled up to the stands, and the police came, and when the mess finally ended, there were hardly any players left to finish the game. Oh, yeah, it ended in a 5−3 Braves victory. But most will remember the two brawls, three hit batters, five arrests of fans, eight brushback pitches, and 16 ejections.

My son Rick, then a pitching instructor for Montreal's minor league system, will remember something else. He was in the Atlanta area before the game, so he'd stopped by to watch and was sitting in the stands with his wife, Sue and her parents, Joan and Don Podgurny, and Norma. During all the fighting Rick got excited and ran down to the dugout, and guess who the TV cameras focused on? After that, Rick had some serious explaining to do to his bosses in Montreal.

Norma will remember something else. Afterward she walked into the Atlanta wives' waiting room, and it immediately grew silent, as most of the Braves wives were staring at her. One finally said, "This was the most disgusting thing I've ever seen." Norma, bless her heart, jumped right in the woman's face and said, "Yes, it is."

Me, I'll remember something else entirely. First I'll remember what Torre said about me after the game: "Dick Williams is an idiot." In the other clubhouse, I replied, "Tell Joe Torre to stick that finger he's pointing."

And I meant it. How dare he get on his high horse and rip me for doing something he did more flagrantly just two innings later? And something he'd probably started by ordering Perez to throw at Wiggins in the first inning? I've been sorry for many things in my career. But my only regret about that "Battle of Atlanta," as one newspaper called it, is that Torre wound up looking like the good guy.

This was cemented a couple of days later, when Ballard and McKeon informed me about my $10,000 fine and 10-day suspension. "Both managers got the same punishment?" I asked. "Uh, no," Ballard said. "Torre only got three days and $3,000."

Now I was really mad. I finally realized that the real villain of that afternoon wasn't me or Torre but McSherry, whose report to the league office likely failed to mention that Torre was guilty of the same thing as me. And certainly didn't mention that his incompetence was the reason the game got out of hand in the first place. And to think that before this game my biggest specific complaint about McSherry concerned the time he was umpiring second base and an opposing hitter bounced a grounder to my second baseman. The ball ricocheted off McSherry's incredible belly and into the outfield before it reached the fielder. I now had a story to top that one.

After receiving the fine, I called National League president Chub Feeney, who had already defeated his purpose by not specifying that I must pay the fine myself, meaning the Padres could, and would, pay it for me. Feeney must have been taking one of his legendary naps when he filled out that form. Anyway, he was awake when I reached him, and I started yelling my side of the story, about how Torre and I were equally at fault. Feeney listened, but he didn't hear. The appeal process for baseball fines and suspensions is nonexistent, as the umpires always get the first word and the league presidents are usually too busy attending New York parties to change their decisions. Particularly Feeney, who was often the life of those parties. Is it any wonder that, after retiring from the league office, he moved his naps and nips to the Padres front office in the capacity (or should I say incapacity) of club president?

So as we entered the final month of the season, my temper came back. And so did my drinking. It wasn't as bad as Boston, but it did have one thing in common with that period: the dreaded scotch whiskey. I don't know why I couldn't stay away from it, but . . . well, I do know. It's a whiskey that works the way I do. Hard and fast.

In 1984, while I didn't drink as much as in previous pennant races, it was worse. Because this time my so-called notoriety placed me in the public eye. And this led to one problem that was made public and blown out of proportion. It may even have helped cost me my job.

It was September 15. We were eight days from clinching the division. Eight days that were an eternity, at least to me. We'd played in Houston on a Saturday afternoon, and I ended up wandering into our hotel bar before dinner. Unfortunately for this part of my life, I wasn't the only Padre there.

Among others, sitting on a stool laughing and joking, was Carmelo Martinez, our young outfielder.

It's bad enough to see a guy in a bar like this during a pennant race if he's young and doesn't know how to take care of himself. But it's worse if that player has been under-achieving all season and recently benched. I liked Carmelo. But I thought he needed a little boot. So I gave him one. "Maybe you'd hit better than .237 if you didn't spend time down here," I said.

Yeah, I know, it came out sarcastic. Sometimes I just don't know any other way. Martinez brushed me off with the wave of a hand, which at that point was like waving a red blanket at a bull. I repeated my statement, laying on the sarcasm even thicker, while finding it increasingly difficult to believe I was saying what I was. I repeated it again and again until Martinez stood up as if to challenge me.

Thank goodness, for me, that my coaches pulled me away before I discovered whether he really was challenging me. I'd have lost not just a fight but the war. I wanted to anger Martinez, but not past the point of common sense. Once again, buoyed by a few scotches and a pennant race, I may have gone one stomp too far.

The next morning, when I arrived at the Astrodome, I put Martinez back in the lineup and batted him sixth, not so much to apologize as to present my own special challenge. This time that challenge was accepted. Just before he left the on-deck circle for home plate in his first at-bat, Martinez pointed to the giant scoreboard in the outfield. Across it blazed his correct batting average: .239. "You see?" he screamed at me. "I told you I wasn't no .237 hitter!"

Touché. Martinez followed that up by going two for five with an RBI and a run scored. He ended the season batting .250, with 13 homers and 66 RBIs. Not bad for a former .239 hitter who wanted to kill his loudmouth manager.

Whatever I did that night in Houston, it worked. But it also worked against him. Shortly after the incident, even

though we were in the middle of winning the first championship in the Padres' 15-year history, Norma received a phone
call at home. I didn't find out about this call until a year later.
Good thing, because otherwise I might not have lasted that
long. It was from my favorite club president, Ballard Smith.
The team was on the road, which made Norma wonder. Here
is how she recalled the conversation.

"Hi, Ballard," Norma answered curiously. "Sorry, but you
know Dick isn't home right now."

"I'm not calling for Dick, I'm calling for you," Ballard
said. "I want to ask you a favor."

"What's up?" Norma said.

"I want you to tell Dick he has to stop drinking," Ballard
said.

Poor Norma. The phone call shook her to tears, meaning
it carried quite a shake. She'd seen me drink in Boston and
knew all about my problems with scotch. But she also knew
that I didn't have the exact same problem here. She never
saw me drink at home, and rarely did I drink much when
she and I went out. She answered Ballard as much in con-
fusion as in anger.

"How can I tell him to stop drinking if I never see him
drink?" she asked. "I know when he's drinking too much,
I've gone through hell with it. But this is not one of those
times."

Before a stunned Ballard could get in another word,
Norma added a final rejoinder: "If I told Dick that you called,
he would quit on the spot."

On the other end of the phone there was silence. Norma
said it was then she knew that was exactly what Ballard Smith
wanted. He wanted me gone. At the time, she didn't know
why. Later we found out it was so he could give the job to
the guy who'd conned him into this entire scheme, Jack
McKeon. Why would McKeon want my job? And in the middle
of a pennant race? The longer I was there, the clearer it became. As anybody who's ever bought a "Trader Jack" base-

ball cap will attest, the man has a stadium-size ego. Listen to him talk, and note how many times he refers to the Padres. Then compare this to how many times he refers to himself. Himself wins by a 10-to-1 margin. He was never happy just being in the front office, because the glory there was never enough. No cameras in the front office. Your average workday is never on television.

He had managed Kansas City and Oakland in the mid-seventies, and many opposing managers (such as myself) considered him a joke. His 286–310 record during that time was only a little better than a joke. But when he had success in the front office—he is truly a good general manager—he got the idea that maybe he was being cheated as a manager. That maybe he needed more time as a manager. That maybe he should be both a manager and a general manager, where he'd be guaranteed that time because he couldn't fire himself. Turns out this is what he thought. A pity for those who disagreed.

Shortly after joining the Padres as their baseball boss in 1980, he tried to get the managing job that Frank Howard eventually took in 1981. Ballard Smith and the Krocs just laughed at him. So a couple of years later, with the team finally playing well, he'd decided to go after me.

The departure of Tolan and hiring of Dunlop was a first step. I considered Ballard's phone call a second step, though again I was unaware of it. Then McKeon took a third step, which, unfortunately, I learned about right away. At an otherwise nice off-day gathering late in that 1984 season, he apparently ordered Dunlop to confront Norma—why do they all talk to Norma instead of face to face with me?—and tell her that I should remove another of my lieutenants (and one of my best friends in the game), pitching coach Norm Sherry. Told her that Sherry wasn't doing me any good. Now, what kind of bullshit is that to be talking during the heat of a baseball season? Among other things, this organization had no idea how to run a pennant race.

Norma was sure Dunlop was speaking for Jack. After hearing the story, I was convinced of something else: everything I'd said in the clubhouse that season had gotten back to McKeon and Ballard via Dunlop. The man I'd suspected of being a spy was exactly that. And it was too late to do anything about it but hope.

Indeed, I had made mistakes in the clubhouse during the season. I'd wrongfully alienated some people and stumbled over protocol with other people. But it was all because I cared about nothing else but the San Diego Padres winning their first pennant. And sometimes it hurts to win. And for every Carmelo Martinez who hated me, a Tony Gwynn and a Goose Gossage and a Garry Templeton respected me. Didn't McKeon and Ballard see that? Wouldn't Dunlop ever report that? I hoped—even prayed—for that.

The race finally ended on September 20. We beat the San Francisco Giants 5–4 in the afternoon and then went to Goose Gossage's house and waited for Houston to lose to the Dodgers that night. They did, 6–2, putting us up 10½ games over the Astros with nine games to go. Finally, amid the tension and bad feelings and everything else that pops up during six months of devoting everything to victory, we were able to relax. And how. The party that night at Gossage's big place in east San Diego taught me a few interesting things about some of the people with this franchise.

Number one, Joan Kroc can get excited. She walked in that night and shouted, "Well, dammit! We did it, didn't we? Dammit!" Hmm, I thought, maybe this lady does know something about baseball. When the players started throwing people into Gossage's swimming pool, even Joan took a dive. Well, sort of. She walked into the water after announcing she was going to. No player had a contract guaranteed long enough to make it worth grabbing her.

The second thing I learned was that Jack McKeon is afraid of the water. As soon as the splashing started, he actually left the party and sat in his car. It was truly unusual behavior for someone who turned out to be a shark.

The final thing I learned was that Steve Garvey really is a god. No, he didn't walk on the water—damn, that would have made McKeon jealous—but he did the next best thing. He arrived with his girlfriend Judy Ross, who insiders know was the one he hurt worst with his paternity problems. He was wearing typical Garvey off-the-field wardrobe: perfectly pressed blue double-breasted suit with the works, including a handkerchief stuffed perfectly into his breast pocket. Of course, he was thrown in the pool. But unlike others, when he came out, he looked the same as before he went in. Not a hair out of place, not a piece of clothing rumpled. Even the handkerchief was still there. All told, it was quite a night.

While partying, I had this brilliant idea. I would spend the season's final series in Chicago scouting the National League East—winning Cubs against the Cardinals. I'd let Ozzie Virgil boss the Padres in their last regular games. Unfortunately, that last series was in Atlanta, so everyone thought I was a pussy and afraid to face the Braves fans. I only wish I'd realized that our last series would be against the Braves, but I get so involved in the season that I rarely look at our schedule more than a week ahead. Otherwise, I never would have gone to Chicago. I'd have gone down there and challenged the entire crowd—all four or five of them—to a fight, just to shut them up.

As it was, I was too busy wasting my time. I scouted the Cubs, I learned a lot . . . and then, when we stepped onto Wrigley Field on a sunny October Tuesday afternoon for Game One of the National League Championship Series, I realized none of it meant a damn thing. It was the first time the Cubs had been in a postseason game in 39 years. Their fans, the most devoted in baseball, had stuck with them—in spirit if not in body—all that time. Now they were prepared to do four decades' worth of partying in two days. Partying right in our faces.

That first game began with the public address system playing the rock song "Jump" by some group called Van Halen. People were dancing and swaying, and the old brick house was trembling. Cubs pitcher Rick Sutcliffe was running to the mound. And I was about to be sick. We had battled all this way, fighting beanballers and umpires and each other, and now it appeared we would finally be overcome by . . . hysteria?

That's certainly the way it looked, as we were set down in the top of the first inning. Then Chicago started their half with leadoff hitter Bob Dernier knocking one of Eric Show's first pitches over the outfield ivy for a homer. From there it got only louder, and worse, as the Cubs took out 39 years of frustration on one record-setting afternoon. Four of them hit home runs, including the pitcher, Sutcliffe. There were 11 other base hits. They scored 13 runs. All playoff records. We scored zero, which I guess is another playoff record.

Afterward I actually didn't feel so bad. I've been around long enough to know that if you have to get beat, this is the way. Quick and overwhelming and leaving no doubt that it was just the other team's day. You lose close, you wonder if you're good enough. You lose big, you figure the next day that score could be reversed. My team didn't quite understand this philosophy, and most of them left the visitors' tiny clubhouse that day with their heads spinning.

Turns out I was wrong. They were right. That big score wasn't a fluke. The next day, wacky Steve Trout held us to five hits in eight and a third innings, the Cubs scored four runs in the first four innings off Mark Thurmond, and we lost 4–2 in a game that wasn't nearly so close as the score made it look. Surely we were done. Us and the series. The best-of-five series—it was the last year for that format—was going to be won by the Cubs. They knew it, and we knew it.

Despite our fine season record, it was obvious that we'd finally charged in over our heads. All the fighting and inspired play wasn't going to beat these long-overdue Cubs. You can beat other ballplayers, but you can't beat destiny. I knew this better than most. Through all of our trials we'd finished the season winning just half of our final 56 games, and it showed. What had once felt like a champion now felt like a .500 team.

That's what we thought as we climbed aboard our charter plane bound for San Diego. Throughout the four-hour trip the team was quiet. If nothing else, I'd taught the dreamy Padres to be realists. So they knew. Only one team—the Milwaukee Brewers—had ever come back from a two-games-to-none deficit to win a five-game playoff series. The odds were hugely stacked against this happening with a team that had just been robbed of its jockstrap. They knew.

Joan Kroc walked around the airplane trying to cheer everyone up, but instead of encouragement it sounded like a eulogy. At least Joan's daughter, Linda, was honest about it. She sat up in first-class and fumed. By the time our plane landed in San Diego about 11 P.M., we were thoroughly bummed. Then imagine our hearts when we stepped into the airport's auxiliary terminal and there was nobody there to greet us. No fans, no banners, nothing. Heck, some teams have airport welcoming committees that even work during the regular season. Boston this wasn't.

Instead of riding from the airport back to the stadium, where most of their cars were parked, some players decided they couldn't face seeing our field until the next day. So they found other rides home. The rest of us took the bus and longed for bed. But something strange happened when we arrived at the stadium. A guard stepped in front of the bus and detoured us to another entrance. We drove there and saw why . . . there were a couple hundred people waiting for us. How nice. We climbed off the bus, and while some of us walked to the clubhouse, Goose Gossage and I climbed up on a roof and thanked the people for their support.

And then I heard a clubhouse guard shouting frantically, "Go to the other side of the stadium, go out the other door, you aren't going to believe what's over there!" Goose and I climbed down from the roof and ran down the concourse and walked out the exit by the parking lot where the players leave their cars . . . and holy Christ. There must have been 3,000 people there. People stuffed along the outside of a fence that surrounded our cars, all of them clapping and screaming, waving brown-and-yellow banners, doing all kinds of crazy things, but most of all just believing. Believing in us. Believing in a team on the verge of getting wiped out. Believing in a team that, a few minutes earlier, didn't know what to believe. Thousands of people in the middle of the fucking night. How wonderful.

Suddenly we believed too. Led by Garry Templeton, who wasn't used to anybody believing in him, we ran to the fence and slapped and shook these people's hands and pointed at the ones in the back. Templeton, in a gesture that would symbolize the weekend, backed off, grabbed a towel, and starting waving it above his head. I had to look twice to make sure this was really Templeton. He unleashed more emotion that night than in probably the rest of his entire career. Later Templeton went home and phoned all of the depressed players who had gone home straight from the airport. He told them what they had missed. He told them that because of this outpouring of faith, their fellow Padres now believed they could finish this series and not be embarrassed.

Indeed, as the rest of us finally left the park after midnight, steering our cars through the masses of fans, we all knew something very special had happened. I firmly believe this set the tone for what happened the next three days. Coming from a hardened baseball man like me, this sounds blasphemous, I know. But all you baseball fans who think you never directly affect a team or a game, you're wrong. That weekend you may just have won us a playoff.

When we took the San Diego Jack Murphy Stadium field the night after our return home, basking in a full house of over 58,000, we realized that the impromptu party had never ended. Templeton, for one, had simply replaced that towel with his cap. He ran to the foul line during the usually staid starting introductions and started waving that brown thing like it was a pom-pom. The crowd's roar grew to a level that I'd never experienced before. Turns out I hadn't heard anything yet.

That night, of course, the game was no contest. And the hero, of course, was Templeton. After the Cubs had taken a 1–0 lead off Ed Whitson, Templeton hit a two-run double in the fifth inning, which was all we needed. Whitson held the Cubs to five hits over eight innings, and we won 7–1.

It's funny how performing so well in a big game can alter a man's career. Whitson had never won more than 14 games a year, and only once finished with an ERA under 3.24. But because of that one fine game, the next season George Steinbrenner's New York Yankees signed him to a multimillion-dollar contract. This October, see which "minor" character steals the show—one of them always does—and then see what riches fall upon that guy. Ironically, in a season of so many games, sometimes all it takes is one.

Our roll continued. The next night, Game Four of the playoffs, was quite simply the best playoff game I have ever witnessed, period. I'll describe it to you in two words, in case you're one of the few to have forgotten it: Steve Garvey. Much as I felt he was never a team leader, on the most important night in Padres history he controlled nine innings of baseball like few other hitters in the history of the game. Maybe Reggie Jackson with the New York Yankees did as much in Game Six of the 1977 World Series. Maybe.

Garvey entered this game having little effect on our pennant race. He hadn't hit a homer since August 15 and had a career low of only eight homers total. So you can imagine my surprise when, in the third inning, his two-out double scored Alan Wiggins to give us a 2–0 lead. After the Cubs scored three runs off Tim Lollar, his two-out single in the fifth inning scored Tim Flannery to tie it at 3–all. And then in the seventh inning his two-out single scored Bobby Brown to give us a 4–3 lead that we later increased to 5–3. Garvey was out of his mind, and we were out of our minds just watching it.

This is where I thought the game should have ended. Up to the ninth inning everything was unforgettably sweet, but what followed has left more than a trace of bitterness in my recollection. Because we never should have needed any more of Steve Garvey's phenomenal bat that night. But fundamentals. Damn fundamentals. The Cubs tied the game back up at 5–all in the top of the eighth against Goose Gossage on a Ryne Sandberg infield single, a stolen base, an RBI single by Keith Moreland, and then, horror of horrors, a two-out RBI double by Jody Davis. Base hits with two out against my pitchers are as pleasant as ripping off a hangnail. With just a little care, such pain could easily be prevented.

Oh, well. I guess somebody had to set up one of baseball's greatest playoff moments. With the score tied and one out in the ninth and Cubs reliever Lee Smith on the mound, Tony Gwynn reached out and poked a fastball into center field for a single. Up stepped Garvey. The crowd rose to its feet. Hell, even I rose to my feet, although I was sure I'd soon be sitting down. After all, a guy who hadn't been a hero for a couple of months couldn't cram so many heroics into one night. He'd already done his part. Now the law of averages would take over and we'd see a double play grounder.

There was no way Garvey could pull us out of the fire once more, and—BOOM!—my thoughts were interrupted by the loudest crack I had ever heard. All those people stomping around on their feet, and I still heard the crack. Then I saw the white ball heading toward the right center field fence, sailing, sailing . . . up against the right field fence leaped Henry Cotto, the Cubs' right fielder, leaping, leaping . . . he seemed so small and the ball seemed so high and . . . shit, it really was going out of the ballpark, wasn't it? It was! After what felt like forever, in what seemed like slow motion, the ball dropped into the stands and Garvey had his homer.

Oh my God. I ran onto the field behind my players, most of whom had leaped to the field as soon as the ball was hit. So this is what it feels like, I thought. So this is how Bobby

Thomson's teammates must have felt. That was my thought for the few seconds it took Garvey to glide around the bases. And then I forgot everything, forgot all dignity, forgot that this win had only tied the series, and forgot that I was supposed to be a tough guy manager. I dodged around several players until I finally got to Garvey, and, by God, I actually hugged him. And I kept hugging. And somebody snapped a picture. Go ahead, I thought, ruin my image. I was keeping this home run forever.

By God, I thought, sometimes all of baseball's bullshit can be worth it. Sometimes your wins really are perfect, with no strings, with nothing but feelings you haven't had since you were a child. Sometimes this game really can be beautiful.

The next afternoon the fifth and deciding game was almost anticlimactic. Sure, the Cubs led 3–0 after five innings with Sutcliffe pitching. But corny as it sounds, our bodies and minds were still flushed and stinging with success, and we all knew we'd figure a way. Sure enough, after we closed the gap to 3–2 in the sixth inning on back-to-back sacrifice flies by Graig Nettles and Terry Kennedy, out of nowhere we were visited by an old friend of mine from Oakland, where he'd gone after living in Boston. This old friend must have figured that once again my team had done all it could and now it was his turn. Even if he did have to walk over sheepishly from the Cubs dugout.

Surely you remember Destiny. Suddenly he was in our dugout. Carmelo Martinez opened the seventh by walking on four pitches from Sutcliffe, who some say was tiring, but how can you be tired with a pennant on the line? Like Cubs manager Jim Frey, I too would have left Sutcliffe in. Templeton bunted Martinez to second, another rather innocent play but one that set up the shot heard 'round Mission Bay. Well, okay, it wasn't really a shot, but it sounded as good. It was a simple grounder off the bat of Tim Flannery that rolled toward first baseman Leon Durham . . . and between his legs, scoring Martinez with the tying run.

Poor Durham. If I'd been his manager, I never would

have said a word to him. A grounder between the legs is a physical mistake over which a fielder has absolutely no control. If Durham was good enough to help the Cubs get that far, then he was good enough to do everything right to catch that grounder. I'm telling you, this game was not decided on a grounder, or because of Leon Durham's glove. That grounder was 95 feet worth of destiny.

While most of San Diego remembers that play as the key to the inning, I prefer to remember two batters later, after Alan Wiggins had singled Flannery to third. Up stepped Tony Gwynn, and down to second base went an inning-ending double play grounder. Except the ball took a crazy hop over the head of maybe the best-fielding second baseman to ever play the game, Ryne Sandberg. Talk about a fluke. This play was much more important, and unpredictable, than a grounder underneath a poor first baseman. The hit scored both Flannery and Wiggins with the go-ahead runs, and then Gwynn scored from second on a Garvey single to give us our eventual 6–3 victory.

So big deal if we won the pennant on a boot and a bad hop. How many games had this franchise *lost* like that? The celebration afterward was as sweet as if Garvey had hit that homer again. We danced on the field and then crowded our suddenly too-small clubhouse and lost ourselves in the champagne and disbelief. This little team from this little town had earned the right to play the best team in baseball, the Detroit Tigers, on a national stage onto which few of them had ever stepped.

The celebration began as perhaps the happiest moment of my life. I looked into the outfield stands and felt that somewhere among those people the spirit of Ray Kroc was watching. That spirit of accepting nothing less than your best had surged through the team. The previous spring we had dedicated this season to him, even wearing his initials, RAK, on our sleeves. Then we'd spent six months putting our hearts out there next to those initials. That was our real dedication.

The title celebration ended, however, with me feeling like the end of my life here was approaching. I guess Dick Williams can never just be totally happy for more than an hour at a time. I guess it's not allowed. While celebrating, Norma and I were inadvertently missing the real celebration. After the champagne was drained, I had dressed and left the clubhouse, curious that I hadn't seen any front office people. I met Norma in the parking lot, where she was futilely looking for some front office wives. We finally drove home with some other friends, figuring we'd find out where everybody was in the morning.

We found out, all right. They were all at an impromptu stadium club party, an event we hadn't been told about, probably by accident because it was planned at the last minute. But accidents like that shouldn't happen to the winning manager, should they? At least one person at this party thought the winning manager was the wrong man. Carol McKeon, Jack's wife, had apparently been drinking when she entered the party, and after a few more pops she made some statements that were heard and repeated to us by Bobby Tolan's wife, Marian.

"Why couldn't Jack have been the manager of this team?" Carol asked out loud, according to Marian's recollection. "It's not fair. That should be Jack down there on the field." Then she added, in direct reference to Norma's wardrobe and automobile, "I'd like a fur coat and Mercedes too." Carol's daughter, Kristi, tried to shut her up. She couldn't.

I entered the World Series finally certain that Jack wanted my job and would stop at nothing to get it. Suddenly I was just hoping to get through San Diego's finest baseball moment before I quit. I knew it wouldn't be as much fun as my other World Series, mostly because I wouldn't be able to see much of the games. After hearing about Mrs. McKeon's remarks, I figured I'd have to spend at least half the time watching my back.

And indeed, the Series was no party. I don't know if the

Cubs could have done any better against the Tigers, but they sure couldn't have done any worse. In a nutshell, the Tigers beat the shit out of us.

Some may point to the broken wrist suffered by our center fielder Kevin McReynolds in Game Four of the National League Championship Series. Without him, experts said, we were doomed. Wrong. McReynolds is very talented, but he goes at just one gait. He's not a big game player, because he doesn't put out big game effort. He may have done okay in the World Series, but he wouldn't have made the difference. Just not enough fire.

McReynolds knew I felt this way about him, and the next year he publicly called me "Mr. Macho" and a "front-runner." What could I say? He was right. I translated the first description as somebody who likes players who are tough and the second description as somebody who likes players who are winners. That's me.

Seeing as how McReynolds's comments didn't faze me, his mother once put a letter in my hotel mailbox in Houston. She said she wrote the letter on her hotel bathroom floor at 2 A.M. praying for my soul because I was so tough on her son. I think she has that backward. Her son, by not playing to his capabilities, was being tough on me. I'll never forget how, in 1985, he played with no pressure in 152 games and still hit just 15 homers with 75 RBIs and had a .234 batting average.

But back to the 1984 World Series. For just a minute. The first game, in San Diego, was a killer not because we lost, which was expected, but because of how we lost. More fundamentals. And not through my regulars but my reserves, which really upset me because those are the guys who need to know fundamentals better than anybody. By the time those guys enter the game, usually in the late innings as pinch hitters or pinch runners, one mistake can cost us a game. In this case, it was two mistakes, both by reserves forced into the starting lineup because of circumstance.

After Larry Herndon's two-run homer off Mark Thurmond in the fifth inning had given the Tigers a 3–2 lead, we began the sixth with singles by Graig Nettles and Terry Kennedy off seemingly unhittable Tigers starter Jack Morris. Up stepped Bobby Brown, filling in for the injured McReynolds in center field. Since we needed to take advantage of every baserunner against this guy, Brown's job was plain: lay down a bunt and move the guys to second and third. Just hit the ball 20 feet. Pull a Jim Lonborg. But Brown was unprepared. He couldn't get the bat out and down. Couldn't execute. The bunt attempt failed, and he wound up striking out to blow our best chance. Traditionally, my teams have either laughed or grumbled when I've spent an hour every spring making them lay down bunts. As the personable Brown came back to the bench, he was neither laughing nor grumbling. He was simply devastated.

The next inning, with the score still the same, Kurt Bevacqua, playing the American League position of designated hitter for us, led off with a double. With none out, he was in a perfect position to score on a bunt and a fly ball and put us back in this thing. Except Bevacqua, who rarely sees things the way other people do, didn't see it that way. He didn't stop at a double. He rounded second and headed for third and was easily thrown out trying to stretch it to a triple. I wasn't too upset. He only broke virtually every baserunning rule known to civilized man. But as he trudged into the dugout, having ended our last chance in an eventual 3–2 loss, I said nothing. Hell, the guy played so little during the regular season that he probably didn't know where third base was. And besides, at this stage of the season either you have the capability to win or you don't. Having watched fundamental mistakes like these, I walked away from Game One thinking that we didn't have that capability.

But in Game Two, trailing 3–2 in the fifth inning, one of our reserves hit a three-run homer and celebrated by blowing kisses to the fans and pumping his white gloves into

the air. We won 5 – 3 to even the Series up. The player? Kurt
Bevacqua. Ain't the World Series great?

Bevacqua really wasn't too smart, though, as the home
run confirmed. What the hell was he doing dancing on the
field in front of the best team in baseball? Why was he trying
to rub their noses in it? I led my team onto the field in Detroit two days later, worried that we had aroused a jungleful
of sleeping tigers.

Soon my fears were erased. The Tigers didn't even need
to wake up. In Game Three they beat us in their sleep. My
three pitchers walked 11 batters to tie a Series record and
turn this thing into an absolute joke, giving us a 5 – 2 loss.
Eleven walks! I've managed hundreds of spring training games
where there weren't 11 walks. I've rarely had nightmares that
involved 11 walks. At this point I honestly wondered if my
season-long methods had backfired. I wondered if, for the
first time, my players weren't trying to show me up by doing
horseshit.

Then I realized who one of my three offending pitchers
was. A guy named Greg Booker. You've probably heard all
about how he wouldn't have been on the Padres if he hadn't
been married to Jack McKeon's daughter, Kristi. This is true.
He isn't really a major leaguer. I could easily have cut him
but didn't, because as a 10th pitcher he wouldn't hurt us much
anyway. Jack wanted him, Jack got him.

But what you may not have heard about Booker is that
he cares as much as anybody who's ever played for me. He
works his butt off and hates to lose and rips himself when he
does lose. He walked four guys in his one inning in Game
Three, and I knew it wasn't for lack of effort. I knew he
must have gone back to his Detroit hotel that night thankful
that he didn't own a gun. With Booker out there, I know my
players were trying in Game Three. But it also was becoming
painfully obvious that, like Booker, we just weren't good
enough.

At least after Game Three, though, I had fun. Norma
and I attended a professional wrestling match at Cobo Arena,

followed by a party at a Greek restaurant with wrestlers Dick Murdoch, Adrian Adonis, and Barry Windham. One of the Greek belly dancers put a veil on my head, and the wrestlers ate and drank like hell, and we all had a good time. I was simply trying to enjoy myself during a World Series, which I'd finally learned was important after all these years.

The next day my starter Eric Show acted like he had spent the night belly dancing. He allowed four runs in two and two-thirds innings, which was actually our second-best starting pitching performance of the Series. However, it wasn't nearly good enough to stop the Tigers, who won 4−2 and entered Game Five figuring they could win the best-of-seven Series right there. And they were right. This time my starter Mark Thurmond couldn't get out of the first inning and allowed three runs, including two on a homer by Kirk Gibson. We fought back to tie it 3−all in the fourth, then they moved ahead 4−3 on Gibson's greatest play of the day.

No, I'm not talking about his eighth-inning home run. Purists will remember more clearly what happened in the fifth inning. Gibson led off with a single, moved to third base two walks later, and then scored on a sacrifice fly . . . to the second baseman. That's right, in what may have been one of the first "sacrifice popups" in Series history, he hustled home after Wiggins caught the ball behind second base. That gave the Tigers a 4−3 lead they later turned into an 8−4 win and the world championship with Gibson's three-run homer in the eighth. That homer happened, of course, after I changed my mind and allowed Gossage to pitch to Gibson with first base open.

Like I said earlier, I'd do it again. I know I signaled for an intentional walk, but then I saw Gossage yelling at me from the mound. He's a pro, and he doesn't yell for just any reason, so I ran out there to hear him better. And if only you could have heard him. He damn near begged me to let him pitch to Gibson. "I can get him out, Dick," he kept saying, "I can get him out."

What he was really saying was "Don't make me give in."

As a manager who had spent his entire life trying not to give in, the plea struck me to the heart. And even after Gibson hit Gossage's second pitch deep to clinch the game, I stuck by my decision. In the dugout Gossage apologized to me, but for once in my career I refused to accept it. No apology was needed from anybody. I've always managed this game hoping that my best pitcher can challenge the other team's best hitter in the game's most high pressure situation. He had challenged Gibson, he had given it his best, and no matter what Gibson did, Gossage's effort wasn't going to be diminished. Even this being the World Series wasn't going to change that.

So we'd lost the Series four games to one. But at least, we didn't have time to stew over it. Right away, while most of us were still wet from the shower, we were hustled outside to our buses. I couldn't figure out why until we saw the streets around Tiger Stadium. They were, quite simply, on fire. People were throwing bricks through windows, overturning cars. I smelled smoke and, I swear, burning flesh. I didn't stick around to smell or see any more. I jumped on the bus and our driver climbed in and we were all set to leave, except for one teeny problem.

The hoodlums using the Tigers victory to start what became an infamous riot didn't want us to leave. They surrounded the bus and began rocking it back and forth, back and forth. We heard several loud bangs and saw several dark spots bouncing off the windows and realized the thugs were throwing rocks at the bus. My first thought was, Some of those guys have better control than my starting pitchers. My second thought was, We're dead. We got down on our hands and knees between the bus seats, and the constant rocking damn near made us sick. Finally the cops showed up—another five minutes and it would have been too late—and escorted us to another bus, which was then escorted out to the highway.

Most of us had finished wetting our pants when we finally climbed on our plane and headed for home. And it was then

I decided, This is it, I quit. It was bad enough to nearly lose my life shortly after my team, on the field, had lost its life. It was bad enough having to endure a season of conflicts and craziness. But here, sitting on the plane, looking at Jack McKeon and Ballard Smith sitting nearby, I wondered, Why am I killing myself? If they want my job even when I win, is this job really worth having? I told a couple of people sitting nearby that I was thinking about quitting, and before I knew it Ballard Smith had cornered Norma and was begging her to talk me out of it. The entire flight home he begged her— obviously just to avoid the bad publicity my resignation would have.

The next morning I woke up to another beautiful San Diego day, with a nice parade planned for that night, with the knowledge that the Padres had just set a home attendance record (1,983,904) and would probably set one the following year. It felt so good to know the fans had never given up on me, no matter what my bosses were doing. So I decided there was no reason to quit now. No reason to stop doing something that still could make me feel this good. And it had been so much fun watching Ballard beg. Fetch, beg . . . maybe if I stuck around I'd see him roll over and play dead.

So yes, I was staying. And no, I've never made a bigger mistake.

No sooner did I begin my winter-long schedule of appearances and speeches and banquets honoring the Padres than McKeon fired my pitching coach Norm Sherry. When I demanded a reason, he told me Sherry had won a workman's compensation decision from his former employers, the Montreal Expos, something about an untreated heart problem. McKeon claimed that the league's ownership suddenly considered it bad business to be with the guy. Bad business, right. I guess that's why, in 1989, Sherry ended up in the World Series with the San Francisco Giants. McKeon thought it was bad business to have Dick Williams's supporters in the clubhouse.

So McKeon had stripped me of Bobby Tolan and Norm Sherry and had added Harry "Mata Hari" Dunlop. I felt like I was being asked to manage in a straitjacket. I entered the 1985 season with one eye upstairs and one eye on my back. Believe it or not, we still got off to a pretty good start. McKeon traded for Chicago White Sox star pitcher LaMarr Hoyt, which helped, and almost signed Cubs free agent pitcher Sutcliffe, who may have just given us the pennant that year and completely changed this chapter.

But, alas, while entertaining Sutcliffe during the mandatory La Jolla wine-and-thin-breadsticks dinner, Joan Kroc shot her mouth off. Not that she said anything bad, she just didn't shut up. She talked with Sutcliffe from soup to nuts, which didn't give him much chance to ask questions of anyone else. It was halfway through dinner, just before the 17 waiters brought us little hot towels for wiping the spittle from the corners of our mouths. McKeon turned to Norma, who at the time was wondering whether he was going to eat his poultry with his fork or his hands—a common speculation among McKeon's dining companions. "Damn it," McKeon whispered to Norma. "All the work I've done trying to sign this guy, and she's going to blow it for me." McKeon was always nice to Mrs. Kroc to her face, but behind her back he always called her "the old lady."

About the minute dinner ended, Sutcliffe returned to the Chicago Cubs and stayed there. But regardless, we still played well in the first half of 1985, thanks to good hitting from Gwynn, Garvey, and Martinez and good pitching from Hoyt. We actually played well enough for me to dust off some of my old-time agitation and put it to work the Friday before the All-Star game.

We were in St. Louis, and Hoyt was facing the Cardinals' Joaquin Andujar. He was having a hell of a first half and would have been certain to start the 1985 All-Star game in Minneapolis, except one person had done even better—Andujar. This all mattered to me because, as the pennant-winning manager the previous year, I would choose that starter.

Hmm, I thought before that Friday night game. Hoyt versus Andujar, huh? What a good time to stir up a little shit, and maybe get the Cardinals off balance. So I made an announcement: "Whichever starting pitcher throws better in this game will start the All-Star game."

Yeah, I know, it was a bullshit announcement. Andujar deserved to be the starter and probably would have been chosen no matter what happened. I just wanted to get this testy player from the Dominican Republic a little upset, maybe give us a little edge. Well, "a little edge" is putting it mildly. Andujar went crazy and refused to pitch in any All-Star game, period. His team went crazy trying to beat Hoyt, and my guy threw a shutout. We won the game 2 – 0, and Hoyt started in Minneapolis because Andujar wouldn't show up.

I was so involved in the 1985 season that I'd put aside my worries about the front office and believed again that winning would solve everything. At the All-Star break we were 49 – 39, in second place, just one-half game behind the first-place Dodgers. Not bad for a team that everyone first said would become fat and complacent, and then said would kill its manager and each other before winning another pennant. We had survived that June disturbance with Wiggins. We had survived McReynolds ripping my ass more than he ripped at the ball. Having learned the value of winning, it appeared, my players were no longer afraid of paying any price.

For a moment I really believed that my San Diego story would have a happy ending. Once again the moment was shattered by McKeon. This time, perhaps worried that things were going so well, he began a chain of events that would finish the job he'd started earlier.

McKeon began the final act of killing me by starvation. We needed another pitcher to carry us through August and September, yet he wouldn't get one—this man known throughout baseball for his ability to wheel and deal players. A number of decent arms crossed the waiver wires, yet he ignored them. Pittsburgh star John Candelaria was available, I remember it distinctly, but McKeon wouldn't give up the prospects needed to acquire him. So Candelaria went up the road to play for the Angels. And we went down the toilet. This is when "Trader Jack"—the emblem he places on all that merchandise he shamelessly peddles—became "Traitor Jack." That's what I call him today. Just be sure and spell it right.

With no pitching, we sank lower and lower and finally fell apart in late August and finished the year 83–79, in third place, six games behind Cincinnati and 12 games behind the Dodgers. I couldn't believe McKeon would sacrifice the good of a franchise for himself. I couldn't believe anybody would do that.

What happened next, you may find hard to believe. This is why I would like to lay it out step by step. Because of a vow of silence that I will explain later, I haven't talked publicly about any of this until now. Therefore I want to do it carefully, so that everyone will not only know the truth but understand it.

BALLARD'S OFFICE

Shortly after the end of the 1985 season I was talking with McKeon and Ballard Smith in Ballard's office—the office where he can open and shut the door by pressing a button under his desk. (The ultimate power broker.) I'd come there to see about a contract extension because I had just one year left. I was working my way up to that request when, out of the clear blue, Smith said, "Dick, if you don't want to come back for the last year of your contract, I'll pay you off."

My jaw dropped. Instinctively I began tugging at my National League championship ring. The damn thing was still new, and here was the club president virtually asking me to quit. Talk about a sucker punch.

"What the hell are you talking about?" I asked him. "Hell no, I don't want to quit."

After I left his office and drove home, I became even madder. The more I thought, the madder I got, until I finally couldn't believe what I'd heard. So I phoned McKeon to double-check this. At this point I still wanted to trust him.

"Did Ballard really say what I thought he said?" I asked McKeon.

"Yes, he did," McKeon replied, sounding strangely distant.

That did it. I'd heard enough. "If that's the way he really feels, who knows—I might take him up on it!" I shouted. "I'm going to call him right now and find out."

I reached Ballard on his car phone and asked him to repeat his original statement. He sounded nervous, like he'd just driven that car to the edge of a cliff. He told me he would discuss the offer when I returned from a Caribbean cruise scheduled to begin in a couple of days. I hung up on him. You bet your ass we would discuss it.

THE CRUISE

Ah, the wonderful Caribbean, a free cruise sponsored by my Miller Lite beer people; no telephone, no mail, no worries . . . but no power to control the demolition of my San Diego career.

While we were relaxing in the sun, Jack McKeon was home on the phone, ringing up my right-hand man Ozzie Virgil in Venezuela, giving him a little news. According to Ozzie, the phone call went like this.

"Ozzie, we're not going to renew you next year," McKeon said to the one man I trust more than anyone in this game.

"You mean I have no job?" Ozzie asked. "What about everybody else?"

"That's right, you have no job," McKeon said. "But other than that, I don't know what is happening."

"What do you mean, you don't know what's happening?" Ozzie replied.

Ozzie then felt this was his first clue that McKeon was executing his plan to force me out. When Virgil finally reached me upon my return to the United States a week later, I was furious. I made him repeat the news to me again, just to make sure I was hearing right. And I could only agree with Ozzie. The man I'd once trusted, running the organization I still loved, was sticking me with a cold knife.

My House

Considering the level of my anger, it was good that the next move came quickly, and not from me. Word of Ozzie's firing finally reached the newspapers, complete with speculation that this was part of a ploy to fire me. Joan Kroc read this and, incredibly, like everything else that was happening, stated that she had no idea what was happening. The owner of the club had no clue that her president and her general manager were fixing to fire the manager.

She was stunned. First thing, she called Ozzie in Venezuela and offered him his job back. One problem. Being one of the top coaches in baseball, Ozzie had already landed another job, coaching third base with the San Francisco Giants. Joan told Ozzie not to worry about that, and one phone call later she fixed it with the Giants so that Ozzie would return to San Diego, making his two-week Giants stay his shortest stop in baseball.

Now Joan felt she had to take care of me. So she came out in the newspaper and said that if Ballard and Jack wanted to buy me out, they'd have to do it with their own money, that she wanted no part of it. Then she phoned me and asked if she could stop by my house. Of course, rich ladies like Joan Kroc never just stop by the house. So up pulled her car with her chauffeur. While the chauffeur parked the car across the street and stayed there, Joan came inside and we began to talk.

Suddenly the conversation was interrupted by the doorbell. I glanced out the window. Shit. There was a reporter at the door, and several more milling around in the street. They'd come to see me about all this job controversy, with no knowledge that Joan was there. As Norma opened the door, Joan flattened herself against a wall and held her breath. Norma shooed the reporter away. Joan relaxed and giggled, and our conversation continued.

"Dick," she said, "I'm very sorry about what happened. You turned this franchise around. I was going to sell it after last season, but you brought us the pennant, and it's never been more valuable or more loved in the community. So I had to keep it. I suppose I should be mad at you for that, but I'm just grateful. And I don't want you to leave."

Then she said something that I can still hear: "Dick, if you want me to fire Jack McKeon, I will. He has always wanted to manage. He has always pushed for doing both jobs, manager and general manager. Even though Ray never thought one man could do both jobs, and Jack knew this, still he's always pushed. Because of this I have decided that as long as I'm the owner of this team, Jack McKeon will never be down on that field. Never. If you want him fired, he's fired."

She caught her breath and continued. "If you also want me to fire Ballard, I will," she said. "I know, he's my own son-in-law, but he's a liar. He's lied to me before and will lie to me again. If you want him gone, he's gone."

I was so surprised that my heart was racing. This lady had just walked into my living room and hit a ninth-inning homer. She'd confirmed all my suspicions and let me know where her loyalties lay: with me. Suddenly I had what I wanted. I didn't need anybody fired.

"Don't take anybody's job over this," I said. "It's just that I need Ozzie. Without Ozzie watching my back downstairs, this kind of thing will continue all next season."

"Fine," she said. "We'll meet at my house and clear all this up." She paused. "You know, none of this would have happened if Ray were still alive. Those people wouldn't try to step on Ray."

As Joan rose to leave, the phone rang. The voice on the other end sounded close, and with good reason. It was her chauffeur, calling from her car across the street. He said there were so many media people outside that if she didn't want anyone to know about her visit, she'd better stay put.

"Oh no," Joan said. "What am I going to do?" I got this idea. I'd pull my van out of my garage and drive away and all the media would follow me. Then Joan could run to her car.

But Joan was still worried that they might not fall for the decoy and that she'd still be seen. "Wait, wait," Norma said, jingling the keys to her car, which was safely hidden in our garage. "Let Dick go, and then you go with me."

And that is how it happened that Joan Kroc exited our house on the floor of the backseat of a car, covering her face and giggling while Norma drove out of the garage. "Shut up," Norma remembers saying to Joan. "You're making me laugh, and somebody's going to suspect something. Just shut up and stay down."

Although all the media had fallen for our fake, Joan stayed down for the entire five-minute drive to the Hotel Del Coronado, where her chauffeur had driven and was waiting for her. Just another billionaire with the shakes in America's Finest City.

Joan's House

The meeting there, several days after Joan's visit, was short and tense. As I was going into her house, carpenters on a nearby roof recognized me and sensed something was up. Working people know about other working people. They yelled, "Give 'em hell, Dick!" I smiled. When I walked inside, an awaiting McKeon looked like he had a stogie stuck up his ass. I already had given them hell.

Right away Joan told Ballard and Jack that I was going to be back. She said, "You want Ozzie back, right?" I said yes. She said, "You want anybody gone?" I said, "Get rid of Dunlop." She said, "Fine, that's the way it will be." End of meeting. Jack never even belched.

That afternoon Ballard Smith held a press conference but invited none of us, and for good reason. The big announcement was this: the manager who had led this team to its first pennant, who had increased attendance by nearly 50 percent, and who still had one year left on his contract, was not going to be fired. I'm no journalist, but this was news? Just another public covering of an ass in America's Finest City.

The Phone Call

A couple of months later, and two days before the start of spring training, after not hearing a word about my problems since that press conference, we received a phone call from Joan Kroc. Norma picked up.

"Norma," Joan said, "I've been thinking. Does Dick drink a lot?"

Norma nearly fell off her chair. She told Joan what she'd told Ballard in his rude phone call more than a year and a half before, that she rarely saw me drink. Norma said it softly, because she knew what was coming next.

"Norma," Joan said, "we don't want another Billy Martin on our hands."

Before Norma could respond, Joan asked, "Norma, does Dick really want to manage?" With her face red, Norma muttered, "Ask him." And then handed me the phone.

What could I say? My reputation with Joan had obviously turned from solid to shambles in the span of two months, and now my unshakable pride was starting to teeter. What could possibly have changed her mind so drastically in 60 days? That's the real question here, one I'll never be able to answer. But I knew this: I couldn't spend the next season monitoring everything Ballard and Jack told Joan. If they could do this much damage to me in two winter months, if they could completely change Joan's mind without me even managing a single game during that time, I didn't stand a chance once the season started.

"Hell, Joan," I told her. "The way I've been treated this winter, I guess I really shouldn't want to manage, should I?"

That crack in the wall of my pride was all she needed. "Fine, Dick," she said. "I'll have a plane waiting for you tomorrow. You're coming to see me in Palm Springs."

And she hung up before I could mention to her that,

hey, spring training was in two days! We already had our room reservations in Yuma! We'd already stopped our newspapers and ordered our mail held in Coronado! Norma was already beginning to pack, for pete's sake. What about team continuity? What about the fans?

If Joan is going to can me, I thought, then this is certainly a hell of a time to do it.

The End

We climbed aboard Joan's Lear jet, Norma and I and one of Kroc's lawyers, this businesslike-looking woman named Beth Benes. Dark hair, dark eyes, weird smile. I heard recently that her picture and biography have been put in the Padres media guide and that she was being touted as a top adviser to the club. Problem is, I don't think Beth Benes knows a wild pitch from a wild hair. On second thought, I guess she'd be perfect for their media guide.

We arrived at Joan's lush Palm Springs house, and the rules had already been made. "Dick, we're going to buy out your contract," Joan said in a friendly manner, as if she really believed she was doing me a favor. She then picked up the phone and made a long distance call to Australia.

She handed me the receiver. On the other end was Ballard Smith. Don't ask me what the hell he was doing in Australia at the start of spring training.

Ballard said, "Dick, we're going to buy out your contract."

I thought, Now, where have I heard that before? What are these two doing, firing me in stereo? I said nothing.

I put down the phone, and Joan spoke again. "We will pay you your final year's salary on one main condition," she said. "You have to make it look like it was your decision to leave. You have to bow out."

Before I could say a word, tough Norma lashed out. "No," she said, her voice cracking. "It has to be mutual agreement. You can't do this to Dick." Suddenly Joan looked cold. "If we don't do it this way, we don't do it at all," she said. Now it was Norma's turn: "Then fine. Dick will go to spring training."

Joan turned white. "Uh, no, we can't do that. We'll work something out," she said, pointing to her woman Benes. But as we found out too late, Benes never did anything. The announcement still made it seem like my fault.

Later we discovered another stipulation in the separation agreement, a clause saying I couldn't talk about what happened for one calendar year. Gee, I thought, the Padres must be really proud of this. I called my brother-in-law Bill Allen, who is a lawyer. We concluded that if I didn't follow the conditions, they would just fire me anyway and I might have trouble getting the $240,000 owed me for my final year. I decided to suck it up. I told Norma we had no choice. She was so mad she couldn't speak. Joan looked distant, like she was unable to feel. I stared at her and said, "You got your wish, Joan."

Joan said, "We'll meet at the stadium tomorrow and make the announcement then."

I protested. "But spring training starts in Yuma tomorrow! Everybody's waiting for me in Yuma! If you're going to screw the fans and players, at least have the guts to do it in front of them."

Joan, acting like she never heard me, repeated, "We'll meet at the ballpark."

This day had one final nasty exchange remaining. On the plane ride back, Beth Benes turned to Norma and said, "I bet you have a huge load off your shoulders."

"What did you mean by that?" Norma snapped.

"Fuck you, Beth," I whispered under my breath, speaking for all the San Diego fans who have been stepped on by the power brokers.

• • •

I don't remember much about making the actual announcement. It lasted 10 seconds or so. Mostly I remember that, in the eyes of the public, Dick Williams picked the first day of spring training to quit. Dick Williams waited all winter knowing he would be quitting, and then finally announced it when the team was ready to play, when it would be too late to get another good manager. Dick Williams was an asshole.

That's how it looked. And that's why it hurt. Because not only were those statements wrong, but they hurt everything I loved, mainly the San Diego fans. I loved their loyalty in the face of losing, their bravery in the face of annual ridicule. I loved them on opening nights, on August afternoons, and during impromptu pep rallies at midnight.

I tried to give the San Diego fans every ounce of me. I tried to give them that competitive urge inside of me that makes me want to kill somebody for not caring as much as I do, and kiss somebody for caring more. I wanted to show them that every night when they put down their money to watch their Padres, they need not worry. The investment was good. In my sweat and through my screams and every other bit of my insides I put into this job, their investment paid off. In short, I tried to be the manager Ray Kroc had hired.

I know I caused some trouble. I wasn't always the nicest manager to watch. But I knew no other way, and because we won, I think the San Diego fans understood. I know Ray Kroc would have understood.

The Padres front office certainly didn't. In return for giving up my entire soul, I was conned by an owner's son-in-law with no guts, who was conned by a fat man with a cigar and a secret agenda.

The son-in-law is no longer related to Kroc and is now removed from the daily operation of the franchise. The fat man, however, is now running the whole show. As of opening day, 1990, Jack McKeon had his manager's uniform. After eliminating me, his agenda cost my successors Steve Boros and Larry Bowa their jobs too. But he finally got that uniform. In doing so, he never had to give up his general manager's desk. Finally he has fulfilled his dream of having both jobs at once.

And that's good. I'm glad for you, Jack. I'm gone, you win. Just a bit of advice, if I may. Most of the people in the

Padres organization are good people, Jack. The ones who don't already have your footprints on their backs, go easy on them, okay? Maybe for once you could step around somebody. They deserve better.

And about the fans, Jack. They're believing in you these days. They love the cigar, they love the shtick. You do a pretty good shtick, I've got to admit. That live radio talk show you host at the stadium each winter, people eat it up.

So one favor, please. Don't let those good folks see the real you. Don't let them hear you whisper behind their backs, as you often do, about what idiots you think they are. Don't act like you're being nice to them when you're really laughing at them for not being as smart or devious as you. And when they come to the park to watch you, Jack, be a pro. Don't let them see you fall asleep on the bench during games and forget to make important pitching changes or defensive maneuvers. I saw this happen in 1989, when the Padres should have won the division. Treat the people better than that, Jack. Give the best fans in the world credit for more intelligence.

(Jack, I know the media will ask for your comments on my words, and I expect a denial—why should you change now? But whatever your comments, I sure feel a weight lifted off my shoulders.)

Funny how I still talk about them as if they were my fans. As if San Diego was my town. As if I was still living that dream. Sorry. Force of habit. I'll get over it one of these years.

MAN OVERBOARD

The sting of getting fired from the San Diego Padres lasted about three months. At that time it was finally replaced by a sting in my bladder.

A bit of explanation: It was May 1986, less than three months after I got dumped by the Padres. I was in Denver being interviewed by George Argyros, owner of the Seattle Mariners, and his president, Chuck Armstrong. They were talking about making me the next manager, just as soon as they fired Chuck Cottier. For me, a man looking for a quick way to erase some bad memories, it was exciting news. Too exciting, in fact.

After the interview George, a self-made southern California millionaire who became rich in real estate and airplanes, offered to fly me back to my southern California home on his Lear jet. Fine, I said, figuring that I could use the extra time with my future boss to learn more about him. As we were boarding the jet, some of his assistants were laughing and telling everyone to be sure and go the bathroom before we left. I laughed too, although I didn't quite understand why.

Then we got up into the air, and I felt an urge to relieve some bodily pressure from my excitement. I turned around in my seat and glanced toward the back of the plane, and suddenly I understood what all the joking was about. This plane had no bathroom. I'm serious. It was then I realized that Argyros, a fine man and friend, was just a little, uh, well . . . let's leave it at cheap.

The most amazing thing about that uncomfortable flight was that several days later, when Argyros phoned and offered me the job as his manager, I accepted it. Part of the reason was that a couple of years earlier Peter Ueberroth, then Commissioner of Baseball, also nearly wet his pants on an Argyros flight. Upon landing and spotting a bathroom in the terminal, he reportedly ran a record 100-yard dash (stuffed shirt division). If Ueberroth could endure that and still be one of George's best friends, I figured, then maybe the man wasn't so bad after all. A more truthful reason I took the Mariners job was that at that point in my life I'd have taken anything to make me forget about the San Diego Padres.

The first thing Norma and I had done after my firing from the Padres was change our Coronado Island phone number so nobody could bother us while we stewed. Then we decided, Why stew? We jumped in our van, turned on the Willie Nelson, and headed north along the California coast.

Our first stop was Hearst Castle, about 50 miles south of Big Sur. We climbed out of the van and prepared to go inside for our tour when we noticed we were the youngest people in the parking lot. All around us were senior citizens, hundreds of them, shuffling slowly toward the castle. Don't get me wrong, they were wonderful people with generous smiles. But they were old. They made us feel old. And we weren't old, were we? San Diego hadn't taken that much out of us, had it? Immediately we jumped back in the van and headed for the nearest hotel, where, upon checking in, I was offered a senior citizen's discount. This was some trip.

The next day we arrived at San Francisco's Fisherman's

Wharf, where it seemed so cold that we wondered why the local fishmongers actually bothered to set out their daily catch on ice. We left after only 24 hours, heading back toward the sun. Two days later we found ourselves in Scottsdale, Arizona. It was warm, but we still felt cold. After a couple of days we realized that the kind of chill we felt couldn't be escaped with a van and Waylon Jennings and a few thousand miles of road. You really couldn't escape it at all. You had to learn to bundle up your psyche and live with it until it passed. And so four days after beginning our escape attempt, we drove home from Scottsdale.

A couple of months later, as I was leaving home for a Miller Lite speaking engagement in Orlando, Florida, George Argyros called and asked if I'd be interested in running the Seattle Mariners. This was baseball's very worst franchise— so of course I listened. At the time, early in the 1986 season, the team was being run by a nice man named Chuck Cottier. Like every other nice man who had managed that team, he was being handcuffed by Argyros's tight wallet and controlled by the pacifier-friendly players, who were completely out of place in the rugged Northwest.

For being such a lousy team, the Mariners were the most pampered group of athletes in professional sports. Because Argyros and Armstrong didn't understand baseball, they lived by the rule that the player is always right. Make the player happy, they figured, and he'll help you win. More important for them, apparently, he'll be your friend. And they made sure they only had players they would cherish as friends. So while the players were a public relations dream—outwardly nice guys with outwardly clean lives—they were a manager's nightmare.

When Argyros phoned me, Cottier was just finding this out. The former Mariners third-base coach had been promoted from interim manager late in 1984 mostly because the players had asked for him. They loved the guy. They proclaimed him one of them. But then he had gone just 74–88 in his debut season of 1985. And late that year, enveloped again by losing, the players turned on him. Took advantage of him. Stopped playing hard for their buddy Chuck.

When George called me early the following summer, the Mariners were in the process of repaying Cottier's devotion by losing 19 of their first 28 games. During that time they were in such a funk that they helped Boston's Roger Clemens to a major league record by striking out 20 times to him on April 29.

Ten days after that night in Fenway Park, I was standing in front of a filled Kingdome dining room, trying to explain why I had become the manager of the only team in baseball that had never had a winning record. Cottier had been fired, and I had agreed to a three-year deal that would pay me $200,000 a year to win. It was a small price for expected miracles. Did I have any left in me? Trying to answer that question was one of the reasons I took the job. Could the pampered players ever be made tougher? Well, I had done it before. Would Argyros start spending some money? I assumed his pride would eventually force him to.

Two years later I discovered that my assumptions about everything in modern-day baseball were wrong. While my little driving adventure after being fired from San Diego had made me just feel old, my two years in Seattle hit it home that I really was old. Almost as if overnight, this game and its standards had changed, and this little voice in the back of my head kept telling me, Old man, you'd better change too.

I tried. From the moment I stepped in front of that first press conference, expecting that this change might be happening, I tried. I announced to the media, "My wife, Norma, told me one thing before I left home—be nice." They giggled, but I was serious. And for the next two and a half years I tried to follow Norma's edict. I smiled. I sucked up the losing. I walked through the clubhouse. I damn near became Chuck Tanner is what I did.

And in the end, despite leading the team to its best record in franchise history in 1987 at 78–84, it cost me. I lost my edge. I was so worried about being cool that I lost my fire. And before I knew it, I nearly became one of them, one of those many Mariners players and front office types who, since the franchise was born in 1976, had accepted losing games as long as they didn't lose too much money or sleep. Seattle, as it turned out, neither wanted nor needed a Dick Williams.

If only I'd known this at the time. But in May 1986 all I could think of was that I should be flattered they wanted me, because they could have taken Billy Martin instead. That's right, Seattle fans, you nearly had an up-close view of Billy-ball. Martin and I had talked about the Mariners at the previous winter's baseball meetings and had agreed that it would be a hell of a club for fundamentalists like us. Ironically, a couple of months later Argyros called us both and met us both in Denver on consecutive days. In the end Argyros was more impressed with Martin, and understandably so. Martin had managed under the spotlight more often than me (in other words, in New York) and would sell more tickets than me and was every bit as good a manager as me. While an awful baseball man, Argyros was a great businessman, so he made the sensible business choice of Martin.

But then Chuck Armstrong talked him out of it. It may have been the only battle Armstrong won during his association with George. Because Armstrong voted for me. I guess he worried that Billy would be hell on clubhouse walls and Pioneer Square barstools. Armstrong must have figured I was more sensible and quieter—meaning he overlooked the fact that scotch is readily available in the Northwest.

The Mariners A-team—Argyros and Armstrong—phoned me at our Coronado Island home shortly after our interview and my in-flight squirm session and offered me the job. The entire time I held the receiver, Norma was in the background shaking her head. She didn't know any better than me how deep this hole was, only that I was stepping too quickly into it. When she realized it was a step I felt I had to make, her only advice was to step lightly.

Turns out she should have told the Mariners to be nice. Beginning with the number of coaches they allowed me to have. They gave me Ozzie Virgil as my third-base coach when I arrived, and the next year they let me have Bobby Tolan for a short time, but that was it. And that was trouble. As I've said, without loyal coaches a manager might as well walk through the clubhouse with a bull's-eye on his back.

Armstrong insisted that the front office name the coaches, claiming it was not only a set policy but a smart one. I wondered how Armstrong had come to this conclusion. I asked him about his baseball experience. That was my second Mariners mistake. He told me, for the first of what would be only about a thousand times, that he'd played baseball at Purdue. Later in my Seattle career I'd match his bravado by saying, "Oh yeah, well, my daughter played softball at Duke." That didn't shut him up. The Mariners president, as you will see, was a frustrated jock.

After a bit of negotiating I was able to bring in one friend, Ozzie Virgil, who would once more be my third-base coach. One friend is better than none, I figured, and I could work on bringing in my other coaches after the season. Thank goodness for Ozzie, because he was able to lend me immediate perspective. In other words, the morning after his first game he walked into my downtown hotel room and announced, "Dick, you have taken over one horseshit team."

I looked at Ozzie and shrugged. "Have I ever taken over any other kind of team?"

"But, Dick," Ozzie said, "these aren't just young guys you can train. There's more here than just Alvin Davis and Mark Langston and Jimmy Presley and a couple of good triple-A players. There are also some guys in that clubhouse who are nearly your age, and nearly the prick you are. How are you going to work with those guys?"

Easy. My first act with the Mariners did not require a

baseball mind but a cold heart. Within days of my first game I met with Argyros and put it plainly. Before I could build this team, he needed to tear it down from the inside out. He needed to knock out five veterans—the team's so-called stability—so I could build this team on something younger and stronger. Only five players were on my hit list: Barry Bonnell. Gorman Thomas. Al Cowens. Steve Yeager. Milt Wilcox.

George looked at my list and said the one phrase that would come to symbolize our relationship. "Dick," he said, citing the players' guaranteed contracts, "I can't afford it."

"What do you mean you can't afford it?" I said. "Because of their guaranteed contracts, you've got to pay them no matter what they do. Aren't they more valuable out of the way so that younger players can have a chance? And, George, those younger players are cheap!"

George thought a minute and said, "Well, yeah, I guess I never thought of it like that."

But of course. George never thought of anything like that. I wonder how many good Mariners years had already been lost because of it. Best I could figure it, George spent too much time talking to the ballplayer from Purdue.

My sharpest impressions of Argyros actually came when I was managing San Diego. During spring training games he would always sit in his club's dugout. I didn't know who he was, but I knew that a polo shirt doesn't belong in a dugout. Umpire Doug Harvey saw him sitting over there and asked me, "You want him thrown out?" I said, "Sure." And an embarrassed Argyros was forced to sit in the stands.

George never came into my dugout and almost never entered my clubhouse. So I was spared the consequences of frequent contact with him. Fortunately, he did agree to help me get rid of some pests. Although it was a bit like breaking up Animal House, within a month of my arrival I began scratching names off my hit list.

The first to go, on June 12, was Al Cowens. Good guy,

fair outfielder, but uglier feet than a clown. And he was always complaining about them. He would be sent to doctors, and their diagnoses were unanimous and brilliant: bad feet. That's all they would say. "The man's got bad feet." Poor guy wanted to play but just couldn't. Finally I told those feet to hit the road.

Next to go, on June 13, was Milt Wilcox. He'd come to the Mariners the previous winter as a veteran pitcher with World Series experience who promised to be a steadying influence on the field and in the clubhouse. Probably would have been too, if he hadn't started 10 games and lost eight. Didn't win a one. Even then, he wouldn't have been so bad except one day I saw him down in the bullpen, trying to help pitching coach Phil Regan work with one of our young pitchers. I steadied my suddenly weak knees. This was like Charles Manson working with young skeet shooters. The only time I listened to him was when he was forced to say goodbye. I only wish he could have pitched for me like he later pitched in the winter of 1989 in the new Senior League, in which he beat my club three out of the four times he faced me.

Next to go down, on June 25, was Gorman Thomas. This was my easiest release. I never even had to leave the clubhouse, because by that time Thomas never left the clubhouse. Hampered by a sore shoulder and what had become a sore attitude, he spent most of his time in front of his locker tying fishing flies. He was one guy who took the nickname "Mariner" seriously.

Thomas hadn't always been like that. He was an old-time, hard-knuckled player brought to the team in a trade in the winter of 1983 as another one of those World Series veterans, one who could hit. And he could. But he finally bagged his career only after an incredible incident that shows clearly how baseball is no longer for old-time, hard-knuckled guys. I remember this because it was the same incident that marked the beginning of the end of my tolerance for the game we'd both once loved.

Thomas, no longer able to play the outfield regularly because his arm was so bad after rotator cuff surgery, could only be a designated hitter. But he loved to play the outfield, so before one game in New York I put him in left. I was just hoping to rekindle whatever feeling for baseball remained in him. And I would have succeeded too. He saw his name in the lineup and got all excited . . . until the phone rang. Back in Seattle, general manager Dick Balderson was watching the game on television and had seen my lineup. He panicked. "Dick," he shouted into the phone, "you can't play Thomas in the outfield, you just can't!" Before I could ask why, he continued, "Because of his operation. If he plays out there and gets hurt, he can sue us!" "Do what?" I asked. "Sue who?" Poor Balderson shouted back, "Dick, my hands are tied." I hung up the phone and put my head in my hands and damn near wept.

Because Balderson was completedly controlled by Armstrong and Argyros, I didn't blame him for that call. Because Armstrong and Argyros were learning this game the way a two-year-old learns not to drink from the toilet, I couldn't blame them for the call. It was baseball that I blamed. And throughout the remainder of my disillusioned Seattle tenure it was baseball that I continued to blame. Baseball let itself be controlled by agents and lawyers. Baseball put itself on witness stands and positioned itself around negotiating tables and transformed pin-striped players into millionaires in suits. Baseball was slowly allowing itself to be stripped of everything but the love of the trusting fans. Yes, it was baseball that I blamed.

I walked down to the dugout and told Gorman he couldn't play the outfield. And he was hurt. I could see that hardened face on the verge of tears. His career was over. It was a damn shame.

On July 16, nearly a month after Thomas's release, I whittled my hit list to one by canning Barry Bonnell. He was another veteran acquired by the club a couple of years earlier in hopes of adding leadership. The Mariners just didn't seem to realize that to be a leader you must first be ready to open your mouth and say the right things and be willing to extend your body. Age in itself doesn't make for leadership. You must make great effort on the field and then follow up with encouragement and advice in the clubhouse. Bonnell did neither. Just before he was released, he spent most of his time walking through the bowels of the Kingdome with a towel wrapped around what he called his aching neck. He walked in silence, wanting like hell to play, knowing he couldn't.

That left one player, catcher Yeager, yet another guy the Mariners had picked up in hopes that some of his World Series experience would rub off. Except the way he rubbed the young pitchers was with such encouraging words as "Get that shit over the plate." So nobody wanted to pitch to him. He was too cocky, which is fine, as long as you're still good enough to be cocky. He wasn't. He insulted our pitchers' pride and, ultimately, their intelligence. So after my first season we offered him the ultimate insult—a release.

And that was that. The "veteran influence" was gone, and entering the 1987 season, I felt I'd brought up enough youngsters and helped make enough moves to put a potential winning team in place. Catching was Dave Valle, an easy choice for the job, considering the other candidates had been Yeager and a guy named Bob Kearney, who had a few problems of his own—particularly with pitching coach Frank Funk. When I arrived in Seattle, everyone was dying to tell me the story about the Saturday morning in Oakland in 1984 when Funk attempted to flush Kearney's glove down a dugout toilet. It started a fight, but it was the only way Funk knew to tell Kearney that he thought his pitch selection was shit.

At first base was Alvin Davis, a former Rookie of the Year whose promotion and nurturing was one of the best moves former manager Del Crandall ever made. At second base was my baby, Harold Reynolds, whom I brought up from triple-A within a couple of days of taking the job. Didn't anybody in the organization realize what a great mix of foot speed and bat speed he possessed? Didn't anybody here know how important that was? When I arrived in Seattle and found a talent like Harold still without much major league time, it was obvious why this franchise was still minor league.

If nothing else, didn't they see what a bad second baseman Danny Tartabull was? Yes, that outstanding outfielder for Kansas City was once a second baseman for the Mariners. When I arrived, he had a blood problem that kept him out of the lineup. After watching him once, I told him he also had anemia in his leather. Out to the outfield he went, where he sulked, quite unlike his father, Jose, who I'd managed in Boston. Tartabull made a good match with another Mariner outfielder, Ivan Calderon, who was plain too lazy to manage. And those two complemented another outfielder, Dave Henderson, to whom everything was funny. I couldn't imagine what it was like to be blessed with such bizarre humor that you laughed even when you lost. Give Henderson credit, though. After leaving Seattle he played in three World Series in four years, with Boston and Oakland. And he played well. And he was still carefree. Looking at him, maybe baseball can be all fun. Nah.

By the time my first full Mariners season started in 1987, Tartabull and Calderon and Henderson had been traded. And I'll admit that today those deals might seem pretty bad—I think the only guys worth a damn that the Mariners acquired for them were catcher Scott Bradley from the Chicago White Sox and pitcher Scott Bankhead from Kansas City. But they were deals that had to be made, because I couldn't discipline any of those three players and management wouldn't help. That was another way baseball had changed. Suddenly I was not only on my own with the players, I was actually fighting my bosses over them. The bosses wanted to baby them, and when I didn't, the bosses told their players it was okay, they were still loved by someone. And I was left hanging, realizing that unless I got players who would listen to me from the start, I couldn't teach them anything. So I worked to trade the babies and find me some men who were ready and willing to learn.

At shortstop was Rey Quinones, who I'd helped acquire via a trade for Spike Owen and Dave Henderson a couple of months after I arrived. Quinones was an asshole with Boston, and became an asshole with us, but I thought that was what we needed, somebody to shake things up in the clubhouse, make things a little tense. And unlike hardworking but limited Spike Owen, Quinones could play. At third base was Jim Presley, who'd had 27 homers and 107 RBIs the previous season—he could play and listen, believe it or not.

My revamped outfield included a legitimate .300-hitter in Phil Bradley, who I didn't really know yet, because he was so quiet, and a couple of hustlers named Kingery and Moses. My starting pitching staff included a couple of guys you may have heard about named Mark Langston and Mike Moore, and I had a couple of hard young throwers in the bullpen named Edwin Nunez and Bill Wilkinson.

So why wasn't 1987 the best year in Mariners history? Hey, it was. Hell, we finished just seven games out of first place. A better question might be, How come we didn't finish closer? And how come in 1988 it all fell apart? And how come Dick Williams failed?

Begin in the winter following the 1986 season, after the club had gone 58–75 under me during the changes. In addition to all these changes, I felt we needed two things to put us over the magical "top" that everyone talks about. First, we needed a pitching coach—any team's most important coach, by far—to handle all of our talented arms. And second, we needed one badass to play the one American League position that requires such a special man—the designated hitter. We could get by with local boy Ken Phelps batting from the left side, but we needed a right-handed hitter with some powers of intimidation.

My choice for pitching coach was a guy who'd taught Mike

Moore everything he knew, a former Dodgers pitcher and Oral Roberts University pitching coach named Jim Brewer. My choice for designated hitter was a free agent who had hit three homers in the Kingdome in one of his last appearances there—Dave Kingman.

Oh, what dreams. Mariners fans may recall that I was unable to acquire either of these talents. Argyros said no. It was that simple. Brewer wanted just $60,000. Argyros spends more than $60,000 a day talking to his buddy Armstrong on the fucking telephone from California. And yet George said the price was too high. That move may have eventually kept the late Brewer's favorite Oral Roberts student, Mike Moore, who actually brought Brewer to my hotel suite for our job interview. Instead, management hired a pitching coach named Billy Connors, a move that hurt me far worse than I could have guessed at the time.

Then, during spring training, Argyros's other alligator-skin shoe dropped. He kicked my butt with Kingman. I had found Kingman at his Lake Tahoe home, and this former star with experience on about 25 teams—Oakland was his latest—was enthusiastic about playing one more year. He was so eager that he paid for his own flight to Tempe, Arizona, where we had breakfast before one of our spring workouts. Kingman said all he would require was $250,000, about as much as San Francisco's Will Clark makes today in a couple of weeks.

I was so excited that I called up Balderson immediately and told him to please ask George to sign this guy. Balderson said he would try. I later learned he was afraid to ask George to do anything. When they finally did have a chat about it, it was a short one. Balderson quickly got to the part about $250,000. George quickly said no. End of discussion. And I was outraged. To deprive the team like that for what amounted to relatively little money was criminal. About as criminal as our designated Ken Phelps driving in 68 runs for us that year.

People often ask me if George was trying to lose so he could keep attendance down, get out of his Kingdome lease, and move the ball club to some sucker city that would give him a billion dollars for it. My answer has always been that George's tenure as a Seattle owner wasn't about winning or losing. It was about making money. He had no concept of a final score, just a bottom line. And he made that line pay off when he loaded his pockets by finally selling the Mariners in 1989 for $75,000,000, close to six times what he'd paid for them.

So no, he didn't try to lose. He just tried to stay rich. And he did. And even though the entire city of Seattle lost, even though their civic pride was damaged and summers were less glorious for nine solid years . . . well, that's emotion. And emotion is for silly human beings. Not bottom lines. Not George. You know what I mean when I say "bottom line," right? Like a sewer.

Management did do one thing for me that winter. Because they knew I felt surrounded by foreign coaches, they let me bring up my buddy Bobby Tolan from the minor leagues, where he was a hitting instructor. With him and Ozzie, I felt like my back was fairly well protected now.

And so the season started. And it was obvious we were good. We were close in every game, winning nearly half of them. But I soon noticed that besides the one big slugger, this team was missing something else. Balls. We never had the balls to put anybody away. We lacked the Dave Kingman—size crash in our bats and our personalities. When I finally discovered why, I also discovered another reason nobody could ever win in Seattle. It had to do with a sacred title many of my players gave themselves: born-again Christians.

I call it a sacred title because it should be used responsibly and with the care it deserves. Talking about it all the time in a baseball clubhouse is not giving it the care it deserves. And I feel that talking about it while putting on their baseball pants turned these guys into nice kids who were afraid to play hard.

You see this God-is-my-batting-coach trend everywhere in baseball now—from the minor leagues to the bullpens, which were once sacred in their own, undignified right. It's rare to hear a game's savior speak now without mentioning the real Savior. It's rare to hear a pitcher say he won a game just because he's a tough bastard.

I wonder if, unfortunately, this rage all started with the Mariners. I wonder because of the story of Ozzie Virgil and his Sunday morning shit. One Sunday on the road Ozzie had grabbed his sports section and was in one of the stalls relieving himself when suddenly, underneath the stall door, he saw many pairs of blue cleats. Turns out our players couldn't find any quiet place to hold chapel, so they were holding it in the john. Before Ozzie knew it, half the team was standing outside his door praying while he was inside crapping. He finished before the players, but no way was he going to wipe and flush with the religious ceremony taking place just a few feet away. Trapped by the Christians. So he waited. And waited. And finally, when both feet were asleep and his butt hurt, the players finished their prayers and left. And finally he could flush.

He waddled into my office and told me the story, and that was it. I laughed like hell. And I remained calm through the early part of the 1987 season until these same meetings were causing players to show up late for Sunday batting practice. And perhaps causing them to accept defeat more easily. To say that losing is God's will is crap. I began hearing that again and again, and finally it was too much. I complained, and Balderson laid down a new commandment: chapel services were to be held either Saturday afternoon before batting practice or much earlier Sunday, early enough so that the services would finish in time for the players to be able to concentrate on the game.

This God rift caused a huge uproar, headlines and everything, and suddenly I was the devil. Steve Largent, a player on the National Football League's Seattle Seahawks, even came out and said, "It makes sense that they got rid of God. They've gotten rid of all their other good players." I resented Largent for saying that. Our edict had nothing to do with getting rid of God. It had to do with getting to batting practice on time and standing up for your actions once the game began. And if wanting those things is being the devil, then I can go to hell. Which, incidentally, by the end of the 1987 season, was where many people were telling me to go.

We played well for the first half of the season, and we were 45−43, just three and a half games out of first place at the All-Star break. But the players were growing impatient with my strong hand, and I with their weak hearts, and then came the one game that, as in all my other managerial stays, marked the beginning of the end. That game typified everything that was wrong about those young, pretty, and nice Seattle Mariners.

It was July 27. We were playing the division-leading Minnesota Twins at a Kingdome that, for once, was not so dreary. It was the ninth inning, and my ace Mark Langston was pitching with a 3−0 lead. Having allowed just two hits, he seemed damn near perfect. Then Twins shortstop Greg Gagne, who batted just .265 that year, hit a single. And center fielder Dan Gladden, who batted just .249, walked. Langston, who looked a little tired, was giving up. Despite having a two-hitter working—do you know how many pitchers dream of taking a two-hitter into the ninth inning?—he was still giving up. Because he was tired. Because he wasn't tough enough. How did I know this? Because all season he had been taking himself out of games. He'd walk past me in the dugout after an inning and say, "I've had it," and be gone. Just like that. No regard for his teammates. And worse, no regard for winning.

In this late July game I saw the same thing happening all over again. After those first two batters reached base, I watched Langston on the mound contorting his face and shaking his head and all but shouting for me to take him out. Fuck him,

I decided—my duty is not to him but to the Seattle Mariners. He was my best pitcher, he had allowed just three hits, he had not allowed a run, and if he couldn't win this game when it counted, then the Seattle Mariners could never win games when it counted. He had to get tough, and his teammates had to get tough. So I would make him tough it out.

But, of course, he didn't. He threw up a fat pitch and was nailed for a three-run homer to Steve Lombardozzi, who finished that year with eight homers total. Unbelievable. I yanked Langston from the game without looking him in the eye, because I was too embarrassed. For the great game of baseball, and the great art of competing, I was embarrassed. We eventually lost the game.

For the rest of my time in Seattle I perceived Langston as I feel much of baseball finally perceived him when he cost the Montreal Expos the pennant in the late summer of 1989 by choking on his final few starts. Gutless, that's how I perceived him. Gutless. Anybody can pitch for a loser, which Langston did very well for the Mariners before I arrived. But let's see you pitch for a winner. That's the sign of a true competitor, which Langston is not. And I don't care how many saddlebags Gene Autry dumped on his head to sign with the Angels in the winter of 1989. C'mon, Langston. Let's see you pitch for a winner. Let's see you be a winner.

So Langston, despite a 19–13 record that year, was one of the reasons we couldn't get over the hump. Another reason was our other ace, Mike Moore, who went 9–19 and allowed nearly five runs per game. You know how many players Moore hit with a pitch in 1987? In 33 starts? None. It is one of the most unbelievable stats of our age. With that many starts, you'd think he would hit a couple of guys at least by accident. But to his credit, he has since turned it around by helping Oakland to the 1989 world championship. He proved he could win with a winner, and I tip my cap to him.

Our pitchers weren't helped that season by a pitching coach

who, because he was hired by management, treated the pitchers like management wanted them treated. In other words, Billy Connors coddled them, and it ruined us. Connors would play favorites, treating some pitchers nice and shitting on others. He had no regard for winning. He wanted to be the manager when I would inevitably be fired, so he tried to be the players' best friend. Once again, if only I'd had my own pitching coach.

The final bit of us that collapsed that season involved my batting instructor, Bobby Tolan, and one of the team's biggest malcontents, outfielder Phil Bradley. Sorry, I shouldn't call him a malcontent without first explaining. But since most of baseball agrees with me, I figured I could cut a few corners.

Tolan, who you'll remember as my good batting instructor in San Diego, was the Mariners' roving minor league batting instructor when I arrived in 1986. Obviously, because of the Padres' success, I was convinced that he was one of baseball's best. The problem was that the team's hitting leader, Phil Bradley, didn't want to be instructed. He was a former all-star quarterback at the University of Missouri, a black quarterback at a place where previously there had been virtually none. He felt, and perhaps rightly, that he'd been a victim of racial prejudice in college. The experience put a chip on his shoulder that he's carried with him ever since. So Bradley didn't want to listen to anybody. Or talk to anybody. The younger players were begging for his leadership, but he didn't give it. All the players were begging for a share of his batting expertise, but he wouldn't give it. Phil Bradley was playing for one person: himself. Just find him today—he was in Baltimore last I looked—and try to talk to him. He'll give you a one-word answer and a scowl. His bitterness has made him almost inhuman. I know I've been tough, but at least I've been human.

When Bobby offered batting tips, Bradley refused to listen. When Bobby wanted Bradley to take extra work like everyone else, Bradley refused. And as the season progressed, Bradley taught the rest of the team not to listen. Because Bobby has a sharp edge like me, the guys were easily persuaded to turn him off. Even Harold Reynolds, in a change of heart that broke my heart, became insubordinate. That tough young player I'd rescued from the minor leagues joined Bradley and turned on Tolan.

Late in the 1987 season, with the club preparing to riot against him for reasons that I swear I still don't understand, the Mariners fired Bobby Tolan. And for me, that did it. The tail had officially wagged the dog, and I officially was gone. I had lunch with Armstrong at Seattle's ritzy Rainier Club and nearly threw my croutons at him while arguing for Tolan's return. Armstrong said no.

And so in Kansas City just before the end of the season, with our team's fine start completely blown by pussyfooting and politicking, I decided, Enough. I announced that I was going to retire following the 1988 year.

Yes, I meant it. I could see no end in sight. I'd come up here with high hopes and been left to burn. Left to die. And that was it. Then, damn it, over the winter I had a change of heart. Once I was away from the field, I mellowed, as I always do when I'm out of uniform. I looked back at our good talent and began to think that with just one more year, maybe two, we could be in a pennant race. I was wavering on whether to renege on this retirement when, that winter in Dallas, my mind got made up. We traded Phil Bradley to Philadelphia. And I decided I had to stay.

And what a fun trade. The Mariners and Argyros were so screwed up that Bradley was traded twice. In the first days of the winter meetings that December we worked out all the details of a deal that would send Bradley to Philadelphia for outfielder Glenn Wilson and pitcher Mike Jackson. Unfortunately, George was on a hunting trip, and when he learned of the deal, he wanted us to wait for him to show up and give his approval. So we had to wait. And wait. When he finally arrived in the middle of the week, he stormed into our

suite, where Armstrong and I were entertaining the Baltimore Orioles while Balderson was downstairs in another suite
finalizing the deal with the Phillies.

Argyros had just sat down across from representatives of
the Orioles, who were also interested in Bradley, when suddenly the Orioles made an offer for him. "Sounds good,"
Argyros blurted out. "We could make that deal."

That sudden bad odor in the room was Armstrong shitting in his Brooks Brothers. We had already effectively traded
Bradley to Philadelphia. We couldn't trade him again, for
God's sake. What were we going to do? I looked at Armstrong. So fearful of his owner that he'd rather compromise
his personal integrity than inform the owner of a mistake,
Armstrong sat motionless.

So I said it. I was embarrassing myself again, but I said
it: "Uh, George, as you know, Phil Bradley has been traded
to another team." I glanced at him and then faced the Orioles as coolly as possible. "Sorry, guys, but Bradley is no longer
available." After the meeting George got filled in on what the
hell was going on. He apologized, and Bradley was sent to
Philadelphia. Me, I was so excited about getting rid of the
poison Bradley that I went to Argyros and flat-out asked for
a contract extension past the 1988 season. George said, "We
will see." He admitted that the Mariners had finished 1987
at 78–84, the best mark in club history. But the best I could
get was "We will see."

From the start I knew he'd never see. Both Norma and I
got our first strong hints in the spring. Her hint came when
Chuck Armstrong's wife, Susan, wouldn't go out of her way
to talk to her. My hint came when Argyros agreed to extend
my contract. It happened over breakfast that spring, when
he finally responded to my queries about a new contract. Over
my bacon and eggs and his pureed something-or-other, he
asked me if I wanted to keep managing. I told him that of
course I wanted to keep managing. We were coming off the
franchise's best year ever, and my insides were beginning to

stir again in hopes that maybe this year my ideas of winning would sink in. No, I told him, bad as things seem, I never give up hope. And yes, if you want me to keep managing after this season, I want to stay. "Then it's done," he said, shaking my hand on a verbal agreement to a one-year contract extension.

Why was this an omen of my departure? Because historically, George's word lasts about as long as a handshake. Knowing this, I still accepted the handshake instead of a written agreement. It proved to be my last mistake as manager of the Seattle Mariners.

In this case, George's word lasted 56 games. That's how long I managed in 1988 before being fired. It took George less than two months to get me. Or should I say it took the Mariners players less than two months to get me? For many of them, my firing was the greatest accomplishment of their careers.

After a typical spring training I started that season praying for the one thing you can't learn in the spring: player maturity. I prayed that finally my guys would realize it would be a lot easier to live with me, and themselves, if they'd just be tough and always try to win. Turns out they hadn't learned shit. In 1988 they started slow and were soon going through the motions. Pitchers crying to come out of games. Batters crying about opposing pitchers not giving them a chance to hit the ball, as if that was the way it was supposed to work. Everybody crying that the umpires were always picking on the poor little expansion Mariners.

The clubhouse had become a Sunday school, with Armstrong running through there like a minister and me being generally ignored by the players, who apparently thought, If we don't listen to him, maybe he'll go away. Seems they were right.

We continued to lose more games than we should, and I took up smoking again, lighting up and sneaking a puff behind the dugout between innings. Local columnists would look for me during those times, not see me sitting in my usual spot, and write that I wasn't watching the game. Of course, they'd never come down and ask me in person if I was watching the game.

As I became more and more pissed off, and began feeling more and more out of control, I called quiet Alvin Davis into my office. This club needed a leader to settle things down. Hell, if the players weren't going to listen to me, we needed somebody to inspire us, and with Bradley gone, Alvin was probably our best position player. I knew the introverted first baseman had the leadership potential of a potted plant and surely wouldn't go diving head-first into our complacency if I asked him. But I expected that he at least had a conscience.

So I asked him to take charge. Dumb request. He told me he'd do his best, but that he didn't think he could give me what I was asking. So right then I told him, "Alvin, if you think it will help the club, I'll resign right now." He was immediately apologetic, as if he didn't want to get blamed for this: "Oh no, oh no, this team still needs you." Turns out that Davis, like every other Mariner on every other day of my managerial stay there, was afraid to get his hands dirty. He wanted to see me fall, but only as a spectator, not as the guy doing the pushing. After I was fired, guess who barked the loudest about what a horseshit manager I was? Guess who helped lead the clubhouse in ripping me? Alvin Davis.

The strange lack of response from Davis got me thinking, so in early May I met George for breakfast in Seattle and laid out my final plea. "If you want me to keep managing here, I can't keep feeling like my players are holding the door for me to leave," I told him. "Please, give me that contract we discussed, give it to me right now, or else fire me." Knowing full well I would never quit, George shook his head. "We'll wait until the season ends and see what happens then," he said.

My season, I understood at that point, was going to end soon. I called Norma after the breakfast and told her, "Start packing, honey. It's only a matter of time now."

And from then on, it was like I was there but I wasn't

there. I tried to keep busting their asses, I tried to stay mean and competitive, I worked as hard as ever. But knowing that I was going to be fired, the Mariners had long since stopped listening to me. Hell, they had long since stopped looking at me. It's like that with some modern-day teams. If they think you're on thin ice and it's no longer to their advantage to work for you, they'll quit playing until you fall through the ice. They'll do their best to get rid of you so they can have a scapegoat for their poor performance. Maybe my performance during that time wasn't great either, I don't know; I was so mad then I couldn't judge. But if I did go downhill, I had plenty of help.

Lucky for me, this limbo only lasted a month. On June 6, after waiting that long for the single incident he could use to explain the firing to the public—even though the firing had been in the works for nearly a year—Argyros was handed his weapon.

It happened in Kansas City, during four awful weekend games in which the Royals swept us and humiliated us. In the Saturday night game Mark Langston wanted to come out of a well-pitched game in the ninth inning. I wouldn't give in to the gutless wonder, so he allowed the game-winning hit and the Royals were victorious again. The next day, Langston publicly ripped me, saying, "It's tough on the players, we don't know if he's trying." He also said, "Leadership has to start with him, and it's not there."

Funny, but it almost sounded like he was ripping me for being too nice. Oh, those wacky Seattle Mariners. They could never decide what they wanted. Treat them tough and you're too tough. Treat them like they treat themselves—don't give a shit about them, in other words—and suddenly you're not tough enough. Those Seattle Mariners, such men of principle and integrity. And guts.

After hearing from a reporter Sunday night that Langston's outburst had prompted the Mariners to fire me, on Monday morning I phoned Argyros to give him a chance to drop the ax. In a scenario typical of the Mariners, I damn near had to fire myself.

George told me, "Dick, I'm flying up there today, we'll talk about your problems then." I balked. "No, George," I said. "Tell me what you're going to talk about now." "Okay," George finally said, "we're going to make a change."

And that was that. On June 6, 1988, after going 159–192 with a .453 winning percentage, the best record ever for a manager of this bad franchise, I was canned. I met Argyros and Armstrong at the Rainier Club for lunch that day to finalize the details. I wasn't bitter, just basic. "Here's my deal," I told George. "I'm going to publicly rip Langston and Connors, and that's it." George said that, in turn, he would ask his players not to publicly rip me. Judging from the newspapers the next day, I guess he never got around to making that request.

Our luncheon ended when George, knowing he had to pay me for the remaining four months of the season, came up with this idea. "I've got it!" he said. "How would you like to be one of our television color commentators? You know, really build up our players over the air?" Sure, George.

As I walked away through a cold rain, away from Argyros and likely my last major league managing job, relieved but nearly reduced to tears at the passing of my career, I suddenly had a thought. You know, this shit might make a good book.

HOME AGAIN

True story. January 1990, an early evening. The phone jangled the tiny office in the bowels of West Palm Beach Stadium. I jumped out of my seat, as I always did when that damn phone jangled. Then I picked it up.

"Clubhouse," I grumbled.

"Excuse me, sir," said the voice on the other end. "Is this the West Palm Beach Tropicals?"

"Tropics. We're the Tropics."

"Whatever. Can you tell me what time tonight's game starts?"

I looked at my watch and remembered how the stands had looked the last time I was outside.

"I don't know," I said. "What time can you get here?"

And you never believed Dick Williams would leave this game with a grin. But after 22 years of fighting in the big one, that's what four months in Florida's new Senior Professional Baseball Association gave me. A reason to smile again. A reason to be happy about the game of baseball again. A reason to be a human being again.

When I first heard about this new adventure in the spring

of 1989, I was wary. After all, a league featuring only players over 35 years old, with catchers over 32? With eight Florida franchises that began play in November, a full month before the snowbirds arrived to buy their tickets? With fewer big name players than bitter ones?

This was either a great idea or a terrible one. I was just curious enough about it to contact Jim Morley, the league's founder, to ask him a few questions, the most crucial being, What are these old guys going to do—play three innings each and drink beer between at-bats?

Morley assured me that the players would be encouraged to endure an entire nine innings, and that alcohol would not be allowed in the dugouts. Then he showed his entrepreneur's giddiness by offering me a job as manager. Hmm, I thought for about 10 seconds. Good enough for me. Bored with retirement and longing to find myself in a baseball-as-it-used-to-be world, I wasn't going to be picky. Besides, being paid $15,000 a month to spend a winter in Florida isn't the worst thing that can happen to a guy. And so in the summer of 1989 I signed on as manager of the West Palm Beach franchise.

Looking back, I can't blame Morley for what was to become one of the most unusual experiences of my life. After all, he was sort of right. There was no alcohol in the dugouts, but outside the dugouts it was a different story. Our team had such enthusiastic drinkers, Sunday softball—type beer drinkers, that my strategy was sometimes affected. I was never sure when they might be overcome by their thirsty enthusiasm. So I had to make my decisions accordingly. Take my pitcher, Tim Stoddard, age 37. Once when he was struggling, I actually went to the mound and told him, "Tim, I'm honestly afraid to take you out. I don't want you drinking all our beer in the clubhouse before the game ends."

And yes, Morley was accurate in saying that most of the players could last nine innings. What he didn't mention was that so could their animals. I'm speaking of the cocker span-

iel puppy that spent every game in our bullpen. She belonged to one of my relief pitchers, Lowell Palmer, age 42. I
didn't much mind it, not that I actually had much of a choice.
Otherwise, little Katy would have taken her daily dump in
my dugout.

The problem was that in convincing me to join this league,
Morley just couldn't have foreseen such sheer silliness . . .
Like a team owner joining us in workouts, uniform and all,
with just one teeny thing missing: a protective cup. Or like
the fistfight on the field between two teammates, who happened to be lawyers, over the kingship of Palm Beach Coun-
ty's legal system.

Morley also left out things like the pitcher who was traded
for 500 teddy bears. And the player who wouldn't be traded
unless his brother was traded with him. And the pinch runner who had no cleats. And the team bus driver who got paid
more than the players. And deserved it.

The Senior League was all of that and more, struggling
through its infancy as something most of the nation only followed by accident. The major leagues ignored it, at least one
national magazine panned it, and yes, crowds were so small
that I really did tell one surprised fan that we'd start the
game when he showed up.

But I think back on it, and I smile. And not because my
West Palm Beach team was the league's best during the regular season, winning 52 of 72 games before losing a silly one-
game, winner-take-all championship playoff. I smile because
I had discovered a remote island in the sporting world where
the players, once again, cared. Nobody demanded a new contract. Nobody demanded to be traded. Nobody yelled when
benched. Nobody gave excuses. They'd even call our trainers
if they were going to be late for early pregame treatment.
And guess what: we did it all with just two weeks of spring
training, one less than 1990's whining major leaguers who
had their camps cut short due to an owners' lockout that was
at least partially the players' fault.

In the safe, never-heard-of-arbitration Senior League, fans discovered 72 games being played at a level consistently above triple-A and just below the major leagues. And I rediscovered, after many seasons of looking, players who were just happy to be there. This maybe even gave me back my soul, after years of watching helplessly while it seemed to drift farther and farther away from me.

Sure, many of these players hadn't crossed anyone's mind in years, ever since their big league careers were over. But thanks to the lessons of age, they were guys who knew that professional baseball isn't a game but a privilege. Something not just to be played but cherished. I'm speaking of guys like—and pull out your baseball encyclopedia here—Toby Harrah and Al Hrabosky and Jim Bibby and Pete LaCock and Butch Metzger and Mike Tyson (the second baseman, not the boxer). And I'm speaking about better-known guys with the right attitude—Rollie Fingers, for instance, and even the reputed prick Dave Kingman, who was wonderful all season.

But I'm getting ahead of myself. None of these former big leaguers were there when I began work in October 1989. I got my first glimpse of life in this league when we had to assemble a full team. Although the league had many rules governing that process, Boca Raton lawyer Don Sider, who owned the club along with West Coast businessman John Henry, decided to get us started at square one by holding a tryout camp. What a lovely idea—inviting middle-aged people in southern Florida (all of whom felt they could have been baseball stars) to take one last chance on proving their athletic greatness.

What a headache. These open tryouts are bad even when run by major league teams. We had 60 people show up, and some of them had lived at least that many years. We had people who could catch the ball but were afraid to bat. We had people who said they were pitchers, but that must have been before the mound was moved back to 60 feet, six inches. Some guys came just for the free caps. Many others came just because they had a free weekend day. Nobody keeled over from exhaustion, although several guys barely made it down to first base before they needed a breather. "What are you going to do if you hit a home run and have to run all four bases?" I asked one such weary soul. "A what?" he replied. No, I didn't ask myself what I was doing there. I asked myself what those other people were doing there. We had construction workers, company presidents, street bums, just about everything but baseball players.

And we had the guy with the cellular phone. Owner of a local charter airplane service, he was my favorite player in the tryouts, mostly because when he tried to play he had this cellular phone sticking out of his pants pocket. It wouldn't have been so bad except the phone would keep going off—beep-beep, beep-beep, beep-beep. Even that wouldn't have been so bad except he insisted on answering it. He took a call once while shagging flies in the outfield, another time while jogging from the field to the dugout. But the final straw came when he was walking from the on-deck circle to home plate to bat. His pants went off—beep-beep, beep-beep—and he stopped. "Sorry," he yelled to the pitcher, "I got to take this." Our hero motioned for the next batter to take his place, and while we all watched with growing laughter, he stood next to home plate and chatted on the phone.

The guy didn't make the team. Really, the sorry thing about it was that, with all those cellular phone shenanigans, he even had a shot at it. So did every damn one of these guys because our owner Sider insisted on a practice game that would give everyone an opportunity to be seen. With pitchers who could barely throw and runners who could barely walk, the game took nearly six hours. After seeing yet another senior citizen boot a grounder down the third-base line, I called it quits.

Actually, I can't kick, because we found two guys at the camp who eventually became important parts of our team, former minor leaguers Felix Pettaway (pitcher) and Alfie

Rondon (plays anywhere you put him). Pettaway was a cement truck driver, Rondon was a house painter, but both agreed to one of the most important contract stipulations of our league: they would get time off their regular jobs so they could play regularly. We also kept two colleagues of our lawyer owner, who'd gently persuaded me to give them a good look. One of his buddies—first baseman Joe Minceberg—was assigned to our nonactive taxi squad; the other—Jim Bonfiglio—became our bullpen catcher. Remember those names, and remember their professions.

Of course, two blue collar guys and two business suits do not a team make. To round out the rest of what would eventually be a 24-man squad, we used a method in keeping with the entrepreneurial spirit of the league's founders: we exploited my name. Back when the league was forming, questionnaires were sent to more than 1,000 older players, asking them if they'd like to play and for which team. Since many knew that I would be at West Palm Beach, and that their only other option involving a former major league manager was to play in Miami for Earl Weaver, many of them picked our team. From that list we could protect rights to 15 players. That's how we got our starting catcher, Luis Pujols, our starting outfield of Tito Landrum in left, Mickey Rivers in center, and Lee Lacy in right, and most of our starting infield of Jerry White at first base, Rodney Scott at second, and Toby Harrah at third. And our designated hitter, Dave Kingman.

That's also how we got our top two starting pitchers, Tim Stoddard and Juan Eichelberger, although in those cases it wasn't so simple. Both had played for me before, so they suffered from the same simple misconception shared by most of my former players: they thought I hated their guts. When our owners contacted them, they both said they wanted to play for me again but only if I wanted them. "Are you serious?" I asked our co-owner John Henry when he called about my problems with Stoddard, who had pitched for the San Diego Padres when I was there. "That was years ago! I've got nothing against him now!" Henry wouldn't back down. "Say it, Dick," he insisted. "Say that you like him, or he won't come." I felt like a reprimanded schoolboy, but I said it. "Okay, okay, I like him, I like him," I said. Later, much to my horror, I discovered I meant it. Not just about Stoddard and Eichelberger but everybody else on my team.

The roster was rounded out with a variety of other free agent signings and discoveries, like the one made by John Henry, who also owns the Tucson Toros triple-A team. He noticed that the team's veteran star, Ron Washington, was supposed to be recalled to Houston at the end of the 1989 season but had been sidelined with a leg injury. He phoned Washington, age 37 at the time, and asked if he was going to be busy over the winter. This is how we acquired our starting shortstop and eventually the league's Most Valuable Player.

The best thing about the acquisition process was that, because the average player made just $7,000 a month, no agents were involved. Well, one. Sort of. Rollie Fingers's agent tried to get him more money at Port Saint Lucie, whereupon the team's management told him to take a hike, and so Fingers came. In other instances, players switched teams for more compelling reasons. Like, the league was afraid that we would go undefeated. Vida Blue wanted to pitch for me, but when the other owners decided my team was so stacked at the time that it wouldn't be fair, he ended up going to Fort Myers.

We had our first full squad workout on October 16 at the site of our tryout camp, Bucky Dent Field in Delray Beach. Due to a lack of available locker space there, we had to get into uniform at our team hotel in West Palm Beach, then travel to the workout in vans. Heaven help any players who were injured at the field. Our trainers' room was set up in— bite my tongue—the press box. The reason for all of these inconveniences was that we had no place else to play. We couldn't have West Palm Beach Municipal Stadium field until just before our season started on November 1, and even then we couldn't have much of it.

You see, the Montreal Expos, who hold spring training there with the Atlanta Braves, didn't want us to have the field at all. It took a plea from West Palm Beach city hall to finally work out an agreement, and we still couldn't go near a major league clubhouse or batting cages. When we were finally allowed inside, we dressed in the visitors' clubhouse underneath the third-base stands. Meaning we had to walk outside from there and up the third-base line to reach the dugout. Meaning if you had to use the bathroom in the middle of the game, everyone knew it. Say this much for the room, though. Don Sider had it recarpeted and repainted and spiffed up almost to major league standards. As if this wasn't impressive enough, I later realized that our other owner had spent $19,000 on a new sound system for the field, a system that will have to remain if the team ever leaves. The owners were like the players—they cared.

My first speech to my team was stern. I told them that, despite what they saw and probably felt, this was not an old-timers' league, not a bush league. This was no place to be fat or lazy. I told them I wanted to build a team around the things that older players can still do well—throwing and catching and smart pitching. I told them, "If you still have your timing and can still hit, fine. But that's not what will win it for us." Upon finishing my speech, I heard an amazing sound. Silence. And I saw an amazing sight. The players were looking at me. Damn, I thought, these guys have actually been listening. And from that point on, the league was an absolute blast. We won our first seven games, and I never had to, nor even wanted to, give them that speech again.

My fun came from seeing things I thought I'd never see again. Like Dave Kingman getting excited over home runs, or Rodney Scott jumping up and down over stolen bases, or Mickey Rivers laughing so loud and long you'd think he hadn't laughed at all since he played for Billy Martin. My fun came at seeing players mix regardless of race or beliefs, which isn't so common in the major leagues. It was great to see two guys in a hotel lobby preparing to go to dinner, asking any player within shouting distance to join them. I enjoyed seeing my guys share everything from their old jokes to new insults while staying around the clubhouse long after games would end.

Don Sider is a man in his mid-thirties with wire-rimmed glasses and a serious face. But although he looked and dressed more conservatively than the rest of us, he was just one of the guys. He'd wear a uniform with his name on the back before every home game and make certain that if any of his relatives wanted to have a little fun, they could also come out early and wear a uniform. I said fine, as long as nobody got hurt.

Sider knew that buying this team was a risk, but he seemed to like risks. Not only did he help put up the nearly $2,000,000 required to buy and operate a franchise, but he also would take ground balls at third base without a cup. I know this because one day a grounder hit him in the nuts. Failing to stifle our laughter, we helped our writhing owner off the ground and into his clubhouse, where somebody had the nerve to tell him, "Don't worry, man, this happens to George Steinbrenner all the time."

Then there was the player who acted like an owner. His name was Jim Collins, an outfielder on our taxi squad, meaning he could be activated to play at any time. But for three straight games, in the sixth inning each time, somebody discovered him in the clubhouse dressed in street clothes and eating from our postgame meal. Eventually I was going to get around to saying something to him—what the hell, the guy probably didn't have the money to eat regularly—but my hand was forced when Sider walked in and saw him. "Is that what happens in big league baseball?" he innocently asked me. "Players eat during the middle of games?" And so Collins was fired.

Funny, but players were allowed to do everything else in the middle of games. Like smoke. Contrary to the big league ban on smoking in the dugout, it was done in the Senior

League. After all, it wouldn't look good if the guys smoked on the field. Soon umpires got wind of this trend, so to speak, and they'd duck into dugouts between innings for a smoke, practically turning our bench into a boys' bathroom. I never got mad at this, and not just because I occasionally sneaked a cigaret myself. I never got mad, because—well, I never got mad at my team for anything.

Not that I didn't try to get mad. Like when the guys would miss bunt and hit-and-run signs, which wasn't often. "I know things are pretty loosey-goosey around here," I shouted to a stunned Alfie Rondon one day after he missed a bunt sign. "But you have to at least try to remember the fucking signs!"

"You're right, you're right," said Rondon, nearly sobbing. "I no look. I no look."

Now, how could I stay mad at that incredibly rare sight? A ballplayer admitting he was wrong! The same sort of thing happened the time I yelled for Mickey Rivers to come into the game as a pinch runner. "Mickey's got no cleats!" yelled one of the players. Sure enough, from down in the bullpen, here comes Mickey, who has the gait of a 70-year-old but runs like he's on roller skates, here he comes sliding toward the dugout in an old pair of tennis shoes. "I'll be with you in a minute, Skip!" he shouts. "I just plain forgot my cleats."

How could I do anything but laugh like everybody else? We did a lot of laughing that winter at the unusual Mickey Rivers, who was as delighted to be back in the game as everyone was delighted to have him. I'll never forget the time he looked at this round hole in our outfield fence and announced, "I'll do anything anybody wants who can throw a ball through that hole." Before most of the players could even figure out how big the opening was, Felix Pettaway casually picked up a ball and—bingo—bounced it right through the hole from 60 feet away.

Pettaway immediately began jumping up and down and screaming that he won. Mickey contested it because the ball was bounced through. But instead of getting into a fight, my guys handled the disagreement like any normal team with three attorneys playing on it. They held a clubhouse trial. It was funnier than hell, witnesses and everything, with Jim Bonfiglio as the defense attorney and pitcher Pete Broberg as prosecuting attorney and Joe Minceberg as the judge. It was finally ruled a draw, because there were no set ground rules for the contest. That meant Mickey didn't owe Pettaway anything, which was fortunate because what Pettaway had demanded, in jest, was a blow job.

Probably the most unusual part of my role was dealing with the attorneys. Until Bonfiglio, I'd never had a bullpen catcher who couldn't catch. I was actually worried about him down there. He was a bit overweight and a bit slow, and one of my former major league pitchers was liable to skull him. Minceberg became the first player for whom I had to make copies of my basic playbook, the one that explains who is the cutoff man, how to steal a base, et cetera.

Both Bonfiglio and Minceberg were thrilled just to wear a uniform and would do anything I said, anything for the team. So you can understand my surprise the day Bonfiglio, just before a game, came running into my office holding a blood-stained towel over his lip. "The 'on of a 'itch 'it me," he mumbled through the towel.

"Which son of a bitch hit you?" I asked, hoping it wasn't someone with a multisyllablic name.

" 'ince-'erg," he said. " 'ince-'erg."

I threw him out and called in Minceberg, who admitted that yes, he'd hit him. "What, you fighting over time in the batting cage?" I asked. He looked at me funny. "Not the batting cage," he said. "The courthouse."

Minceberg said that Bonfiglio was running around the courthouse telling everyone what a horseshit lawyer he was, so when he could no longer take it, he decked him. After hearing this, I called Bonfiglio back in. He was still bleeding from a cut that would require 16 stiches.

"Yes," Bonfiglio admitted, speaking clearer now. "I called him a horseshit attorney."

"Why?" I asked.

"Because he is one," Bonfiglio said.

No ordinary baseball fight, this. Minceberg screamed at him, Bonfiglio did his best to scream back, and finally I stood up and pounded on the desk. "You're in my courtroom now!" I shouted. "I want to say I'm disgusted with both of you. Here we are, going almost the whole year without any problems on this team, and now two horseshit attorneys making 2,000 chickenshit dollars a month as chickenshit ballplayers want to kick each other's ass. One of you guys is lying about this fight, and because Bonfiglio is the only one with blood on him, I'm going to believe him. You, Minceberg, I'm throwing you off the team. Pack up your stuff."

Both players silently trudged out of the office, stepping carefully over the other players, who had hunched down watching and then literally rolled on the floor in laughter. I thought about it a few minutes and decided that Minceberg's roster spot was much more important to him than any statement I could make to discourage fighting among teammates who (except for the lawyers) loved each other. So I found Minceberg before he finished packing and told him to forget it, that I was wrong, and that he should stick around. What the hell. It was funny.

After the season I received a handwritten letter from Minceberg, this lawyer who probably makes about $250,000 in a bad year, more than I've ever made a year in my life. Part of the letter read: "I want to express my gratitude for giving me the opportunity to be a member of the Tropics. Although I have achieved many goals in my life, nothing compares to the day you told me I had made the team." At the risk of sounding like someone nicer than I am, I thought that letter was neat.

As our season continued, despite a daily game like every other game I've ever managed, with bats cracking in your ears and chalk dust in your mouth and the sun in your eyes, you were still never allowed to forget that this league was different. I remember talking with Bradenton manager Clete

323

Boyer about acquiring infielder Graig Nettles. "We'll trade him," Boyer said, "but you have to take his brother Jim with him." Other teams had players who wouldn't leave the area, simply because they lived there; if they were traded, they just quit. Poor Luis Tiant. When he was traded from Winter Haven to Miami, even if he'd wanted to quit he couldn't. What would have happened to those 500 teddy bears he was traded for? The Miami owner was in the toy business, Winter Haven needed a good promotion, teddy bears were cuddlier than Tiant, and a deal was made.

All you needed to do was turn away from the field for one second to actually see how this league was different. Take a look at the stands—almost empty. There was nobody there in the beginning, in November, when the publicity people claimed the snowbirds would soon fill the seats. There was nobody there in the end, in January, when the snowbirds clogged the roads outside the ballparks, all of them heading for the early bird special at some fish joint.

My West Palm Beach franchise will proudly say it led the league in attendance with just over 50,000 for 35 home dates, but a lot of those tickets were freebies. How hard is it to attract people when you hand out tickets at a shopping mall? Or at the end of a grocery checkout line? Pretty soon we were handing out nearly as many as we sold, which played hell with our printing costs. But I never complained, because I'd witnessed the alternative: places like Orlando, tourist capital of the country, where there'd be only 300 people in the stands. In Orlando you should be able to draw more people than that just by accident. Or places like Winter Haven, where there were even fewer people, where you could walk outside on a winter night and hear nothing but the equipment rattling and the players quietly muttering and the fat guy yelling, "Your son should be out here instead of you!" Players on those teams told me they hated playing in those places. Some nights they didn't even feel like leaving the clubhouse.

I'd walk away from those conversations feeling lucky. I

hated to leave the clubhouse, only because I was having so much fun there. And as the season was ending, our team players got closer and closer to one another. United in this journey through baseball the way it used to feel, we grew to not only work together but think together.

Once when I was wired for a cable television game, I had run to first base to check on Ron Washington, who had just been hit in the leg with a pitch. "Exactly where did it hit you, Ron?" I asked. He winced. "It hit me in the fucking leg, Skip." I smiled. It was showtime. "Ronnie, you know I'm wired for TV, so I'm going to ask you, on what part of your fucking leg did it hit you?" He smiled back, suddenly feeling better. He grabbed his calf. "On this part of my fucking leg," he said. "Oh, shit," I said, "you just said fuck." He laughed. "Oh, fuck, you just said shit." At this point we'd even outraced the guy pushing the censor button in the production truck. I apologize to all those families who, I later heard, were forced to turn down the sound on their televisions. On second thought, I don't apologize. After all these years, I figure I deserved a little fun.

And like somebody's giddy grandmother, I had fun. I actually baked chocolate chip cookies and brought them to the clubhouse. Before you think I became a complete pussy, understand that I only related to them because they played hard for me. And it wasn't like it was the first time in my life this had happened. It was the second. Surely you remember Oakland. Didn't I hug Reggie Jackson, and worry about Mike Andrews, and drink with Sal Bando? You see, you doubting fans, I can be nice—the A's and the Tropics proved it.

Because of the players' age and priorities, I found myself doing other little things I wouldn't have dreamed of doing during real live pennant races. For instance, after we'd clinched our Southern Division title with a week left in the season, I allowed pitcher Will McEnaney to participate in a fantasy camp. No, not as a customer but as an instructor. I was also very attuned to injuries, so that by the final month of the season I would check every man in every day's lineup to see if he was physically able to play. Of course, in this league, because of their age, I had little choice. I didn't force Dave Kingman to play a day game after a night game, because of sore leg muscles. I let Mickey Rivers miss the final two weeks of the regular season because he could hardly walk. I saw as much of Tito Landrum's chronically bad back as his doctor and never hesitated to sit him down. In every case, in a big league pennant race I might not have even asked them how they felt.

In return, my players were by far the best team in the league, winning their division by 15½ games. Pete Broberg said we were the best team he'd ever played for, period. And he was only half-joking, considering he'd spent most of his career with some terrible Washington Senators and Texas Rangers teams. I remember telling fans they were seeing better baseball than they would in the spring, particularly because the big leaguers only take a couple of at-bats during spring games, while the pitchers only go a couple of innings.

Hell, the team couldn't be too bad. We had four minor league instructors in Toby Harrah, Ray Burris, Jerry White, and Luis Pujols. And we had two other guys sign new major/minor league contracts during our season: Ron Washington with Texas and left-handed reliever Paul Mirabella with Milwaukee.

Our year climaxed on January 19 in Fort Myers, when we beat the Sun Sox to clinch the division 12 days before the end of the season. There were no fans, no television cameras, and half of my players were already in the clubhouse when cement truck driver Felix Pettaway retired the final batter for the win. But it was still special, even if just us boys knew it. The nine players on the field and the few left in the dugout hugged and jumped across the diamond like always. We ran back to the clubhouse and joined our celebrating teammates by pouring champagne in our hair like every major league pennant-winning team.

But typical for this league, even the celebration was some-thing different. Because after all of us had been soaked, and everyone had finished screaming . . . we stayed together. From midnight until nearly 3 A.M., in that tiny Fort Myers clubhouse, we all remained, drinking beer and leftover champagne and dancing. Yes, the guys actually took turns dancing to some loud music from this huge radio, getting up on a table in their underwear and boogying. Texas Rangers fans beware, even Toby Harrah was boogying. It wasn't as intense as my other title celebrations, it wasn't as elaborate or expensive. But none has ever lasted as long or made me feel—as I sat there in soaking-wet long underwear—any happier. I wish New York Mets baseball announcer Tim McCarver had been at that final game. He ripped our league after ad-mittedly seeing just parts of three games. Said we were tar-nishing baseball. I guess Tim McCarver is such a big deal now, much bigger than when he played, that he can rip any-body. But I wish he could have seen one full game before he said anything. Nine innings. Is that too much to ask of some-body before they pass judgment on a thing that's so impor-tant to so many people?

That night was the season's highlight, and not just be-cause, still high on victory, we took the field a couple of hours later for an afternoon game. It was also because, with their screwy playoff system, it never got any better than that. In the Senior League playoffs—at least, this is how they did it that first year—the team with the best record in the league was forced to wait while other top teams played each other in an elimination round. The winner of that round played that best-record team in a one-game finale. One game for the title? You're talking to a guy who thought a five-game pen-nant series was too short. It might not have been so bad with-out having to take three off-days after the regular season before we played.

The championship game was in Fort Myers, against St. Petersburg. Beforehand I told my guys, "This is no way to run a playoff system, but hey, it's been a hell of a year. Go out and have fun." But by then we'd already had our fun. The first ball hit in the game went between the legs of Ron Washington at shortstop, and next time I looked we trailed 9–0 after about six innings. I give my guys credit, though. Even then, with our dreams of a championship gone, they remained cool realists. "Hey," several guys would shout at once, "let's get this son of a bitch over with!" And so we did, as fast as we could, still managing to score four runs in an eventual 12–4 loss.

Afterward the players jumped on a bus and got the hell out of town. Norma and I went to the hotel room of John Henry's mother, Sue. We ordered a couple of Domino's Pizzas. Soon we were joined by St. Petersburg manager Bobby Tolan and his wife, Marian. And that's how the first season of the Senior Professional Baseball Association ended, with the winning and losing managers of the final game sharing a large pepperoni.

Well, it didn't quite end with that. There was the small, very small, matter of playoff money. Each player on the runner-up team, meaning us, was entitled to $500, which came out to about $300 after taxes. The players could vote on who received a share, and typically, they voted one for everybody. Running out of shares before they reached the bus driver, they decided to do something different for him. After all, he had spent the winter driving us around at an average speed of 70 miles per hour. And after all, in front of the entire team, he did once talk a state trooper out of giving him a ticket. So the players took up a collection for him, and at $15 a head from us he became the first bus driver in the history of sports to make more off a postseason game than the players. With that announcement, the season ended.

• • •

So what next for the Senior League? The league certainly needs to make some changes to even have a "next." First, get rid of the name "Senior." Two of our season ticket holders told my wife that they couldn't convince anybody in their trailer park to attend the games, because they thought they'd be watching actual senior citizens run the bases. Second, get better umpires. A single one of my six ejections—Earl Weaver was tossed out 11 times—took them 23 minutes. And I spent the year in a good mood, remember? They cut corners by hiring high school and college umpires, and they paid the price. The umps were intimidated and inconsistent and just plain rotten. Next winter, when good young pro umps are changing planes in Miami en route to Puerto Rico and the Dominican Republic to work those leagues, collar them. And pay them more to stay. Also, make it easier on everyone by making the league shorter—cut it down to, say, 60 games.

There's only one thing I think they shouldn't change. The players. Forty-five minutes before the championship game, I gathered the team together for a meeting. But just as I was ready to begin, Ray Burris stood up and stopped me. He called for Mirabella, who came walking around the corner with a plaque. "This is for you, Skip," Mirabella said, handing it over and then quickly turning away. Here's how the plaque read: Presented to Dick Williams in Appreciation for All Your Hard Work During the Season! 1989–1990 West Palm Beach Tropic Players.

I read it. I held it. And I cried. Right in front of my team, I cried. And then I hugged each one of them. And then, as if my reputation wasn't already totally ruined, I ran outside and grabbed Norma and showed her the plaque, me in my uniform, my face all tearstained.

How about that. When everything's said and done, after all these years, Dick Williams is the one left shivering in his cleats.

On one of our last bus trips a couple of players asked if we'd all be together again next year. It was the hardest question I answered all season. How could I say that I was fairly sure about them but not about me? Because late in the winter

I was contacted by George Steinbrenner about possibly being a special assignment adviser for the New York Yankees for 1990. I told him I was interested, and as of early spring I guess I'm still a candidate. And I guess it would be nice. It would be baseball without the all-encompassing feeling of competition. I could love the game and not be devoured by it. And I could stay married. Norma's words still ring in my ears: "If you manage again, it will be without me."

Oh, hell. If the right money and the right team came along and offered me one more chance to kick somebody in the ass . . . Norma would be grabbing my arm and hanging on for dear life like always. In other words, if Steinbrenner or somebody else asked me to return to major league baseball as a manager, I would . . . oh, hell.

There's only one certainty here. If I did leave the Senior League and returned as a big league manager, one thing would be for goddamn sure. One thing these modern-day players could take to the bank. One thing these millionaires will be crying on their mommies' shoulders about. One thing they better get straight before they come walking into my clubhouse with their briefcases and their attitudes. One thing you can bet your slouching, uncaring ass on. No more Mr. Nice Guy.

INDEX